Burden
of Dreams

Post-Communist Cultural Studies
Thomas Cushman, General Editor

The Culture of Lies
Antipolitical Essays
by Dubravka Ugrešić

Burden of Dreams
History and Identity in
Post-Soviet Ukraine
by Catherine Wanner

*Gender Politics in
the Western Balkans*
Women and Society in
Yugoslavia and the Yugoslav
Successor States
By Sabrina P. Ramet

Burden
of Dreams

History
and Identity
in Post-Soviet
Ukraine

Catherine Wanner

The Pennsylvania State University Press
University Park, Pennsylvania

Library of Congress Cataloging-in-Publication Data

Wanner, Catherine.
    Burden of dreams : history and identity in post-Soviet Ukraine /
Catherine Wanner.
        p.   cm.
    Includes bibliographical references and index.
    ISBN 0-271-01792-9 (cloth: alk. paper)
    ISBN 0-271-01793-7 (pbk. : alk. paper)
    1. Nationalism—Ukraine.   2. Ukraine—History—1991–   .
3. Russification—Ukraine.   4. Narodnyĭ rukh Ukraïny.   I. Title.
DK508.846.W36   1998
947.7—DC21   97-49170
                                                                      CIP

It is the policy of The Pennsylvania State University Press to use acid-free
paper for the first printing of all clothbound books. Publications on uncoated
stock satisfy the minimum requirements of American National Standard for
Information Sciences—Permanence of Paper for Printed Library Materials,
ANSI Z39.48–1992.

For my parents,
James R. Cowhey and Maureen Duffy Cowhey

Contents

Illustrations

*Photos by Tania Mychajlyshyn-D'Avignon. All other photos by the author.

Acknowledgments

This book has been many years in the making, and it is a genuine pleasure to acknowledge the many people who have contributed to it. I first traveled to Ukraine in 1980 as part of an undergraduate study abroad program. Since then I have remained captivated and enraptured by the culture and people of what was then the Soviet Union. My interest in doing ethnographic research in Ukraine was initially sparked by a small Ukrainian cultural elite espousing a nationalist agenda within the confines of a multinational Soviet socialist state. Pre-glasnost stays in 1980 and again in 1984 gave me some idea as to how burdensome their dreams were and what was at stake for those who dared to wage such a struggle against the Soviet state. Fast-breaking historical developments greatly influenced the course of my research and the final form this book has taken. Had I done my fieldwork at a less turbulent and conflicted time, a vastly different book would have emerged.

Over the course of many trips to Ukraine since that initial visit in 1980, I was graced by the insight, wit, and generosity of innumerable individuals as I struggled to understand the workings of Ukrainian society. Conducting research for this book was made incomparably more interesting and enjoyable thanks to Andrii Alexandrovich, Ludmilla Asmalovskaia and her entire extended family, Alla Banderchyk, Natalia Bochakarevaia, Natalia Chernysh, Anatolii and Anna Kuks, Ludmilla Kovalchyk, Tatiana and Rostislav Pasternak, Valentina Pavlenko, Svitlana Slipchenko, Vitalii Timofiiv, and Olena Yahodovs'ka. Special thanks are due to Ludmilla Lapchyk and Nina Lapchyk, who truly *lived* with this project more than any friends should have to. I thank them and each person who took the time to speak with me and share their dreams over the years.

To research the meteoric rise of political opposition in Soviet Ukraine, I received funding from a MacArthur Pre-Dissertation Fellowship, the Harriman Institute, and the Sheldon Schepps Memorial Fund of the Anthropology Department, Columbia University, to travel to Ukraine for three months during the summers of 1990 and 1991. However, nearly all of the data presented here were gathered immediately following independence during fieldwork from 1992 to 1994. During this period, I spent seven months in Kyiv, three in L'viv, and two months in Kharkiv, from August 1992 to August 1993, and returned in spring 1994 to spend an additional three months in Kyiv. This research was funded by a Fulbright-Hays Doctoral Dissertation Award and by a grant from the International Research-Exchange Board (IREX). I also benefited from a Social Science Research Council Dissertation Writing Fellowship and from participation in two SSRC workshops in post-Soviet sociology and anthropology in 1992 and 1994. I subsequently returned to Ukraine for brief visits of three weeks each in October 1995 to Kyiv, in January 1996 to Kharkiv, and in May 1996 to Kyiv, made possible by a Columbia University Traveling Fellowship and a Harriman Institute Junior Fellowship. During the final revision stages I benefited from a Neporany Post-Doctoral Fellowship, administered by the Canadian Institute of Ukrainian Studies.

Portions of this book have appeared elsewhere in a different form and I wish to thank the publishers for granting permission to incorporate the materials here:

"Nationalism on Stage: Music and Change in Soviet Ukraine," in Mark Slobin, ed., *Retuning Culture: Musical Changes in Central and Eastern Europe* (Durham, N.C.: Duke University Press, 1966), pp. 136–54, now part of Chapter 5.

"Educational Practices and the Making of National Identity in Post-Soviet Ukraine," in Nancy Ries, guest editor, *The Anthropology of East Europe Review* 13(2):8–18, now part of Chapter 4.

Tania Mychajlyshyn-D'Avignon very graciously shared many of her lovely photographs with me, some of which appear in this book. Victor Marushchenko very kindly gave permission for one of his exquisite photographs to appear on the cover of this book.

I am very grateful to the members of my dissertation committee for their thoughtful comments on an earlier version of this manuscript: Elaine Combs-Schilling, David Koester, Alexander Motyl, Mark von Hagen, and most especially to my adviser, Katherine S. Newman, whose dedication to her students sets the standard that I strive to live up to. Graduate school was made immeasurably more interesting by my friendship and very long conversations with Kate Dudley and Daniela Peluso.

Several friends and colleagues read earlier versions of chapters or contributed to this book in other ways. I would like to thank Dominique Arel, Helga Duffy, Nancy Ries, Mark Slobin, Corinna Snyder, Amy Stambach, and Michael Taussig. Tom Cushman, Jane Dawson, Kate

Dudley, Bruce Grant, Oleksandr Hytsenko, and Marian Rubchak read the manuscript in its entirety and offered detailed and insightful comments for which I am grateful.

Marina Kohl was with me when I first traveled to Ukraine in 1980 and over the years I have enjoyed her unwavering encouragement and inspiration in all my endeavors, anthropological or otherwise, and for this I offer heartfelt thanks.

And lastly, my parents have been an unshakable source of support and encouragement in this project and in so much else that I have undertaken, and it is to them that I dedicate this book. Much of the revision of this manuscript was written with my young daughter Elizabeth on my lap. Her patience and good nature provided the mental space and the inspiration to work. My husband, Adrian Wanner, accompanied me to Ukraine for fieldwork during the summers of 1991 and 1993. He read every word of this book. Always generous with his time, keen intellect, and eye for the absurd, he has contributed to my research, and to my life, in ways too numerous to mention.

Note on Transliteration and Translation

I use the Library of Congress system of transliteration from Ukrainian when rendering quotations spoken in Ukrainian and general terms, except when another spelling has become accepted usage in English (e.g., "Chernobyl" rather than *Chornobyl*, "glasnost" rather than *hlasnist'*). Place-names in Ukraine have been transliterated from Ukrainian (Kyiv rather than Kiev, Odesa rather than Odessa, and Dnipro rather than Dnieper). When quotations, citations, or bureaucratic designations are given from Russian, and not Ukrainian, I have indicated so and used the Library of Congress system of transliteration except in such instances, once again, where other spellings are likely to be more familiar to the reader (e.g., "Yeltsin" rather than "El'tsin," "Trotsky" rather than "Trotskii"). All translations are my own, except where otherwise noted.

Introduction

Ukraine is the largest new state to appear on the map of Europe this century. With a population of over 50 million and a territory larger than France, it promises to change the dynamics of the region. This new political entity also represents the first internationally recognized Ukrainian state in the modern period. In the age of the nation-state, the dissolution of the Soviet Union was partly achieved through a multitude of groups asserting their nations' right to self-determination. In Ukraine, this principle underwrote efforts to institutionalize Ukrainian culture after independence. This book details some of the sites where distinctly post-Soviet Ukrainian histories and myths are being institutionalized in an effort to create a culturally based allegiance to the new Ukrainian state.

Unlike traditional ethnographies, which focus on a "people" or a "community," this book is a multi-site ethnography of processes, specifically the processes and dynamics involved in converting a nationalist ideology into an institutionalized national culture and a meaningful national identity in the aftermath of the socialist experiment. The state has a vested interest in such processes because their success or failure directly affects perceptions of state legitimacy. As such, this ethnography becomes an anthropological study of the state, of how the state, through a negotiated settlement among competing interests and visions, attempts to establish the categories, periods, and events that give meaning to individual and collective experience, and of how such attempts by the state are challenged and even overruled by individuals through everyday practices.[1]

Max Weber defined the state as the unit that has a monopoly on the use of violence within a territorially circumscribed space (1968: 54). This succinct definition of the state has been widely embraced for decades by scholars of various disciplines. Yet when we look at the fifteen new states that emerged from the collapse of the former Soviet Union as they head into the twenty-first century and take stock of the power of mafias, transnational capital, and culturally based challenges to established borders, I am tempted to suggest that such a concept of the state has become analytically insufficient.[2] The nature of state power is changing. In the age of the nation-state, a state's ability to craft a nation out of a diverse population and cultivate allegiance is perhaps more likely to ensure its survival than a monopoly on violence.

Indeed, the Soviet regime possessed a monopoly on the use of violence and took every opportunity to display its might and power over its own citizenry during its seventy-four-year existence. Yet this did not stop it from crumbling before our eyes in a matter of days. Its disintegration gave birth to (at least) fifteen new states, each asserting its legitimacy in terms of a nation's right to self-determination. The stability of many of these states remains imperiled because they have been unable thus far to institutionalize a national culture and forge a national community. Just as the Soviet Union broke apart along ethnically based political subunits, there is no guarantee that these new states will not see regions attempt to break away in spite of vast arsenals of nuclear and other weaponry.

"Ukraine means borderland." This is how Orest Subtelny (1988) begins his seminal work on the history of Ukraine.[3] Ukraine's position as a "borderland," a buffer zone between larger states and empires, has shaped its history considerably. Its frontier location left it open to many outside influences. Yet shifting state borders left Ukraine in an amorphous space. The legacy of statelessness, combined with the mosaic of influences it produced and comparatively close cultural and geographical proximity to Russia, makes the process of articulating a national culture and a sense of national identity to reflect new political realities particularly complex.[4]

Economically speaking, Ukraine is blessed with rich soil, an expansive industrial base, and a highly educated population, and yet paradoxically remains mired in economic crisis. Poverty is on the rise, and it is possible that post-Soviet Ukrainian society will develop a permanent underclass. Ukrainian political leaders cannot promise economic well-being, except in the long run, and this is likely to be beyond the lifetime of many. Yet in the age of the nation-state, culture provides a vast repository for the legitimation of political authority.

Nationalist leaders in post-Soviet Ukraine argue that since they agitated for a Ukrainian state on the basis of the internationally recognized right of national self-determination, a top priority for the new state must be to protect the collective right and cultural heritage of the nation. This was the rationale for launching a "nationalizing" project, an effort to convert a nationalist ideology into an institutionalized national culture, so as to incorporate this heterogeneous population into a newly defined Ukrainian nation.

Nationalizing efforts in Ukraine face two potential obstacles. First, Ukraine has the largest Russian diaspora of all the former Soviet republics, numbering 11.4 million out of 52 million, and lives within earshot of Russian nationalists pledging to protect "Russians in the near abroad" from cultural oppression even though they are now Ukrainian citizens. Second, one-third to one-half of Ukrainians are considered "russified" or "denationalized," as evidenced by the widespread use of the Russian language. Efforts to "renationalize" Ukrainians, who often do not feel "denationalized," has triggered intraethnic discord, even more than interethnic tension, and has provoked a heated debate about the meaning of contemporary Ukrainian identity.

Many look to the past to understand the present and to shape the future. Ukrainian-speaking Ukrainians tend to see their Russian-speaking Ukrainian brethren as "victims" of oppressive imperial and Soviet cultural politics. Nationalists frequently depict the historic relationship between Ukrainians and the Russian and Soviet states in terms of cultural subjugation, economic exploitation, forced assimilation, and genocide. Russified Ukrainians, on the other hand, often feel that through intermarriage, mobility, and the media, they freely assimilated to Russian culture. They do not necessarily see themselves as "Little Russians," but rather quite simply as Ukrainians who speak Russian. Even though the new Ukrainian state has not resorted to coercive means, many efforts to promote Ukrainian culture in russified regions have met with resistance, suggesting that nationalizing "the people of Ukraine" (*narod Ukrainy*) into the "Ukrainian people" (*ukrains'kyi narod*) will be an uneasy process.

I define nationalism as an ideal which posits that the political should be congruent with the national, that a nation should be united under its own state.[5] From this ideal, an ideology may emerge. This makes nationalism a project of the modern state and an integral part of the process of state-building. In taking such an approach, I give greater prominence to the role of the state (actual or potential) as a powerful agent in nationalist struggle than do other anthropologists, who often focus on nationalist ideologies in terms of the production of "peoplehood" (Dominquez 1989: 11; Fox 1990: 3). Within the Soviet and post-Soviet contexts, I have found it of paramount importance to take into consideration the role of the state in creating conditions that inform everyday practices and in which cultural production takes place.

Going beyond an elite's construction of symbols of the nation (Geertz 1973) and of the means by which a nation is "imagined" into a community (Anderson 1991), I propose to examine the sites at which a national culture is articulated, contested, negotiated, and perhaps, institutionalized. This process involves cultivating a sense of belonging, stemming

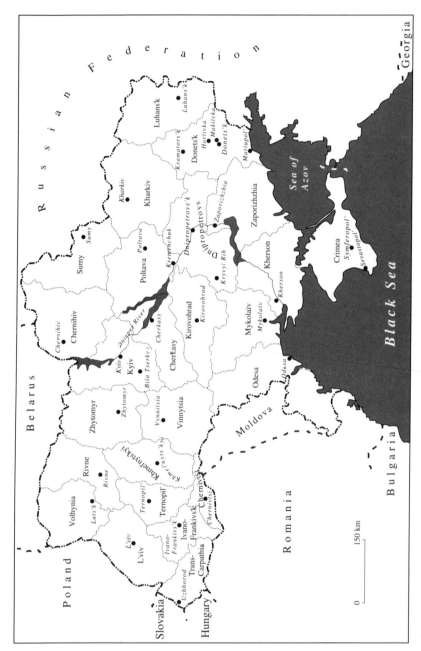

Ukraine: oblasts and cities with population over 200,000. (From Martha Bohachevsky-Chomiak, *Political Communities and Gendered Ideologies in Contemporary Ukraine* [Cambridge: Harvard Ukrainian Research Institute, 1994]. Created by Adrian B. Hewryk and Robert A. De Lossa.)

from individual experiences cast as collective experience within the boundaries of a particular state. By embracing a nationalized culture as a meaningful element of the social person, an individual is linked to a state. This embrace fundamentally informs national identity and makes it salient. The institutionalization of a national culture is a project of paramount importance for Ukraine, a new state steeped in economic crisis legitimating itself against a culturally oppressive multinational empire.

I do not wish to argue, as has been done in the popular press, that the breakdown of the Soviet system merely lifted the structural constraints holding in check ethnic animosities that were fermenting all along—the so-called ancient hatred theory. Rather, particular historical circumstances, which produced cultural diversity and shaped perceptions of self, other, and belonging, all of which I address in this book, explain the sources of collective attachments and animosity among nationalized groups seen today throughout the former Soviet Union.

I believe the essence of the Soviet system reveals itself most clearly during this period of transformation, as parts of it slowly disintegrate and others tenaciously endure and impose themselves on post-Soviet society. In the Soviet Union, official state-sponsored historical narrative was overtly manipulated to legitimate the system and the regime. Events difficult to integrate into the teleological development of a "bright future" were simply ignored and denied public expression. The practice of tight state controls on historiography has left a powerful legacy in its wake.

The residual memories, which were able to withstand the onslaught of official historical narratives and give meaning to individual experience, are what Michel Foucault called "counter-memory" (1977). For some, Soviet state-sponsored historical narratives did not lend context and meaning to personal experiences because of the disjuncture between individual recollections and official historical accounts. Individuals struggled to safeguard memories against the multitude of forces in the public sphere that attempted to shape private recollections to coincide with official historical narratives. Although denied acknowledgment in official historiography, narratives of events and experiences that did not match state-sponsored accounts were often sequestered in kitchens across the country where they were passed down from generation to generation. Counter-memories endured over time, formed a base of resistance to state power, and inspired passive-aggressive sabotage of the system. Such atomization of alternative historical experience, and the ensuing discomfort it produced, undermined the cultural authority of the state and in large part provoked the sweeping, popular interest in historical inquiry once the tight controls on public discourse were relaxed in the final years of Soviet rule.

Although it was the policy of glasnost (introduced to aid in the process of economic restructuring) that made such historical revisionism possible, it was Chernobyl that linked historical inquiry much more firmly with a reexamination of the legitimacy of the Soviet state. From a Ukrainian perspective, Chernobyl perhaps more than any other single factor set the Soviet system on the path to demise. The initial denial and subsequent cover-up of the accident spurred fierce popular resentment of a system that proved itself to be unashamedly self-serving.

Shortly after the accident at Chernobyl, members of the Ukrainian Writers' Union issued a stinging critique of the Soviet state's environmental policy and the ecological devastation it was inflicting on Ukraine. They likened this ecological aggression to the Soviet state's attack on Ukrainian culture and language. As writers voiced concern about damage to the environment, Oles' Honchar, a leading literary figure and soon-to-be leader of the nationalist movement, encouraged them to consider the destruction of Ukrainian historic and religious monuments as well.

Under the guise of glasnost, the Ukrainian Writers' Union actively began to promote a Ukrainian cultural revival. They created language societies to foster interest in the Ukrainian language and Ukrainian literature, agitated for the rehabilitation of suppressed and persecuted Ukrainian writers, and began to publish historic works with interpretations that challenged standard Soviet accounts of Ukrainian history. The writings of Mykhailo Hrushevsky and Volodymyr Vynnychenko, early-twentieth-century cultural and political leaders, suddenly began to circulate and were devoured by a public starved for a more honest depiction of its past.

In late 1987 disgust and angst over Chernobyl also prompted the foundation of an independent, grassroots association called Zelenyi Svit (Green World), which eventually emerged as the dominant organization uniting a variety of environmental groups. Zelenyi Svit sought to establish a nuclear-free Ukraine and to initiate ecological reform and clean-up.[6] By 1990, Zelenyi Svit's vigorous protests, in the form of strikes, unauthorized commemorations, and station blockades were carried out by the approximately three-hundred local chapters registered under the Zelenyi Svit banner. Environmental protests gave encouragement to Ukrainian intellectuals striving to discredit the Soviet system by equating environmental destruction with cultural destruction.

Nineteen eighty-nine proved to be a watershed year for nationalists. A host of developments worked in favor of delegitimizing the Soviet system and advancing a Ukrainian cultural revival. Nationalist advocates cheered when socialist regimes fell in Poland, Hungary, Czechoslovakia, Romania, and East Germany. Dmytryo Pavlychko founded the Taras Shevchenko Language Society to improve the status of Ukrainian and make it the official language of Ukraine—a demand that was met in December 1989. With considerable help and involvement from the diaspora,[7] the Ukrainian national churches, the Ukrainian Catholic Church and the Ukrainian Autocephalous Orthodox Church, both of which had been outlawed and driven underground decades earlier, were allowed to regain their parishes, which had been confiscated and handed over to the Russian Orthodox Church. And finally, Volodymyr Shcherbytsky, the hard-line Communist Party leader of Soviet Ukraine, retired from his post in September 1989, and hostility against the burgeoning nationalist movement thereafter subsided.

In September 1989, Rukh (Ukrainian Popular Movement in Support of Perestroika), an umbrella organization uniting a variety of nationalist, environmental, religious, and professional groups under the banner of independence held its founding congress with over 30,000 members in attendance. Although its first program, published in February 1989, called for the "rebirth and comprehensive development of the Ukrainian nation," it was not until 1990 that the movement became sharply politicized and agitated directly for independence.

Rukh and other opposition movements garnered support by launching attacks on the legitimacy of the Soviet state in historical terms. This proved to be an effective strategy, and Rukh made steady gains in popular support. However, it was the bungled coup attempt in Moscow, only two years after Rukh was founded, that paved the way for independence far more quickly than many had ever expected. On December 1, 1991, a referendum on Ukrainian independence received a sound, popular mandate with a majority in every oblast, including the heavily russified Crimea, voting for independence. And with this, a new era began for Ukraine and for the 52 million people who live within its borders.

Rukh's strategy of tapping into individual memories to conjure up images of a collective past was so effective in generating anti-Soviet, pro-

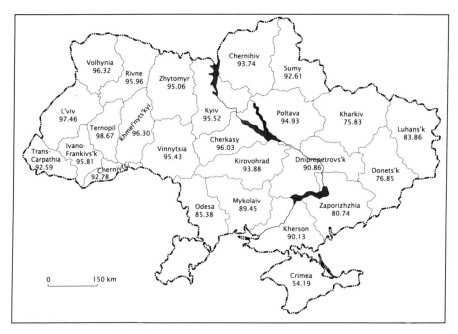

Map showing results of the referendum on Ukrainian independence on 1 December 1991. Each number represents the percentage of citizens who voted for independence in each region.

independence sentiment that it was maintained once independence was achieved—but with a new purpose. History supplies a vast reservoir of raw materials from which to craft a post-Soviet national culture and underscore the legitimacy of a state. New historical myths and a revised historiography encapsulated in historical representations are now the cornerstone of the new Ukrainian state's efforts to expand a sense of nation based on common historical experiences among an otherwise highly diverse and disenfranchised population.

Historical representations function as rhetoric of the state, used during the Soviet period to construct state socialism and now used to deconstruct the same in favor of a Ukrainian nation-state. Because they are imprecise and emotionally suggestive, representations, more so than narratives, which in all their detail invite dispute, have the potential to be embraced by a greater portion of a vulnerable population reassessing its collective past. The use of historical representations to articulate a particular historical narrative can transform historical consciousness, which, in turn, can shape national consciousness and form the basis of a national identity.

It is impossible to survey all historical representations of the Soviet period in post-Soviet Ukraine. I focus on popular and state-sponsored representations of four key events: the Revolution of 1917, the Famine of 1932–33, the Soviet victory during World War II, and the Chernobyl nuclear accident. Chernobyl and the Famine were initially mobilized by cultural and political opposition leaders as a justification for Ukrainian independence, as symbolic of the victimization of Ukrainians under Soviet rule.[8] They have now become the foundation of a Ukrainian national charter to legitimate the Ukrainian state. The Revolution and the Soviet victory during World War II were key events glorifying the Soviet system and the Soviet state. Just as the Revolution created the Soviet state, the victory over Nazi Germany and its ensuing superpower status sustained the Soviet state for nearly five decades thereafter. Specifically, I look at how such events are interpreted at four key sites, schools, festivals, the state calendar, and monuments, in an effort to institutionalize a new national culture in keeping with post-Soviet political realities.

The re-crafting of a nation to reflect political change involves not only issues of historical reinterpretation and representation, but the authentication of these constructions as well. They need to be shrouded in an aura of the "really real" in order to mask their very fabrication. All historical representations are, of course, multivocal. By no means do I intend to suggest that there is a single type of historical representation conveying a certain meaning. Rather, to the extent that the state is able to articulate a particular interpretation of the Soviet past, this represents a negotiated settlement among competing groups espousing nationalist, socialist, and prerevolutionary views, to name only the most obvious visions of the past and designs on the future. I do not focus on the jockeying and competition among political parties in formulating these representations but rather on the divergence of reactions each representation produces as it emerges as a site of cultural contestation. Representations can divide the population by forcing a debate about their meaning and the experiences which stand behind them. Yet along with a polyphony of responses, representations have the potential to craft consensus and solidarity across national, class, religious, and gender lines by recognizing a commonality of experience. It is this uneasy tension of potentialities that the (re)makers of historical representations must confront. As we will see, crafting consensus of historical experience in post-Soviet society is a complicated process, albeit one which reveals aspects of how post-Soviet society functions.

Nationalism in Ukraine is often conceptualized in overly stark terms, such as "diaspora Russians in the east versus nationalistic Ukrainians in the west," with language as the sole criterion delineating group membership. I will argue that the fracturing of Ukraine goes beyond an east-west dichotomy and creates national and linguistic divides that are far more blurred than the national allegiances that are assumed to follow linguistic lines. By challenging some of the dominant paradigms and rhetorical conveniences when discussing contemporary Ukraine, I hope to illustrate the distinctiveness of the Ukrainian case as compared to other former Soviet republics and socialist societies. By analyzing how the Soviet system imbued nationality with meaning in Ukraine, we will see the extent to which this resulted in far-reaching ethnic mixing and in the emergence of comparatively strong regional identities. Although Russia is highly centralized with most resources in Moscow or St. Petersburg, Ukraine is certainly not. Ukraine has several powerful and diverse regional centers. Distinct regional cultures testify to variations in the experience of Soviet rule and to the multitude of interpretations of Ukrainian history and Ukrainian identity that this variation has produced.

Attempting to redefine a national identity in keeping with contemporary political realities through the institutionalization of a revised national culture engages other aspects of identity as well. National identities are intertwined with gender, religious, and regionally based conceptions of self and society. Given the interdependence of the factors contributing to a person's sense of self, any attempts to encourage reexamination or reformation of one will trigger a domino effect, shifting all others.

The paradoxes, ironies, and absurdities that color life in post-Soviet society make Ukraine an excellent site to undertake an anthropological study of the post-socialist state and its relationship to nationality. The long history of Soviet manipulation of historiography, compounded by state domination of the public sphere, leaves nationalist leaders in post-Soviet society in a delicate bind. How can a revised historical narrative be accepted as authentic if it is presented in a public space that has been discredited as a forum of lies? By analyzing how a formerly colonial and socialist society institutionalizes a reformulated national culture, which hinges primarily on a revised interpretation of the experience of Soviet rule, we see how the Soviet system imbued nationality with meaning, how a national identity automatically engages other aspects of identity, and how individuals in a formerly socialist society strike a balance between resisting state power and complying with it, and in the process change the social order while not directly overturning it.

Chapter 1 gives an overview of how a sense of nationality was constituted by the Soviet system and analyzes other, non-national forms of allegiance and identity the Soviet system engendered. Both factors intrude on efforts to institutionalize a post-Soviet national culture. Chapter 2 analyzes why national opposition to the Soviet system made rapid strides in the final years of Soviet rule and focuses on the role of historical revisionism in generating support for independence. Chapter 3 discusses Soviet-era patterns of discourse and practices that remain salient and give life to the values and practices embodied in Soviet culture even though the Soviet Union has collapsed.

Chapter 4 is the first of four sites we will examine. Schools were one of the first social institutions to undergo rapid reform. We look at the forms this change has taken and at how it has been received. Specifically, I turn to the emergence of private schools and analyze how their curricula differ from those of state-sponsored schools. Chapter 5 details how attempts to promote Ukrainian pop culture via a music festival have evolved in tandem with political change. Chapter 6 looks at how the official state calendar of commemorations and celebrations has been altered. Chapter 7 looks at how public spaces, and specifically monuments reflecting a particular historical interpretation, have been defaced, dismantled, or left untouched.

During this period of painful transformation and adaptation, state and cultural leaders supportive of Ukrainian independence continue to reinterpret the past in tandem with perceived levels of national consciousness to knit together a diverse people into a nation. By refashioning and reinstitutionalizing a national culture, they exploit the potential to provide a vital link between individuals and the state via the nation. Collective histories are suggestively and emotively revised to foster solidarity and a feeling of belonging. The articulation of a culturally distinct Ukrainian nation and national culture, which will be used to justify an independent Ukrainian state in the face of sharp economic decline, amounts to a second social experiment with consequences every bit as great as those which followed in 1917.

Part One

The Legacy
of Soviet Culture

1

Nationality in Soviet and Post-Soviet Ukraine

The mayhem and confusion that color life in post-Soviet society and animate the ethnographic context of this book are perhaps best illustrated by a personal narrative. While doing fieldwork in Ukraine from 1992 to 1994 I frequently traveled by train alone. I was constantly warned by friends and recent acquaintances alike never to say that I was American. In today's strained economic climate, the word "American" means only one thing: dollars. With no consumer banking system to speak of, travelers in Ukraine carry cash. As basic items of clothing have become either unobtainable or unaffordable, theft has become a significant problem on the trains. Some cars have two beds to a compartment, others have four, and still others, called "cattle cars," are completely open barracks-style. My friends convinced me that I had to travel incognito. By publicly acknowledging that I was American, I was told, I would conjure up the ascribed status of Americans as wealthy and make myself vulnerable to unnecessary risks by alerting everyone in the car, if not beyond, that before them was a passenger with imported clothes, an American passport, and dollars.

The whole issue of assuming another identity to hide my nationality arose because it is inconceivable that a passenger could sit in silence over the course of an overnight train ride. It is not only custom to chat with others in your compartment, but to share your picnic dinner in a communal meal as well. Inevitably, someone produces a bottle and the drinking and banter begin. The need to talk, to exchange, to trust, is particularly acute during a period of such unbridled confusion and dislocation.

Of course, I have somewhat of an accent when I speak Ukrainian and Russian which limits where I can say that I am from. A good friend suggested that I say that I am from the Baltics and specifically from Lithuania. Like all Lithuanians of my generation, I studied Russian from age eleven up through college. My hair and skin are fair enough to pass for a Lithuanian. I figured that I could probably pull the charade off, but still I had deep reservations about concocting a bogus biography.

I said to my friend, "But what if they begin to ask me questions about what life is like now in Lithuania? What can I say? I only know what I've read in the newspapers and they know that too and even more."

"Haven't you learned yet? The answer to that question is always the same: things are bad, bad, bad," she retorted.

"I know they'll ask me about inflation, about the price of eggs, a kilo of butter, or a liter of milk. I can't even keep up with the prices here in Kyiv. What should I say about the prices in Vilnius?"

"Very simple," she said. "You just tell them that you're fed up, that you can't bear going into stores any longer. Your husband does all the shopping. You no longer have any idea how much things cost. All you know is that it is all frightfully expensive." A woman proclaiming this kind of exhausted resignation and cowering at the prospect of shopping was entirely believable. For every objection, she had an answer. "You have to lie," she said flatly. "It's for your own good."

And so my fictitious biography was launched on a train to Kharkiv one night. My standard story became that I was a Lithuanian ethnographer from Vilnius traveling to see my mother's sister in whichever Ukrainian city I was bound for.

But my cover was nearly blown one night in March 1993 on a train traveling from Moscow to Kyiv. During the week I was in Moscow, an official border and border check on the train had been established. The train would be held up at the new border an extra three hours so that Russian and Ukrainian customs officials could check the train. Of course, we only learned this once the train stopped in the middle of nowhere en route. It was entirely irrelevant that an unannounced three-hour delay might inconvenience some of the passengers. Abrasive intrusions into everyday life in post-Soviet society were so frequent that they had ceased to be remarkable. One was forced to wonder whether a "transition" was occurring at all or if these eruptions were provoked by individuals and states waging random, frenetic, and sometimes incompatible struggles to survive.

Upon hearing the news of a border check, I began to squirm in my seat. Noting the anxious expression on my face, one of the men in my compartment tried to reassure me by saying that I had nothing to worry about. The border guards were really only interested in two things: illegal trafficking of goods and foreigners. To the three middle-aged men with whom I was traveling, a Lithuanian was clearly not a foreigner.

The trafficking of goods was another issue entirely. In nearly every compartment someone was transporting goods produced at some state-subsidized factory to be sold elsewhere, preferably beyond the borders of the former Soviet Union, for a profit that could be turned into hard currency. Previously, I had traveled with men transporting tires, crates of drinking glasses, boxes as tall as myself of Marlboro cigarettes, and suitcases full of Bulgarian-made men's shirts. The endless stream of individual entrepreneurs clogging train lines with their wares was enough to suggest that the haphazard collection of goods offered for sale at the sprawling flea markets that sprang to life in cities and towns across Ukraine existed solely because a small army of individuals had managed to obtain goods, import them by hand, and haul them to market for sale. If nothing else, the sheer tenacity, dogged determinism, and monumental effort involved—fitting of a people who eat ice cream on the street in subzero temperatures—promised that this nascent form of capitalism was unlikely to die. (What it will grow into is another question entirely.)

In spite of considerable experience on trains, I had to concede that this trip with "speculators," as such traders are called, had plummeted to new depths. Much to my horror, the men two compartments down were transporting gasoline. Beyond the fear of train wrecks, nearly every adult is a heavy smoker, and I could imagine someone, after a few drinks, dropping a not entirely extinguished cigarette on one of the canisters and POOF! We'd be finished. The conductor, who did nothing to stop them from loading their aromatic tanks into the compartment, in spite of shrieking passenger complaints, had obviously been paid off.

In addition to the duty taxes that these traders should have paid for transporting their wares (which were no doubt illegally obtained) across state lines, the border guards were interested in foreigners because selling visas is an expedient way to earn much-needed hard currency for the state. When I heard this my heart sank. I thought for sure when the guards came round and we all had to surrender our passports, not only would I be shown up for the impostor that I was (and I still had five hours of travel together with these men), but I was likely to incur great "unpleasantness" (*nepryiemnisti*), a vast understatement for the difficulties one is inevitably subjected to by the authorities for not having one's papers in order. Having (unknowingly) crossed a border, I was required to have Ukrainian and Russian entrance and exit visas, and I did not have the Russian ones.

Several months before, I had heard rumors that a border check would soon be instituted, but as usual, no one knew exactly when. The dilemma became whether to chance it and hope that I would cross the border before it was created or to perform miraculous contortions and actually get a visa to be on the safe side. Having learned that one must expect the unexpected, I made earnest efforts in Kyiv before I departed for Moscow to get a Russian visa. As was recommended, I arrived on foot at the Russian consulate at 4:30 A.M. while it was still dark (public transportation begins working only at 5 A.M.) one early March morning to become number 22 on the list, which a Sri Lankan was keeping, of applicants for Russian visas. The list determined the order in which we would be admitted to the Russian consulate, and this man, having arrived first at some unimaginable hour, had taken it upon himself to secure his place on line by regulating everyone else's. After hearing from a Bolivian studying film in Kyiv that they usually take only ten to twelve people before closing at noon, I knew that my chances for getting in were slim.

I tried to confirm this with the head guard, a young man lording over the entrance in army fatigues. Astonished to hear that I was from the United States, he dismissed my question and insisted that Americans never wait in line. (Indeed, virtually all applicants were from the so-called Third World.) Eight months earlier the guard had been in Baltimore visiting a childhood friend who had emigrated. He spoke of cruising the strips of shopping malls and fast-food joints with his friend in a big car. Filled with nostalgia for the "terrible freedom" he found in Baltimore, he waved his hand in a gesture of certainty and said, "Don't worry. I'll get you in."

Getting a visa is not as simple as filling out a few forms and paying the fee. One needs to have an invitation from an approved institution, which takes quite a lot of running around for someone in Russia to procure, before one can even apply for a visa. A childhood friend of my husband's was now working in Moscow for the Swiss bank Crédit Suisse, and he had obtained an invitation for me which I was to use to get a Russian visa. Technically, the Central Bank of Russia was inviting me to Moscow on official banking business on behalf of Crédit Suisse. There was an invitation in the consulate replete with the appropriate signatures and stamps to prove it. It was all fiction, of course, but this was the best means I could contrive to get into Russia legally.

My back-up plan was an offer from a friend who lives in Russia just east of the Ukrainian city of Kharkiv. Her husband is the director of a hospital not far from the Russian-Ukrainian border. She suggested that if I could get to Kharkiv, she could send someone to pick me up there in the ambulance. As we approached the border, she explained, the driver would let the sirens and lights fly. "They won't be so stupid as to check the documents of someone who's dying," she assured me. When it came down to deciding how best to get into Russia legally, my choices amounted to leaving Kyiv as a banker on business to Moscow or leaving Kharkiv in an ambulance surrounded by medics as a dying woman. I obviously opted for the first.

As the sun began to rise, the Russian consulate seemed strangely modest and unassuming in the early morning cold. Located in the back half of a large, white building that houses part of the Communist Party archives, the consulate looks out onto a narrow alley and is marked only by a small black panel and the almost invisible typed instructions taped to the inside window on how to apply for a visa. Guards are posted to keep the back entrance and alley clear of foreigners for the rare car trying to get through. With nothing else to do but wait, the guards busied themselves by forcing the foreigners to stand on the far side of the alley. Yet this early in the morning, the traffic on the snow-covered streets was so minimal that the crowd inevitably disobeyed, wandered off the sidewalk, and dispersed into small circles speaking a cacophony of languages and cursing the enduring idiocy of Soviet-style bureaucracy, which continues to hinder and complicate basic living.

At nine o'clock my newfound connection, who promised to catapult me to the head of the line to honor his nostalgia for the lovely city of Baltimore, disappeared into the consulate. When he returned to face the ever-growing crowd of visa-seekers, he announced that it had yet to be decided whether the consulate would open its doors at all. "Today is a holiday. And a holiday is a holiday," he nonchalantly explained with a bureaucratic indifference to which nearly all residents of the former Soviet Union had grown hardened.

What holiday? No one had heard of any holiday. There had been no posting. The guards and consulate staff themselves had only found out five minutes earlier that today was a holiday. They had all dutifully reported for work. Everyone stared in disbelief, especially the African students, expensive plane tickets in hand, who absolutely needed a Russian transit visa to be able to fly out of the Moscow airport.

"Today is Russian Independence Day," the guard explained.[1] Russia celebrating independence from the Soviet Union?!? It was absurd. Even after waiting five hours in the early morning cold, a smile cracked across my frozen face at the surreal nature of my predicament. My plan to dutifully obtain proper documentation by concocting a fiction replete with official stamps to legally cross a previously nonexistent border had been foiled by a spontaneous celebration of a state's withdrawal from the very empire it created.

The crowd grew agitated and annoyed over the arrogant indifference and disrespect exhibited by the consulate staff's decision to shut down essential services without warning. The foreign students began shouting and cursing and even threatened to smash the windows and storm the building if necessary. To quell the growing furor, the consulate staff agreed to process a few of the most urgent applications. The head guard, true to his word, tried to add mine to the handful to be considered that day; however, the consulate staff informed him that there was no invitation for me. Case closed. This bald denial of a file that I knew existed dismissed even the dimmest of hopes for getting a visa. I decided to travel to Russia anyway. The train ticket, which a friend had obtained for me the day before, was for that evening. I couldn't forgo the ticket. It had been too hard to get.

This is how, sitting on a train from Moscow to Kyiv in the early hours of the morning, I came to be not only a liar, but a liar whose papers were not in order. As expected, it was only a matter of time until the border guards thrust open the door to our compartment and barked, "Any foreigners here?" I held my breath.

"We're all Ukrainians!" one of the men shot back.

The guards surveyed the three men in gray suits, all over fifty, and a lone woman drinking tea. Without a word, they slammed the door and proceeded to the next compartment.

The older man leaned over to me and said sheepishly, "I decided that you're one of us" (Rus., *Ia reshil chto vy nasha*). I smiled back.

"Of course, you're one of us," the others agreed in unison, evoking the familiar term *nash*, literally translated as "ours," to designate a certain collective created by the Soviet state. Of course. A woman who admitted to them that she is so strung out that she can no longer cope with the not-so-basic task of buying bread: that's a woman whose psyche has been mangled by the Soviet system. Of course, she's *nasha*.

Cultural and linguistic diversity aside, citizens of the Soviet Union considered—and in this instance even years after the crumbling of the state still consider—each other "ours." The sense of solidarity encapsulated in the expression *nash* or "ours" is contingent upon a shared experience with an oppressive state apparatus. This common experience remains, as unsavory as it is to most, decidedly Soviet. "We" bond together against "them," the enemy, the state. The unspoken agreement to mount a low-level assault on the efficient functioning of the state and state institutions has created a cultural commonality and solidarity, a sense of "us," among vastly different peoples. These bonds are capable of superseding allegiances to ascribed national designations. This is why the men were willing to help mask the nationality I had devised to mask my true nationality. They were honoring the old social contract that held that all citizens should band together to stymie the state.

Feeling that the explosive situation had only been momentarily diffused, I still could not relax. As luck would have it, the Russian border guards never showed up. In the end, I was spared further scrutiny when they discovered the gasoline, and two Vietnamese and a Bengali without visas, who patently could not be passed off as "ours."

The fall of the iron curtain and the emergence of new borders, and the army of border guards ordered to block their unauthorized transgression, have altered the meaning and implications of previous forms of state-ascribed identity. Because of the *suspected* implications of nationality, an American looking to avoid problems poses as a Lithuanian and the Ukrainian passengers, refusing to recognize her foreignness because they believed her to be a former Soviet citizen, try to spare her scrutiny by the Ukrainian border guards by claiming that she is Ukrainian. The topsy-turvy play of deceptions upon deceptions illustrated in this train episode colored the atmosphere following the fall of the Soviet system. In a society tumbling into chaos, confusion lends itself to the unbridled twisting and manipulating of situations—especially those that involve encounters with the state. Cavalier indifference and disdainful sabotage mark popular attitudes toward the state as much as they characterize government policies toward its citizenry, with the distinction between the Soviet and post-Soviet states only faintly shining through. Like a bickering couple, they somehow manage to live together without killing each other. But this tension between the state and its citizenry, which manifests itself in their duplicitous relationship, gives birth to unforeseen paradoxes, ironies, and absurdities as each pushes and pulls to affect change to their advantage.

During a period of shifting state borders, nationality becomes an infinitely malleable designation. It can be strategically deployed by capitalizing on collectively ascribed notions of status and rights created either in the new sphere of the nation-state or in the old and familiar "imagined community" of Soviet citizens. The overarching question this book seeks to address is: Given the hybrid and highly crosscutting forms of identity created by the Soviet regime, how does a new and beleaguered state forge a sense of nationality in keeping with new political realities when its citizens have been long accustomed to thinking of themselves as citizens of socialist superpower extending across eleven time zones? To begin to answer such a question, we must look at how the Soviet system created a sense of nationality and imbued it with meaning, for this is the legacy that each of the fifteen successor states, Ukraine included, has inherited.

The Fifth Point: Nationality in the USSR

When contrasted with the Western experience of nation and state building, the specifics of the Soviet system become readily apparent (see Borneman 1992). In the West, the processes of state formation and nation-building have evolved in tandem to such an extent that the terms "nation" and "state" are often used interchangeably. Indeed, the term "nationality" in the West is frequently used to connote a person's citizenship. "Ethnicity," in the language of Western social scientists, often connotes a minority, "not yet assimilated" status to members of a cultural group in relation to a particular state, its national culture, and official language.

These terms were used quite differently in the former Soviet Union. Although Brezhnev's regime began to refer to the *sovetskii narod*,[2] or Soviet people, as a supranational "new historical community" that had emerged as a result of socialism, Soviet discourse never directly evoked a Soviet nation.[3] Rather, the Soviet administration used the Russian term *grazhdanstvo* to refer exclusively to citizenship, to a relationship to the Soviet state, which did not necessarily carry connotations of shared cultural or linguistic identity. In contrast, the term *natsional'nost'*, which is frequently translated into English as "nationality," was primarily reflective of an individual's ancestry and determined independently of an individual's citizenship and residence in a particular sub-state political entity (republic, autonomous republic, etc.).

In the Soviet Union, an individual was tagged with citizenship and nationality, meaning that he or she was at once, for example, Soviet and Ukrainian or Soviet and Lithuanian—hence the connection my fellow travelers felt with me. We supposedly shared an identity and an experience in common although we lived in vastly different cultural traditions. In other words, the Soviet state distinguished itself from other ethnically mixed states by institutionalizing multinationality through the codification of nationhood and nationality as social categories separate and distinct from statehood and citizenship. Nationality was institutionalized exclusively on a sub-state, rather than a state-wide level (Brubaker 1994: 50). The contradiction involved in recognizing national differences with sub-state political structures and nationally based social institutions—a policy Slezkine (1994) characterizes as "ethnophilia"—while forging a supranational integrationist nation with a superseding political apparatus was highly problematic. Simply translating *natsional'nost'* as "nationality" glosses over the multiple nuances, fluidity, and implications of nationality that are understood by every Soviet citizen (Shanin 1989: 410). In order to highlight the tension and contradiction within the Soviet system—which would have been greatly diminished if the different peoples of the Soviet Union had seen themselves as ethnicities or subgroups—I have chosen to use the term "nationality," rather than "ethnicity," to refer to the different cultural groups, such as Ukrainians, Russians, and Jews, within Ukraine.

I define nationality as the link between an individual and a particular state based on that individual's membership in a nation.[4] This link takes the form of a politicized social identity. When a national culture is internalized and made a meaningful element of the social person, it can potentially inform nationality in a powerful way and prompt a feeling of belonging to a particular place as delineated by boundaries of some kind.

As a multinational state, the Soviet Union was forced early on to grapple with the sticky issue of cultural politics. This prompted an articulation of what constitutes nationality and what it means.[5] As early as December 1926 the first Union-wide census was undertaken. Given the culturally diverse nature of the newly created country, such a census was of critical importance (see Anderson 1991: 163–70). The fourth question inquired as to the respondent's nationality. The instructions to polltakers clearly articulate how Bolshevik leaders understood nationality to be constituted and begin to explain why nationality over time grew to have such elastic meaning:

> *In case that the respondent should find it difficult to answer this question, greater weight should be attached to the mother's nationality.* Considering that the census aims at determining the ethnic (ethnographic) composition of the population, one should not substitute for nationality religion, citizenship or the fact that the respondent resides in the territory of some Republic.[6]

This suggests a conception of nationality based purely on ethnic origin or ancestry, and not on residence. However, additional instructions to the same question on nationality quickly add:

> The answer to the question about nationality need not be the same as the answer to question number five about native language . . . *the determination of one's nationality has been left up to the respondent himself/herself* and one should not change the statements of the respondent during the interview. Persons who have lost ties with the nationality of their ancestors may indicate the nationality which they consider themselves to be members of.[7]

This tells the interviewer that a person's nationality is a matter of opinion, a subjective allegiance, and that no verifying criteria are necessary other than a stated belief.[8] This contradictory understanding of nationality as something inherited/inalienable and elected/experienced existed throughout the Soviet period and contributed to the weakened and fluid nature of the concept within Soviet politics.

The results of this census, with its two categories of nationality and language, revealed the extent of "denationalization" among certain nationalities. Ukraine had one of the highest levels of non-Russian Russian speakers, or russified Ukrainians, living within its borders. Of course, this reflected a pattern set in place long ago. For centuries Ukrainian gentry assimilated to the culture of the ruling class, be it Russian in the east or Polish in the west, leaving the Ukrainian language and culture closely associated with the peasantry. Even though the Soviet Union was never organized as a Russian nation-state per se, Russians were the dominant nationality. They controlled the key Party and state positions in the government. Russian was the lingua franca of the state, the media, education, and printing, and this created formidable pressures to assimilate to the Russian language. Ukrainian, a Slavic language far closer to Russian than the Turkic, Baltic, or Finno-Ugric languages spoken elsewhere in the Soviet Union, was particularly targeted for and vulnerable to assimilation.

National designation was commonly referred to as the "fifth point" and appeared on virtually all Soviet documents. It was a key category of bureaucratic statistics used to inform social and political policy. Nationality was an ascriptive legal category, chosen at age sixteen from one of the parents' nationalities. Each national identity could have important implications, affecting one's life course in terms of access to higher education or employment opportunities. For some, nationality over time reflected little more than ancestry. The practice of assuming the nationality of one's ancestors regardless of experiential, cultural, linguistic, or residential considerations, linked the concept of nationality to blood, casting it with an aura of perpetual, ahistorical eternity. For this reason, one could find people in the Soviet Ukraine of various nationalities (Armenian, Hungarian, Belorussian, etc.) who did not speak their national languages and had never lived in the respective republics or countries. Even more commonplace are people of Ukrainian nationality who speak no Ukrainian (although they have a passive understanding) and have minimal knowledge of Ukrainian history and cultural traditions. Yet they consider themselves Ukrainian.

Paradoxically, alongside this view of nationality as ancestral, inherited, and eternal was the practice of electing one's nationality. It was not uncommon in the Soviet Union for members of the same family to have different nationalities. There was clearly an ethnic hierarchy of nationalities under Soviet rule and this accounts for some of the intrafamilial variation. Russian nationality was the first among equals and the nationality that carried the greatest benefits in terms of social mobility. Ukrainian and Belorussian nationalities were close seconds, considered harmless and almost as good as Russian.

In some instances, intrafamilial variation of nationality was due to sharp stigmatization of some nationalities. Jews, Gypsies, and Chechens, to name only a few of the most discussed examples, were frequently discriminated against in education and career opportunities, often in spite of extensive linguistic assimilation to Russian and, depending on the region, high rates of intermarriage with other nationalities. Most notably, children of Jewish or mixed Jewish parentage did their utmost to hide their Jewish origins by taking the nationality and the last name of the non-Jewish parent. An identifiably Jewish name is an invitation to "unpleasantness," meaning overt discrimination. Of course, this dynamic was in part reversed beginning in the early 1970s when it became possible to emigrate "as a Jew." Suddenly being Jewish carried enormous possibilities, and many people made elaborate efforts to document their Jewishness. If no one in the family was actually Jewish, through bribes and "canals," or connections, archival documentation of one's Jewish ancestry could often be manufactured.

According to the 1989 census, approximately 73 percent of the 52 million residents of Ukraine are Ukrainian, 22 percent are Russian, and 5 percent are of various nationalities, with no single group constituting more than one percent of the population.[9] Looking at the situation strictly in terms of official "nationality" designation, which is what many social scientists have done, obscures more than it reveals. The inherited legacy of using blood ancestry and language as distinguishing factors to determine who belongs to which nationality are problematic guidelines because rates of intermarriage between Russians and Ukrainians are high and the percentage of non-Russians who speak Russian as a first language is very significant as well. These factors are particularly prominent in Belarus and Latvia, too. The Soviet practice of privileging blood ancestry in bureaucratic national designation over actual cultural practices, in keeping with the policy of "national in form, socialist in content," served to undermine the experiential meaning of nationality. An exclusive look at nationality in terms of national designation does not in any way portray the very intricate, contradictory, and multiplex nature of national consciousness, nor does it offer reliable guidelines to political allegiances among Ukrainians, both under Soviet rule and continuing today in post-Soviet society.

This spliced sense of nationality, at once something inherited/eternal and chosen/malleable, has created a powerful legacy. Paradoxically, the arbitrary selection of nationality, especially when it fell into one of the extreme categories (highly stigmatized or not politicized) often weakened the emotional meaning of nationality in favor of a sovietized and/or localized identity. Every Soviet citizen was—and as of this writing every Ukrainian citizen still is—required to have a *propiska*, or resident's permit stating exactly in which apartment an individual lives. This bifurcating macro-micro orientation, at once to a vast empire where a far-off city named Moscow was omnipresent and to a cramped apartment where one was pinned down (often for life), was a tension that was never mediated. These are contributing factors which explain why people of all ages living across Ukraine, save in a few provinces in western Ukraine, in the early years of independence, claimed that their nationality had "no meaning" for them and never did. And yet, although gutted of meaning, nationality was an ascriptive and descriptive self-attribute of which every individual was powerfully aware. The irony is that although many were cognizant of their own national origins, it wasn't until the late 1980s that individuals began to inquire about the ancestry of their spouses, friends, and neighbors.

The Ethno-Political Structure of the Soviet State

The reasons why the Soviet Union broke down along national lines are multiplex. I will focus on what I consider the three most significant historical factors: Marxist philosophy, imperial nationality policy, and the ethno-political structuring of the Soviet state. Following Marx, Bolshevik leaders assumed cultural differences to be an epiphenomenon of economic conditions and assumed such differences would wither as modernization would shape the living conditions for workers in similar ways.[10]

The ramifications of the Marxist underestimation of the importance of nationality as a basis for social identity were compounded by the legacy of tsarist nationality policy. In the nineteenth century, the principle of the unity of autocracy-orthodoxy-nationality informed the political and social policies of Imperial Russia and legitimated the tsar's dynastic rule. Religious affiliation was the primary informant of identity in Imperial Russia. For monarchists and Slavophiles, Ukrainians (Little Russians) and Belarussians (White Russians) were the same *narodnost* (nationality) as

Great Russians, owing to their shared Orthodox faith and the prevalence of Russian-speakers among their elites.

Finally, the ethno-political structuring of the Soviet state was based on the premise that by developing national cultures (*nasazhdat' natsional-nuiu kul'turu*) the various peoples of the Soviet Union would meld together more quickly into a universal culture (*obshchechelovecheskaia kul'tura*) by accepting the Revolution and communism sooner (Slezkine 1994). To generate goodwill toward the Soviet Union, which was urgently needed among some groups, Ukrainians included, after the oppressive experience of imperial rule, Lenin advocated the creation of national autonomies, complete with national languages, schools, cultural institutions, and cadres. This 1920s policy of national development and national self-determination was called *korenizatsiia*, literally meaning "taking root" or indigenization. The republican institutions, run by elites defined as "national," functioned to perpetuate regional cultural practices and, paradoxically, a non-Soviet source of identity (Verdery 1996: 86–87; Brubaker 1994: 50; Motyl 1990). Academies, cultural institutions, and artistic unions, to name a few examples, were all organized on a republican level in supposed recognition of national cultures. "Native language education" became the cornerstone of the Bolsheviks' nationality policy. Language, they reasoned, was the soul of a people, and protection for minority cultures began with institutionalizing national languages. Public life was organized socially and politically to preserve ethnic heterogeneity, which helped produce an intelligentsia who saw themselves as national, as the protectors of a national culture.

While the Soviet state did indeed recognize and institutionalize national cultures, this is not purely attributable to Bolshevik initiative. In some regions of the Russian empire, such as Ukraine, a form of nationalism inspired by Herder had already taken root in the nineteenth century among the cultural elite. When Ukraine became part of the Soviet Union in 1922, Ukrainians were extremely vocal in their insistence upon recognition as a distinct nationality after decades of culturally oppressive imperial policies. Concessions to protect national cultures was in part a response to local demands for some form of assurance that oppressive tsarist cultural policies would not be replicated by the new Soviet state. Aware of the threats that national unrest posed, the imperial policy of a "Russian" state was indirectly perpetuated under a different name with another justification during Soviet rule. The Soviet leadership thought it was possible to contain nationalist sentiment in nonpolitical spheres by offering cultural autonomy to republican elites, while shoring up political power in a Russian-dominated, highly centralized, federated government. The simultaneous celebration of multinationality and the unrelenting efforts at sovietization, which mobilized aspects of Russian culture, continued on a collision course for the next seven decades.

In recognition of the agricultural, mineral, and industrial wealth of Ukraine, the process of russification operated with exceptional efficiency during the Soviet period, most notably under Stalin. As a result, an informal category of national designation emerged in Ukraine. Today many eastern and southern Ukrainians have become "russified Ukrainians." This term, which is commonly in use in Ukraine, refers to people who consider themselves Ukrainian, yet speak cither Russian or *surzhyk*, a dialect blending Russian and Ukrainian, as their first language and have varying degrees of proficiency (at least passive understanding) in Ukrainian. Even though the term is loosely applied in scholarly and journalistic writings, there is no accurate way to indicate who is "russified" or to what degree they are "russified." Many Russian-speaking Ukrainians also speak Ukrainian, and depending on the context, are quite willing to do so. Many are the children of mixed marriages. Motyl (1993: 80) estimates that no less than one-third of Ukrainians are russified. Arel (1995a: 161–67) presents survey data showing that in eastern Ukraine 72 percent of ethnic Ukrainians claim Russian as their "language of preference" and politically favor a positive "orientation" toward Russia as demonstrated in voting patterns. Szporluk (1975: 212) goes so far as to speak of two Ukraines, one russified and the other essentially Ukrainian.[11]

"Russified Ukrainian" contrasts with the formal national designations "Russian" and "Ukrainian." Russian nationality refers to individuals whose Soviet passport designation was Russian and who speak Russian as a first language. Many have some competence in Ukrainian too, and they are all considered Ukrainian citizens because they reside in Ukraine. When I refer to Ukrainians, I mean people of Ukrainian origin who speak Ukrainian as their primary language. Virtually all Ukrainians are perfectly fluent in Russian. Although there was only one national designation on Soviet passports, and even people who are bilingual have a primary language, the cultural and linguistic proximity between Ukrainians and Russians nonetheless means that many people have cultural and linguistic fluency in both spheres. This, compounded by the hybrid third category of "russified Ukrainian," truly blurs distinctions between Russians and Ukrainians in Ukraine and indirectly gives currency to a sense of self as Soviet.

Narratives of Soviet Nostalgia[12]

National identification is so contingent on the consolidation of a collective self, a process in flux in Ukraine today, that the arbitrariness of national categories is heightened. The confusion over reorienting oneself to another cultural (non-Soviet) identity is compounded by overall social and economic chaos and the subtleties of identity choice. Changing a sense of self and redefining one's relationship to the greater society calls for formidable imagination. As we will see, individual and state-driven efforts to align a sense of nationality based on citizenship with a newly redefined cultural base are often at odds. Political borders were quickly redrawn following the fall of the Soviet Union, but the historical legacy of the Soviet system and the identity-forming cultural practices, values, and orientations it created are not so easily dispelled.

For a variety of reasons, several of which will be explored below, nostalgia persists for a bygone way of life, even one that was almost universally lambasted as unacceptably bad. In spite of unrelenting criticism, attachments in the form of identities, practices, and values developed over time to the Soviet system and to the Soviet Union itself, and for some they tenaciously endure. In the narratives that follow, we will see four commonly cited reasons that complicate individual efforts to reorient to new political realities. Attachments based on cultural (broadly stated), familial, professional, and ideological grounds constitute residual aspects of Soviet culture that are difficult to shed and continue to inform a sense of nationality.

Sofiia Mikhailovna, a Russian literature teacher in Kyiv, who teaches at a Russian language school, said, "I have Armenian and Jewish roots from my father's side. My mother is Ukrainian. And that makes me Russian, as the saying goes." Conventional wisdom had it that when ancestral mixing was too extensive, the nationality a person chose was usually Russian. When Ukraine became independent in 1991, there were two Ukrainian language schools out of twenty-five in Sofiia Mikhailovna's district in Kyiv. One year after independence, only two were slated to retain Russian as the language of instruction; the rest were to switch to teaching in Ukrainian. Sofiia Mikhailovna is afraid that she will be unemployed soon. Russian teachers who refuse to pursue "higher qualifications," or retraining, which includes learning Ukrainian, and in her case, supplementary training in Ukrainian literature, will be dismissed, she fears. Sofiia Mikhailovna knows Ukrainian passively but doesn't want to teach Ukrainian literature in Ukrainian. "Russian is what is close to me," she explains. "I will resist to the end. I live alone with a child. I have to feed the child. If it comes down to it, I'll teach Ukrainian literature. But I will resist to the end. I don't know how you can compare the richness of Russian literature with Ukrainian literature. Which Ukrainian authors do you have? Shevchenko, Lesia Ukrainka, and Franko. Only Shevchenko is known abroad." Sofiia Mikhailovna has lived her entire life in Kyiv and now is a Ukrainian citizen. But culturally she is Russian, and this impairs her willingness to alter her professional life in response to new political borders and the ensuing shifts in cultural and educational policy based on a doctrine of the nation-state. Sofiia Mikhailovna resents the reality of her cultural status reversal and yet recognizes that changes are imminent and irreversible.

A colleague of hers, who is Ukrainian, also has difficulty reorienting himself, but for different reasons. His cultural allegiance to Russia is based on familial ties and his experiences in the Soviet army. Ivan Nikolaevich, a retired army officer, teaches "War Preparation," a mandatory class for boys in the tenth grade. His job is to prepare young men for their impending two-year military service by teaching them such basics as gun maintenance, how to use hand grenades, and the skills of marching and saluting. (Girls in a parallel class learn about first aid.) Unable to live on his pension, he began, as many retired officers do, to teach military conduct in school. Speaking in 1993, four years after the Berlin Wall came down, he said, "Most officers don't agree with the break-up of the army. Our responsibility begins in Germany and ends in the Far East. We don't care what a person's nationality is. The whole idea is strange to us." With a sigh he adds, "I can tell you one thing: the ukrainianization of the army won't be happening anytime soon [Rus., *ochen' ne skoro budet*]."

He is Ukrainian, but his wife is from Russia. His two sons, born and raised in Kyiv, went to Russian schools where they studied Ukrainian as a second language. His only sister, as well as his wife's entire family, live in Russia. With the cost of train tickets spiraling, a dysfunctional postal system, and rising telephone rates to the "near abroad," maintaining contact with family members is strained to levels that were previously un-

Celebration of the demise of the Soviet Union and the socialist system it supported
varies by generation. For these retired women living in a rural area to the north of Kyiv,
there is little to gain from the massive political and economic changes. When this photo
was taken in 1993, their monthly pensions were not even sufficient to purchase a loaf of
bread a day.

imaginable. New borders between former republics amount to another
iron curtain. Only this time, rather than separating them from the "bourgeois capitalist enemy," it separates them from their children, from their
brothers and sisters. "They split up but they can't split us up," he insists.
"I wouldn't split us up. I would keep Russia and Ukraine together. Belarus doesn't have as much meaning, because there aren't as close family
ties as with Russia. I think they should split economic links only, not
political ones." This is a common wish: independence from the Soviet
system and its faltering economy but not independence from Russia.[13]

In other words, although there is widespread agreement that the society was in dire need of massive political and economic reform, the cultural changes accompanying such reform are embraced, if at all, far more
slowly. Vera Ignat'evna, a Russian-speaking Ukrainian and sociologist
working at the sociological research laboratory at Kharkiv University,

likewise laments the separation from Russia (and ignores the loss of the other Soviet republics) for professional reasons. In terms of intellectual activity and research opportunities, she says Kharkiv was the third most important city in the Soviet Union after Moscow and Leningrad. She claims her university was probably the best in the Soviet Union for sociological research. Of course, political restructuring and economic collapse since the break-up of the Soviet Union have halted collaboration with her Russian colleagues and canceled projects that were slated to be carried out beyond Ukrainian borders. Now she is afraid that Kharkiv will become a provincial city and that her institute will be relegated to the task of furnishing statistics for Kyiv's bureaucrats.

In an attempt to try to redeem the Soviet system, she said, "It's true that we weren't able to travel abroad but we could go to the Baltics and that was like visiting Europe. Central Asia was certainly very exotic for us. We could visit the Far East where the climate, the landscape, and the way of life were very different. Even though we couldn't travel abroad, this was such a huge country that we still, in a way, could visit the whole world. Now where can I go?" Indeed, she spends virtually every weekend and the entire summer farming at her dacha, trying to keep food on the table through the long winter. Rather than seeing improvement in her life after the fall of the Soviet system, she sees her personal and professional life slipping. Nostalgia colors her memories of life under the Soviet system, favoring those elements which are sorely lacking today. Although virtually no one seriously advocates resurrecting the Soviet Union, Vera Ignat'evna included, this nostalgic longing becomes an influential factor in shaping the process of rethinking post-Soviet identities.

A vice principal of a Russian language school in Luhansk also has a rather positive assessment of the Soviet system—at least in hindsight. Political change has discredited much of what she believed in and worked toward. Although she says she is a committed communist and atheist, she speaks of Gorbachev in biblical terms: "He is for us Judas the betrayer. He destroyed this great land of ours and we will never forgive him." She laments, "I was born and raised in the Soviet Union. I am Russian. I have lived in Lugansk [this is the Russian name for the city] for decades and this is my home but I don't want to live in Ukraine!" The irony is that she came to Luhansk from Russia over thirty years ago when she married and has no desire to leave. She is a citizen of a slain system and longs to live in a country that no longer exists. The territorialized part of her sense of self has come undone following the break-up of the Soviet Union.

Luhansk is her home and yet she is not Ukrainian, although she is a Ukrainian citizen.

The intermingling of cultures and weak reliance on nationality as a means of self-identification is particularly common in eastern Ukraine where in and out migration to Russia and intermarriage with Russians are common practice. Familial, professional, and ideological investments in a system and the culture it supported are not easily relinquished. The cultural identity of many Ukrainians today is multidimensional as a result of the highly cross-cutting attachments a Russian-based Soviet culture bred. This, combined with the fluid and bureaucratic, nonexperientially based meaning of Soviet passport nationalities, is why some scholars have argued that the post-Soviet nationalizing project in Ukraine is not targeted to assimilating an ethnic minority, but rather a linguistic minority, the Russian-speaking community (Arel 1995a, Motyl 1993).

Given the relatively low level of national consciousness and the rather weak appeal that Ukrainian cultural revival has for large sectors of the Ukrainian population, a critical question then arises: how did Rukh, the umbrella opposition movement advocating a nationalist platform, manage to rapidly marshal support and mount a serious challenge to Soviet authority in the final years of glasnost? We now turn to an examination of how nationalist ideologies arose in the final years of Soviet rule and to an analysis of the cultural elements they incorporated.

The Rise of Nationalist Opposition

When Gorbachev came to power in 1985 following a series of official funerals for preceding general secretaries of the Communist Party, he was greeted as a young and dynamic leader. Brezhnev had ruled for eighteen years, a time that under Gorbachev became known as "the period of stagnation." Brezhnev, in turn, was succeeded by former KGB chief Andropov, who ruled for fifteen months. Andropov's funeral was followed in short order by that of his successor, Chernenko, who held the highest post in the land for a mere thirteen months. Announcements of the leaders' deaths came in the form of uninterrupted radio and TV broadcasts of classical music. Although this gesture was meant as a sign that the entire country was in mourning, it soon became the occasion for black humor.

In spite of the quick turnover in leadership, Soviet nationalities policy in the early 1980s remained steady, focusing primarily on improving and

expanding the teaching of Russian in schools and universities in the republics. This was particularly so in Ukraine, where various decrees celebrated "internationalist" values as the police apparatus rooted out
"bourgeois nationalism" and "hostile foreign influences," Soviet labels
for national and religious sentiments and activities (Nahaylo and Swoboda 1989: 225). Over the nearly fifty years of Soviet rule in western
Ukraine, a region annexed during World War II, nationalism remained a
potent force, where it overlapped with strong influences from Poland,
including the Solidarity movement.

In addition to pockets of nationalist and religious-based dissent in
western Ukraine throughout Ukraine there was growing concern over
the mounting casualties from the war in Afghanistan and widespread dis-
satisfaction with the faltering Soviet economy. Although the economy
had grown at an incredible rate of 10 percent during the 1950s and 1960s,
it slowed in the 1980s to 2–3 percent annually. Production peaked in
1989, faltered in 1990, and spiraled downward in 1991. Across republics
the availability of various goods and services became sporadic, especially
after the Eastern European countries abandoned socialism. Virtually all
residents of the former Soviet Union experienced a decline in their
standard of living. Ukraine, however, was hit particularly hard by the
economic slowdown and political changes because of the heavy concentration of inefficient smokestack industries in eastern Ukraine.

Blessed with rich, fertile soil, Ukraine was once called the "breadbasket of Europe." Now it was plagued with incessant food shortages. Industrial production (steel, coal, and iron, in particular) had steadily drawn
workers away from rural collective farms to factories in the cities and
weakened overall agricultural output. The sense of deterioration of agricultural and industrial production was compounded by a popular perception that highly industrialized and agriculturally rich Ukraine was
exporting more to Moscow than it was receiving back. Along with the
Baltic republics, Ukrainian complaints were among the most bitter of the
unequal, even exploitative, exchange with Moscow. To some degree, this
was true. In the final years of Soviet rule, Ukraine produced 23 percent
of all agricultural products with only 19 percent of the Soviet population;
40 percent of Soviet steel; 34 percent of its coal; and 51 percent of its pig
iron (Subtelny 1994: 527–28). Popular perceptions of Ukraine's contribution to the Soviet economy were nonetheless inflated, and this, compounded by the drop in the standard of living, deepened resentment over
the failures of the system and fueled disdain for the Soviet state.

One of the many coal mines in the Luhansk area. Visible in the foreground is a cafeteria for the mine workers. Many of the mines in the Donbas are no longer profitable without generous state subsidies and are currently slated to be shut down.

Gorbachev's response to the growing malaise upon assuming the post of general secretary in March 1985 was to advocate the "restructuring of the economic mechanism," or a policy called perestroika (Ukr. *perebudova*), to reinvigorate the economy. To accelerate "restructuring," Gorbachev also called for glasnost (Ukr. *hlasnist'*), or "openness," as a means to expedite the articulation and implementation of viable solutions to alleviate the multitude of problems plaguing Soviet industrial and agricultural production.

Within the socialist context, it made sense to introduce a policy on public dialogue to implement an economic policy. In contrasting the transformation of consciousness and the process of cultural production in Western and Eastern European societies, Katherine Verdery (1991b) notes that the transformation of consciousness in Western Europe has been influenced more by practice than by discourse precisely because change has evolved gradually over centuries. In contrast, Eastern European societies were subjected to more convulsive political and social change, which mandated rapid transformation and heightened the importance of discourse. She argues, "Eastern European communists came to power with the intention of rapidly revolutionizing consciousness and with precious few means of doing so. Popular resistance to many imposed practices made language the principal arena for achieving this end. The social power deriving from control of the representations of reality became truly vital for rulers who disposed of relatively few means" (1991b: 430). In other words, when socialist leaders sought to induce rapid change that was likely to encounter resistance, they also needed to control discourse in order to suppress dissent and protest that might prevent such change from coming to fruition.

Gorbachev's attempt to actualize a mass reassessment and reorientation to production to spur output entailed imposing changes on popular consciousness and popular practice. To do so, he also turned to discourse as the primary means. By relaxing the rigid censorship on public discourse—and by extension the control of perceptions of reality—he was able to introduce changes in practice. Although perestroika and glasnost were policies approved by the Party and were slated to operate within the confines of socialism, they nonetheless represented a radical break from past responses to accelerate production, which usually incorporated coercion and terror. These novel solutions bespeak the severity of economic decline and the perceived urgency of the need to change labor practices and revive the workers' commitment to and enthusiasm for the system as a panacea to the ills plaguing Soviet production.

Through the written and spoken word, Gorbachev hoped to reinstate the credibility and legitimacy of the Soviet system and trigger new values and patterns of behavior to boost the sagging economy.[1] Slowly the tortured process of de-Stalinization of Soviet society, which began with Khrushchev's thaw more than three decades earlier, resumed and rapidly took on a force all its own. Greater openness in public discourse, which tended to be extremely critical of the Soviet system, created an atmosphere in late-Soviet Ukraine that contributed to the rapid rise of a grassroots movement that chose to challenge the legitimacy of Soviet rule on the basis of a nation's right to self-determination and was buttressed by a reexamination of the Ukrainian historical experience of Soviet rule.

Ultimately, nationalism, while influenced by economic concerns, is most importantly the outgrowth of processes of history. Following Kapferer (1988), I believe that there is not one universal pattern of nationalism. Kapferer argues against Anderson (1991), who presents a theory of the cultural origins of nationalism, by advocating a comparative study of nationalisms arising in different cultural traditions, namely, an egalitarian Australian aboriginal society and a hierarchically based Sri Lankan one. The preexisting cultural base, itself a product of historical forces, has significant influence in shaping the form and type of nationalism that arises in a particular society. As will become apparent, not only did the culture of socialism construct nationality in a unique way, which contributed to the articulation of conflicts in national terms from Czechoslovakia to Siberia, but local cultures shaped the type and intensity of nationalisms that emerged throughout the region. The experience of nationalism in Ukraine differs from that found in other former Soviet republics in several significant ways.

Chernobyl and the Political Fallout

The key factor that subsequently gave the policy of glasnost unusual relevance in Ukraine was the cover-up of the world's worst nuclear disaster, ' 'ch occurred at the V. I. Lenin Chernobyl Nuclear Power Station in Ukraine on April 26, 1986. The authorities' initial denial of the accident, which released more radioactive fallout than the bombing of Hiroshima, and their refusal to divulge information of critical importance to the health of their own citizenry shone a harsh light on the system's penchant for manipulating information to maintain power. A centralized Moscow-based regime was revealed as blatantly self-serving, as displaying total disregard for the well-being of its own people and a supreme commitment to preserving the facade of normalcy in the proletarian paradise over all else. The anger, frustration, and disillusionment triggered by the Chernobyl accident and its cover-up readily found voice in a less censored media and was devoured by a public eager for an honest depiction of its suffering. Ironically, it was an invisible, odorless, yet deadly, radioactive fallout that landed on Ukrainian soil that played a key role in promoting the view of Ukraine as an exploited colony of Moscow.

For those near the reactor at the time of the accident, the event constituted a surreal type of trauma. A sculptor who was in Kyiv at the time said:

My wife was at our dacha to the north of Kyiv. She was out walking our two-year-old daughter when she saw what she thought were soldiers with gas masks doing some kind of maneuver. She had no idea what it was so she kept on walking. When she finally learned by word of mouth what had happened, she was petrified. She went to her relatives' house in the south with the child for a few months to get away from the radiation. But I stayed behind in Kyiv. That year all the trees bloomed early and the whole city became a terrifying beauty [Rus. *strashnaia krasota*]. Lots of people left so there was almost no one around. Only bands of men roaming the streets drunk on free red wine. It was utterly surreal.

As part of the massive efforts to "normalize" the situation, cases of red wine were shipped in to affected areas under the belief that alcohol consumption would slow the absorption of radiation. Residents of northern central Ukraine were instructed to keep the windows closed and to scrub the floors everyday, under the meek illusion that one could somehow wash away the harmful effects of radiation with a bucket and a scrubbrush.

As with all accidents of this magnitude, Chernobyl was an unfortunate compilation of human error, technological malfunction, and plain old bad luck.[2] Almost thirty-five hours after the explosion, the 23,000 citizens of Prypyat, the town where the reactor is located, were told that they would be evacuated for three days (Marples 1988: 29). Ukrainian Communist Party leaders received orders from Moscow that the schools and stores in the region were to remain open. This, along with a media blackout, was implemented in the interests of stemming panic. Most controversial of all, on May 1st, the order was given to carry on with the traditional May Day festivities during which hundreds of children, unaware of the danger, were paraded in front of the Ukrainian SSR Communist Party leadership in downtown Kyiv, only seventy-two miles south of the disabled reactor.

News of the accident reached Kyiv by word of mouth the next day. The rumors were only partially confirmed by the Voice of America, which began broadcasting the few details it had about the accident. With no independent confirmation from officials, it was difficult for many people—including Western reporters—who had heard the rumors of 15,000 immediate victims and fires burning out of control at the reactor to grasp, let alone gauge, the danger, real or imagined, of exposure to radioactive fallout. Under mounting international pressure, Soviet authorities began to acknowledge that the "unthinkable" had occurred. Two weeks after the accident, details of the radioactive fallout were finally released. Eventually, over 500,000 people were evacuated from sixty-five villages, and a

The abandoned town where the Chernobyl nuclear plant is located.

thirty-kilometer area, now commonly referred to as "the zone," was cordoned off as irretrievably contaminated. The legacy of lies, disinformation, and cover-up created by the Soviet regime has left in its wake a readiness to believe the worst about the magnitude of the accident.

Individual responses to the angst created by Chernobyl range from becoming a weekend farmer to be assured of "ecologically clean" fruits and vegetables, to relocating, and even to emigrating. Chernobyl is held responsible for a multitude of illnesses and discomforts, from nosebleeds to cancer, even among those who evacuated for months following the accident or who live a considerable distance from the plant. As the years go by "radiophobia" seems not only to endure but to grow in the minds of Ukrainians. My intention is not to judge whether these widespread worries of health hazards brought on by Chernobyl and popular diagnoses of all types of illness as "radiation sickness" years after the accident are justified or not.[3] I do want, however, to illustrate the pervasive fear and the sincere conviction among the Ukrainian population that the "genetic fund of the nation" has been irreparably damaged because of Chernobyl.

Chernobyl rapidly became a *cause célèbre* for the independence movement. Cries for restitution and compensation for the victims became political ammunition for opposition leaders as they ever more cogently rallied against the Soviet regime before an increasingly receptive audience. Opposition leaders cultivated popular anger by using Chernobyl and the bungled attempt at rescue and evacuation to discredit the Soviet regime. They cited Chernobyl as evidence that Ukrainians would never be entirely safe as a colony of Moscow and that an independent state was needed to protect and to maximize prospects for the well-being of Ukrainians.

Lesia, an artist living in Kyiv, who was pregnant at the time of the accident and who later became an ardent and vocal supporter of Rukh, said, "In a strange way Chernobyl was a good thing for Ukraine. It created a lot of support for independence and for Rukh. It showed the extent to which they will lie, how this system was built upon lies. With Chernobyl we saw the human price that Ukraine has to pay for these lies."

The Chernobyl Gen

Much as Robert Wohl (1979) argued that World War I was a "magnetic field" creating the "Generation of 1914," Chernobyl is the primary orienting experience for a generation who experienced the accident, the terror of contamination, and heightened cynicism toward the Soviet regime. A traumatic historical event can crystallize as a defining experience, dramatically affecting the life history of individuals and fundamentally informing their sense of identity and values. Chernobyl provides a sharp example of how the process of identity formation can first and foremost be shaped by cataclysmic historical circumstances and the disjunctures and interruptions to anticipated life trajectories they produce, rather than by a series of experiences leading to a gradual evolution of identity. Those who have firsthand experience of the Chernobyl nuclear accident have become isolated from those who cannot imagine what they have endured. Women of childbearing age were particularly traumatized by the nuclear accident and plagued with worries about damage to their childbearing abilities or harm to their small children.

As Gorbachev's regime was publicly and internationally shamed for denying and covering up the accident, Gorbachev rebounded by extending glasnost to regain credibility for his regime and the Soviet system. Yet the damage had been done, and glasnost, rather than redeeming the regime, produced only a barrage of angry protest. Chernobyl generated more anti-Soviet, pro-independence sentiment among the Ukrainian population than could ever have been dreamed of by the small group of Ukrainian nationalist intelligentsia struggling to create a ground swell of support for independence. Although there was a growing interest in historical revisionism and national revivals across the Soviet Union, Chernobyl gave such projects extra relevancy and urgency. The fear of retribution for publicly criticizing Soviet policy receded as the outrage over official suppression of the extent of the accident mounted. Members of the intelligentsia, primarily writers with political ambitions, cultivated a sense of victimization and betrayal at the hands of an unjust Moscow-based regime by using Chernobyl to symbolize party incompetence, national suffering, and environmental destruction.[4]

In his book on Chernobyl, Zhores Medvedev writes that "the imagination often plays a more important role in history than simple facts" (1990: ix). Indeed, the historical imagination has proved to be a more durable force than any kind of "fact" when the discussion involves Chernobyl. No matter what teams of experts claim or predict, one of the more powerful legacies of the Chernobyl accident is a pervasive angst which Ukrainians call "radiophobia."

Sally F. Moore argues that certain kinds of events are a preferred form of raw data for ethnographers because of their ability to reveal contestation and competing cultural claims (1987: 727–36). She writes:

> An event is not necessarily best understood as the exemplification of an extant symbolic or social order. Events may equally be evidence of the ongoing dismantling of structures or of attempts to create new ones. Events may show a multiplicity of social contestation and the voicing of competing cultural claims. Events may reveal substantial areas of normative indeterminacy. (1987: 729)

Using Moore's term, we could describe Chernobyl as a "diagnostic event," that is, an event which reveals "official" and competing contradictory interpretations as well as the internal connections among groups affected by the event (Moore 1987: 730). In analyzing historical events and their representation I do not argue, as Geertz did in his famous essay on the Balinese cockfight, that events are a reification of an essential cultural system (1973: 412–53). Rather I have chosen to view the representation of historical events as embedded in a process of identity reformation where power relations and the ability of various groups to advance their interests is revealed. By examining the representation of events as an event in and of itself, we see how perceptions of self and other are transformed when nationalism and historical memory intersect. Numerous artistic depictions of the aftermath of Chernobyl in film, plays, and books have forged a consensus about the magnitude of the atrocity (see Onyshkevych 1989).[5] For many, even those who at the time were not in favor of Ukrainian independence, Chernobyl symbolized the exploitative nature of the system and the victimization of Ukraine under Soviet rule.

The release of two highly critical and emotionally charged films, *Dzvin Chornobylia* (in Ukrainian, *The Chernobyl Bell*) and *Chernobyl: Khronika Trudovykh Nedel'* (in Russian, *Chernobyl: A Chronicle of Working Weeks*), fueled and sustained the terror of radiophobia. *The Chernobyl Bell*, made by V. Sinelnikov and R. Serhienko, was filmed shortly after the accident from May 28 to June 26, and features eyewitness accounts portraying the shattering effects of the disaster on the lives of individuals. Considerable efforts were made to suppress the film, but it was finally released in March 1987.

Chernobyl: A Chronicle of Working Weeks was produced and released under dramatic circumstances, creating a story about the story. The film was shot immediately after the accident from May to August 1986. During the filming, several members of the crew, including the director and producer, Volodymyr Shevchenko, lived in close proximity to the reactor in some of the most highly contaminated areas. Shevchenko died of "radiation sickness" after the film was completed and did not live to see its premier. His camera had to be buried because it could not be decontaminated. This not only underlined the danger of radiation, but the supreme sacrifice he made to chronicle the tragedy conferred something of a martyr status upon him. These films and others added to the insatiable thirst for information about something so real and yet so unimaginable.[6]

One of the initial attempts to portray the disaster in the theater was Vladimir Gubarev's play, *Sarcophagus*, named after the covering used to seal the leaking fourth reactor. Written by a science correspondent for the Communist Party newspaper *Pravda* (Truth), the play chronicled the unfolding of the tragedy. In September 1986 excerpts of the play were printed in the newspaper *Sovetskaia Kul'tura* (Soviet Culture). The story centered around a "Mr. Immortal," an alcoholic worker in a nuclear power plant. The play implies that technological progress is still laudable but human error is to be guarded against. Indeed, following the accident there was a demonizing of one Anatolii Dyatlov, the worker on duty at the time the test of the cooling system occurred. He was initially blamed for making the error that first led to the meltdown. The artistic director of the play summed up the relationship of Chernobyl to changes in the political climate: "Before glasnost, *Sarcophagus* would not exist. Before Chernobyl, it would not have had to."[7]

Glasnost allowed a forum for critical commentary to open up because Chernobyl generated so much anger, frustration, and resentment that *had* to be expressed. The atmosphere of official tolerance for such dissent and a public forum in which to vocalize it were newly won freedoms brought on by glasnost that the population was not likely to give back. When states retell narratives of history in categories and meanings that match those of their constituents, then chances are greater that these states will be accepted as legitimate. The coincidence of state-sponsored historical narratives of national experience and personal narratives of individual experience is a compelling component in perceptions of legitimacy. Chernobyl powerfully and irrevocably destroyed the legitimacy of the Soviet state in the minds of many Soviet citizens who were taken aback by the bureaucracy's blatant subservience to image over real people and real injury. The Soviet authorities' efforts to shape public perception of the "normalcy" and "innocuousness" of the accident, when challenged by far more meaningful artistic and popular commemoration of the tragedy, produced widespread anger and distrust. The legacy of lies, disinformation, and cover-up has left in its wake a readiness to believe the worst, not only about the accident, but about the whole Soviet experience.

During the aftermath of Chernobyl, many Russians and russified Ukrainians agitating for change in Ukraine, who could not relate to the charges of exploitation and cultural oppression that drove the independence movements in other areas of the former Soviet Union, saw their republic as a colony for the first time. For many, Chernobyl was the most significant and traumatic event in their lifetime. The failure of political leaders to take responsible steps to mitigate the negative consequences of the accident served more than anything else for russified populations to discredit the Soviet regime and generate support for an independent state.

The Ascendancy of Rukh

In September 1989 Volodymyr Shcherbytsky, the hard-line communist leader of Soviet Ukraine, was finally ousted from power. He was one of the three last Brezhnevites to serve on the Central Committee of the Communist Party Politburo. Without Shcherbytsky's neo-Stalinist rule, press restrictions, prohibitions against informal groups organizing, and harassment of dissidents all began to abate. Oppositional tactics quickly shifted from the rather innocuous gathering of signatures to highly visible strikes, protests, and blockades as it became apparent to protesters that such actions would not be punished as they had been in the past.

Within the Writers' Union, the program for the "Movement for Perestroika," or Rukh, had formed, a seemingly innocuous organization with the stated goal of supporting Gorbachev's program of perestroika. It was finally able to explore its potential as a budding political opposition group by holding an inaugural congress on September 8–10, 1989. Nearly half of the 1100 delegates were from western Ukraine. Delegates railed against socialism and the Communist Party and openly called for Rukh to assume power in Ukraine.[8] By 1990 the movement had become highly politicized and openly opposed Party rule and advocated independence for Ukraine. The destructiveness of Chernobyl to the environment was equated with the destructiveness of Party rule to the Ukrainian nation and to Ukrainian culture. The demands of environmentalists for greater autonomy and greater rights of self-determination overlapped with those of nationalists and proved to be mutually reinforcing. Support was also forthcoming from labor leaders, even striking coal miners from the heavily russified Donbas region, who were disgruntled over sagging wages and deteriorating services. They demonstrated their power to challenge the Soviet state by organizing a seemingly endless stream of strikes and demonstrations.

The emergence of Rukh also coincided with a formidable religious revival, which instantaneously focused attention on a long history of religious persecution and oppression. In particular, the fate was highlighted of the two distinctly national churches, the Ukrainian Catholic Church (Uniate) and the Ukrainian Autocephalous Orthodox Church, both of which had been forcibly disbanded, their property confiscated and their clergy and parishioners persecuted. These two churches and a multitude of others became vocal advocates of change, particularly after Gorbachev's meeting with the pope in 1989.

To unite these varied interests, Rukh articulated its rationale for an independent state in terms of a nationalist historiography. To reform the present system involved engaging, if not discrediting, the past. The Soviet state had always made a steadfast and unwavering commitment to control historical representation and public discourse about historical events. Rukh consistently sought to challenge official Soviet interpretations of Ukrainian history and to replace them with national myths and symbols in an effort to generate national consciousness and support for an independent Ukrainian state. Several works, long banned by Soviet censors for violating established, state-created norms and limits of historiography, finally saw the light of day during glasnost and were voraciously read by a public craving a fresh perspective on the past.

In particular, these works share an intense critique of the excesses of the Stalinist regime. When Gorbachev and his colleagues allowed for a critique of the Stalinist past in the late 1980s, they assumed that it could be contained and controlled, like previous historical inquiry, and ultimately used to strengthen and legitimate the Soviet state. Harsh reappraisal of the Soviet past had enormous implications. Dialectical materialism's scientific theory of history, upon which Soviet ideology was based, had provided the underpinnings for the legitimacy of the Communist Party and the entire Soviet system by plotting society's past on the way to a "bright future." Marxism-Leninism had justified itself as the final and most glorious phase of teleological historical development. In the end, much to Gorbachev's horror, the critical reexamination of the Stalinist past reached beyond to include a scathing critique of Marxism-Leninism and the Revolution of 1917 and a repudiation of the colonial nature of the Soviet Empire.

De-Stalinization

Because of the strategic and highly politicized nature of history writing, historical work was much more closely scrutinized by the censors than literary writings were (Verdery 1991a: 215–55). This explains why the initial reexamination of history was not led by professional historians, but rather by writers and artists who used forums such as cinema, literature, theater, and music to vocalize a scorching critique of the past.[9] Many long-banned literary and historical works were published or serialized in the press in the late 1980s, which caused circulation and subscription rates to skyrocket.[10] The widespread popular interest in reexamining the past so dominated public discourse that the changes induced in Soviet society by perestroika and glasnost in the late 1980s took place in tandem with a transformation of official discourse on the past. Gorbachev himself on several occasions encouraged greater historical inquiry and even linked renewed historical debate to the realization of perestroika (Davies 1989). This turn to the past animated history in the present. A plethora of critical opinions suddenly became accessible to the public through an increased flow of information, profoundly altering the intellectual and cultural climate in the final years of Soviet rule.

The public acknowledgment of a history filled with tragedy, terror, and sorrow only fueled an already insatiable interest in the past. Reformers made furious efforts in a multitude of public forums to recognize the full weight and import of history in everyday life in the Soviet Union. This thirst for historical debate was driven by a long-standing and widespread popular rejection of official Soviet histories, which had been blatantly and unapologetically written and rewritten to legitimate and coincide with current political concerns. The erasure of historical figures, the denial of significant events, and the minimization of the system's excesses and failures frequently created a disjuncture between the official discourse and individual recollection. Often there was no reflection in the public sphere of an individual's memories of events, either based on firsthand experience or on secondary retelling by friends and relatives. Expressions of such counter-memories were mostly confined to the kitchen, the usual fortress against the hostility of the outside world. The very absence of representations of an individual's memories in the Soviet public sphere had one of two results: those memories either became disproportionally prominent in constructing an interpretive framework or over time they withered away.[11] In view of the sharp politicization of history, individual recollections were one of the few trusted sources of information about the past. With the advent of glasnost, an anxious public, demanding the externalization of these memories and a sincere public acknowledgment of their suffering, propelled forward a radical reinterpretation of their history.[12]

Partha Chatterjee asserts that the principal task of nationalist historiography has been to claim for the indigenous group the privilege of making their own history, to shift from being passive objects of history to subjects of history (1993: 37). The ability to represent oneself is a potent form of political power. For seventy-four years the Soviet regime placed strict controls on the scope and dissemination of historical writings, favoring Soviet state and institutional histories at the expense of broader social or cultural themes. As the authority and responsibility for interpreting history shifted away from professional historians to the experiential recollections of individuals and to the interpretive renditions of artists, the priorities and emphases of historical representation changed. History was reclaimed for oneself and for one's cultural group and was couched in terms of an endless litany of victimization.[13]

Between History and Memory

The writings of Walter Benjamin help to explain the precarious connection between political stability and historical (mis)interpretation. Writing in Germany on the eve of World War II, Benjamin saw the present as a moment of historical crisis, fueled by the fear that the future would be forsaken if a "lost past" were not recovered and redeemed. Benjamin (1968) asserts that remembering is a means of actualizing the past in the present, hence the coveted value of history and public remembering for nationalist leaders.

The renaissance of nationalisms and post-Soviet identity politics have raised the consequences of historical interpretation and representation to a premium. If we consider history as an institutionalization of memories—and remember that many of the historical events under reexamination in post-Soviet society were personally experienced by vast sectors of the population—then a nationalizing project that squarely harnesses history to its cause will also mandate that national subjects selectively remember and forget certain events. Ernest Renan's oft-cited claim that collective forgetting of the past is an essential factor in the creation of a nation reveals the intimate and dependent relationship between nationalism and history.[14]

I view memory as individual knowledge of the past, as distinct from institutionalized memories, or history. Once institutionalized, history becomes *public* knowledge of the past. Memories find their base, not in institutions as history does, but in individual experiences of historical events. Ukrainian nationalists who seek to recast popular understanding of the Ukrainian experience of Soviet rule are confronted with "living memories" of the very events they seek to reinterpret. Memories distinguish themselves from historical narrative in that they are composed of a kaleidoscope of images that frequently ignore chronology and accuracy. They often were the only available source to fill in the "white spots" of events, personalities, and details deleted from official Soviet historiography.

The intentional use of historical representation to produce a consensus of collective memories of historical events as a means of galvanizing Ukrainian nationalist sentiment and challenging Soviet authority on Ukrainian soil was blatant during the final, volatile years of perestroika. A collective look back, together with Benjamin's Angel of History, at a senseless pile of human tragedy otherwise known as progress, was meant to inspire those living in Ukraine to imagine their futures without the Soviet system and without the Soviet Union (1968: 257). The commemoration of key historical events allowed opposition leaders to showcase an alternative historical interpretation based on victimization and tragedy to garner support for their new vision of the future, which centered on independent statehood.

Each commemoration of historical events was used to revive memories of suffering and destruction on a colossal scale that had been previously denied or minimized in official discourse. In each of these instances, the past was presented as an undesirable other. From among the smashed bits and pieces, nationalist advocates scoured the past for events that could redeem the hopes of the present. Commemorations of various historical events served as a platform from which to interpret the Ukrainian-Russian historical experience in terms of victimization and betrayal in order to make more cogent their calls for an independent Ukrainian state.

The nationalist use of public commemoration to advance a revised history began most significantly in 1988 with the celebration of the Millennium, the 1000-year-anniversary of Christianity in Kievan Rus'. Soviet officials chose Moscow, not Kyiv, as the site for the most important commemorations because this flourishing period of history is viewed as the birthplace of Russian culture in spite of the fact that the political entity known as Kievan Rus' was located in part of what is today Ukrainian territory. The multitude of festivities, parades, and ceremonies noted the illustrious and deep history of Christianity in this part of the world— which flew in the face of the Soviet state policy of atheism—and served to encourage the religious revival already under way. They indirectly shone a glaring light on the repression suffered by religious institutions during the Soviet era as well. In particular, the clergy of the two Ukrainian national churches, the Ukrainian Catholic Church (Uniate) and the Ukrainian Autocephalous Orthodox Church, had been arrested, imprisoned, or executed after the Revolution. After a brief period of tolerance during World War II, both churches were officially outlawed in 1946 and driven underground.

During glasnost a strong interest in religion, be it Orthodoxy, Catholicism, or Islam, arose across the Soviet Union, alongside, and often in tandem with, an enthusiasm for nationalism. The gains by nationalist movements were often far outpaced by a widespread religious revival and newly forged commitments to organized religion. The redefinition of nationality that was under way frequently integrated a religious component, thereby creating a mutually reinforcing effect between a religious and a national revival. The commemoration of the Millennium spurred on the religious revival and by extension cultivated anti-Soviet sentiment, which often found a voice in the growing nationalist movement.

The festivities surrounding the Millennium were followed by a round of fiftieth anniversary commemorations of various Nazi atrocities beginning in 1989. Each ceremony revived memories of suffering and destruction on a colossal scale. The devastation sustained in Ukraine as a result of World War II was massive: an estimated 5 million killed, 2 million deported to camps in Europe, 3.5 million evacuated to other parts of the Soviet Union, and over 10 million left homeless. Yevtushenko's famous poem, "Babii Yar," immortalizes the immense suffering sustained at this one place, where over 200,000 Jews were executed, by describing the atmosphere as "one massive, soundless scream."

This tragic chapter of history was followed in 1990 by the commemoration of the anniversary of the Ukrainian People's Republic's declaration of independence on January 22, 1918. Rukh organized a human chain from Kyiv to L'viv and on to Ivano-Frankivs'k in which over 750,000 people participated to highlight how the nascent Ukrainian state had been struck down by zealous Bolshevik ideologues following the Revolution. Although never internationally recognized, the state existed briefly, weakened by war, disease, and brutal pogroms.[15] The state lost sovereignty during the civil war and collapsed in 1920 when its leaders were forced to flee. This commemorative event served to highlight a (frustrated) tradition of statehood and buttressed claims for independence. In this wave of intense popular interest in history, attention turned to another tragic event in twentieth-century Ukrainian history that had been falsified and even denied by the Soviet regime.

A commemoration of the fiftieth anniversary of the massacres that occurred at Babyi Yar in Kyiv during World War II.

The Famine of 1932–33

Hosking (1989: 120–22) argues that mass collectivization of agriculture, beyond the monumental consequences for those who experienced it, was also a pivotal event for Soviet historiography. Collectivization was a failed policy whose ramifications were so catastrophic that they had to be concealed at all costs. For historians and political leaders, he argues, this event set in motion the state-sponsored distortion and suppression of historical truth for decades and hardened the habit of "two personalities," as former Soviet citizens call it, of secretly knowing one thing and publicly saying another.

Stalin's harsh campaigns of collectivization and dekulakization, or the policy of eliminating rich, hence exploitative, peasants, culminated in the Famine, which became one of the defining events of twentieth-century Ukrainian history. Some intellectual and cultural leaders proclaimed the Famine the Ukrainian holocaust, a national symbol of oppressive Soviet rule, Ukrainian suffering, and a justification for independent statehood (see Kovalenko and Maniak 1991). Stalin understood that nationality and nationally based threats to the state hinged on the peasantry. The Famine not only contributed to the death of an estimated six million Ukrainians, it also effectively destroyed the essence of a peasant-based, rural Ukrainian culture. The terror, brutality, and grave consequences of the Famine have made its representation emotional and highly charged.

There were numerous factors contributing to a famine this crushing and vast.[16] For a variety of reasons, the harvest yields in Ukraine declined sharply from 1930 to 1934: in 1930, 23.1 million tons of grain were produced; in 1931 only 18.3 million; 14.6 million tons in 1932; in 1933 production rose considerably to 22.3 million tons; but by 1934 it had fallen once again to 12.3 million tons (Krawchenko 1985: 126). In 1933, at the height of the Famine, production levels were up. By the time the Famine was over in 1934, production levels hit a new low. How is it possible that when grain was available, there was a horrific famine ravaging the Ukrainian countryside, leaving in its wake scores of starved skeletons? And when production levels fell to nearly half the levels produced at the peak of the Famine, there was no starvation?

The sources of this paradox are multiple. Yet the highly unrealistic and zealous goals Stalin set for industrialization triggered many of them, which is why the Famine is often described as man-made. The First Five-year Plan called for rapid industrialization. To accomplish this, the regime needed hard currency to import equipment manufactured in the West. With little else to sell, more grain had to be produced and sold to finance industrialization if the Soviet Union was to overtake the West. Steep grain quotas were imposed on the peasants of Ukraine. In Stalin's view, the best means of radically increasing the amount of grain the Soviet government had to sell was through "total collectivization." This involved coercing peasants to leave their individual farms, come together, and work collectively on state-owned and managed collective farms (*kolhospy*), and deliver directly to the state all of their marketable grain. Failure to do so carried severe penalties. Needless to say, there was widespread resistance to this plan among the Ukrainian peasantry. Many peasants joined collective farms only at gunpoint. In spite of peasant opposition, Stalin ordered *all* peasant households to be collectivized by the fall of 1930.

To accomplish such an ambitious goal, Stalin ordered a program of "dekulakization," which involved the elimination of kulaks as a class of richer, hence exploitative, peasants. Initially, a precise definition of "kulak" evaded authorities. Indeed, some peasant households had more land than others, but depending on how many people this land supported, it did not necessarily mean they were wealthier. Eventually, a haphazard set of criteria was put forth to determine who was a kulak and who was not. Anyone employing labor was considered a kulak. Therefore, injured, ill, or war veteran farmers became kulaks overnight. Anyone owning motorized equipment was considered a kulak. In the end, any peasant actively against collectivization incurred the risk of being classified as a kulak. By 1929, 71,500 households in Ukraine had been classified as kulak (Krawchenko 1985: 122).[17]

Although the tide of collectivization ebbed and flowed, by 1931 famine conditions were building to catastrophic levels. The earlier slaughter of animals to protest collectivization and mandatory surrender of livestock to the state eliminated draft animals for plowing. Mechanized forms of harvest were either ineffective or totally unavailable. Incentives for peasants to farm had been killed off too. The collective farms became bureaucratic, taking orders from centralized authorities. Negative factors affecting production were greatly aggravated by high grain requisition quotas. In 1931, 7.7 million tons of grain were requisitioned from Ukraine. The same amount was requisitioned in 1930, but the harvest had been 20 percent greater. Obviously, there was resistance among the peasants to turn over so much of their grain. Armed troops were employed to identify peasants storing grain and to raid their supplies. Molotov and Kaganovich set up a special commission in Kharkiv (the capital of Ukraine at the time) to ensure that the grain was collected regardless of the means employed to do so. In 1932 the infamous law against "theft of socialist property," a crime punishable by execution or internment in a labor camp, was introduced. Anticipating resistance, armed brigades were sent into the villages to collect grain from peasants and to punish those who failed to cooperate. Peasants were shot for as little as stealing a sack of grain. Every third person holding a high-level position at a collective farm was purged (Subtelny 1994: 414). A system of internal passports was introduced in 1932 to prevent peasants from leaving collective farms in search of food.

Vigilant collection of grain to finance industrialization, combined with production problems as a result of resistance to collectivization, ignited the Famine in early 1932. Had requisitions been lower in 1931 and 1932, most likely nowhere near six million Ukrainians would have perished from hunger in a region ravaged by mass starvation. Although 1933 was a record harvest, the requisition levels were lowered and the mass starvation which had begun in 1932 slowed. The Famine was over in 1934 in spite of the fact that the harvest that year was particularly bad. When the Famine was raging at its peak in 1932–33, the Soviet Union exported 1.7 million tons of grain to the West. Famine conditions were produced more by the regime's inflated demands for grain and seed than by the size of the harvest in any particular year. The victims of the Famine were primarily poor peasants. The kulaks, or wealthier peasants, had already been executed or exiled by 1932 when the Famine began. The devastating blow the Famine dealt to the Ukrainian peasantry was manifested in sharply reduced vocal opposition to Soviet policies and a new-found facade of compliance.

A Peasant Nation

The tragedy of the Famine extends beyond the lives lost, nationalist advocates argue. The Ukrainian countryside, rural peasant communities, and, by extension, the base of Ukrainian culture, had been irreversibly sapped of life by Soviet plans of grandeur through rapid industrialization financed by campaigns of collectivization and dekulakization. The destruction of the peasantry and of a rural way of life sent many scurrying to the cities in search of factory work. As the industrial bases in the Donbas and Dnipro regions were building, this rapid expansion of the working class at the expense of the peasantry was acutely felt.[18] Peasants who left the countryside for the cities were exposed much more directly to Soviet propaganda and ideology. Furthermore, those living in the cities, even then, tended to be Russian speaking. Many Ukrainian-speaking peasants over time assimilated to the Russian language or to *surzhyk*, a dialect blending Russian and Ukrainian, and a Soviet way of life.

The abuse of power during the Famine inspired cultural and political leaders in the final years of glasnost to mobilize the Famine and to hold it up, along with Chernobyl, as a symbol of the Ukrainian experience of Soviet rule. The Famine savagely killed off peasants as Chernobyl viciously poisoned the land. For a peasant-based people, this meant the nation and its "soul" had been destroyed. The lesson drawn was that genocide of a particular people could occur only under conditions of statelessness and colonial rule.

A claim to this effect had been voiced nearly a decade earlier by the Ukrainian diaspora community in the United States as they commemorated the fiftieth anniversary of the Famine in 1983. The National Committee to Commemorate Genocide Victims in Ukraine 1932–33 organized a commemorative rally and march in Washington, D.C., in October 1983, which drew 18,000 participants. In addition to symposia, monuments, and publications, the diaspora community successfully lobbied for the formation of a U.S. congressional commission to study the Famine. In April 1988, the commission issued a report indicting Stalin and his cruel policies for the loss of seven to ten million Ukrainians. Two years later, the Oral History Project, which captured the last "living memories" of famine survivors, by interviewing Ukrainian immigrants now living in North America, was published (Mace and Heretz 1990).

History and Growing Support for Independence

In addition to publicly acknowledging individual and collective trauma, the intense interest in exploring the history of the Soviet period was also a means to examine power relations, a sensitive point in a country with a non-elected regime. It called into question the received mythology of Soviet grandeur incessantly promoted in the public sphere. Advocates for independence tried to pierce the divide between individually held memories and official historical narratives by publicly voicing historical memories and calling for new historical investigations to reassess the past. Anti-Soviet sentiment and rapidly increasing disgust with the failures of the Soviet system, both of which were widely discussed in a decreasingly subservient press, combined to generate mounting support for Ukrainian independence. A key means of capturing support was the portrayal of aspects of the Ukrainian historical experience of Soviet rule from a national (victimized) perspective. These representations were by and large well received because they, far more so than official Soviet historiography, reflected individual experiences and memories. Because nationalist advocates were able to retell narratives of Ukrainian history in categories and meanings that matched those encapsulated in individual memories much more closely than official Soviet narratives, they created legitimacy for themselves and support for their quest for an independent Ukrainian state.

In doing so, nationalist advocates made history into a critical ideological battleground in the final years of Soviet rule. History was used to override such potentially divisive cultural factors as language, religion, and localized allegiances to unify the people of Ukraine against Soviet rule and for independence. In the heady years of glasnost, collective memories became a well-spring of inspiration from which newly revised histories drew.[19] Quite simply, there was nothing else: historians were considered lackeys of the system and official records were thought to be shrouded in self-serving lies.

Comaroff and Stern (1994) argue that ethnic consciousness can be viewed as a universal potentiality that is objectified as a political identity when a population recognizes a common threat. They argue that collective identities are "an imminent capacity" that take a multitude of forms in response to specific circumstances (1994: 39). Individual memories intersect with attempts to shape collective memories of historical events in the process of crafting national identities. Collective attachments to the histories people imagine they share take root when they have a base in memory, that is to say, in the collective practice or representation of history in the public sphere. In this way, the public is made private, historical knowledge becomes experiential knowledge, and a national designation becomes a nationalized identity.

Memory becomes an essential factor because, as Appadurai has argued, history is not "a limitless and plastic symbolic resource" (1981: 201). It cannot be invented and reinvented out of whole cloth. Rather, there must be some independent social criteria for evaluating and eventually accepting or rejecting rival interpretations of the past. The popular rejection of various Soviet state-produced accounts of the past affirm Appadurai's argument by demonstrating that propaganda, suppression of alternative interpretations, and coercion are insufficient to ensure that particular interpretations will be accepted.

Yet relying on memories as an embodiment of experience can be highly problematic. Not only are memories to a degree recalled in terms of the present, as Maurice Halbwachs (1975, 1980) and, more recently, Pierre Nora (1984) have argued; memories are sustained in various sites and need to be encapsulated in some form in order to be kept alive through recall, particularly as they move further away from personal experience over generations. Sequestered in individual consciousness, memories may be erased or significantly altered.[20] This is one of the many reasons why individuals crave expression, recognition, and an externalization of harrowing and haunting images of the past, even as these images elude articulation and even as the individuals concerned try to forget them.[21]

The plethora of visual images circulating in society meld together and encroach upon individual memories. Collective memories that result from the melding of publicly created visual forms and individual memories form a collage of images, a narrative of the past that often dispenses with chronology, narrative structure, and historical accuracy. Yet given its base in memory, these alternative narratives are often held to be true by virtue of the visceral reaction they prompt. The vast popular rejection of official Soviet historiography and of a manipulated and blatantly politicized public sphere made collective memories a vitally important source of information for individuals about the past.

Reassessing the past during glasnost led to reimagining the future. This, compounded by deteriorating economic conditions and a slide in the overall standard of living, contributed to the remarkable results of the March 1991 referendum. The referendum demonstrated that 80 percent of the population supported Ukrainian sovereignty, meaning Ukraine would have it own currency, army, and foreign policy, within a confederation.[22] Months after the breakup of the Soviet Union, the majority of the population—even in Crimea, the only region in Ukraine with an ethnic Russian majority—voted overwhelmingly in support of total Ukrainian independence during a state-wide referendum on December 1, 1991, and thereby provided a broad, popular mandate to initiate sweeping political and cultural change.[23] Much of Rukh's program was included in the Declaration of Sovereignty adopted ten months later (Kuzio and Wilson 1994: 113).

These results of these referenda are all the more remarkable given that before the creation of Rukh in 1989 nationalist activity was largely centered in western Ukraine among a cultural elite in dissident organizations. Support for independence rapidly soared when it was understood to be a lifeboat off the Soviet Titanic. Even Leonid Makarovych Kravchuk, a former leading antinationalist, head of ideology, and chairman of the Supreme Soviet in Ukraine, began to swiftly "restructure" himself into a proponent of nationalism in 1990 in time to campaign to be the first president of independent Ukraine by adopting 90 percent of the Rukh program.

Political Borders, Cultural Barriers

Political borders were quickly redrawn following the failed coup, but cultural barriers are not so easily dislodged. In spite of widespread support

Rally to demonstrate support for Ukrainian independence outside the Verkhovna Rada, the Supreme Soviet, government building in Kyiv after the failed coup in August 1991.

for an independent Ukrainian state, many living in Ukraine are less supportive of the cultural changes that have followed new state formation. After independence, in addition to advancing a revised, nationalized historical narrative of a common experience based on the tragedies of the Famine and Chernobyl, political and cultural leaders began to engage the icons of Soviet historiography, a practice that was not possible until the fall of the Soviet Union. This meant addressing two specific events highly charged with symbolism: the Revolution of 1917 and the Victory of the Red Army during World War II. The Revolution gave birth to the Soviet state and articulated the unique mission of the Soviet people. The Soviet victory in World War II holds enormous significance, not only because it represents a victory amid tremendous suffering and enormous casualties, but because it accorded a significant expansion in the Soviet sphere of influence and a superpower status on a country the West previously viewed as "backward." Attempts to institutionalize a historically based national culture not only recast the Ukrainian experience of Soviet rule but also began to engage the icons of Soviet mythology.

Maintaining momentum for the cultural revival set in motion during the final years of Soviet rule has proved difficult. Having acquired a state, nationalist leaders have tried to forge a link between individuals and the state via a national culture. This link has been inadvertently challenged by the residual appeal and habit of seeing oneself as Soviet. Before turning to an examination of the sites at which a national culture is being institution-alized in an effort to develop national consciousness and a Ukrainian na-tional identity, it is important to look at several factors that complicate an already complicated process. Practices and values spawned by the Soviet system and nostalgia for the security of a Soviet way of life persist and compete with a nationalist redefinition of self and society by providing alternative, non-national points of orientation for individuals reassessing their values and identities. Thus the process of institutionalizing a na-tional culture must operate within the confines of tenacious aspects of a Soviet way of life and the allure of local allegiances.

3

On Being Soviet

The tradition of all the dead
generations weighs like a
nightmare on the brain of
the living.

—Karl Marx, *The 18th Brumaire
of Louis Bonaparte*

There was a hit song in the 1970s which went like this: "My address isn't a house or a street. My address is the Soviet Union. . . . Today the individual is not important, but the result of the working day."[1] The process of stripping down the individuality and dignity of every citizen to create *homo sovieticus* (Rus. *sovetskii chelovek*) was parallel to the process of peeling back the histories and cultures of the many nationalities in the Soviet Union to create the Soviet people (Rus. *sovetskii narod*). The system wanted individuals to identify with being Soviet, to see themselves as residents of a vast eleven-time-zone country on a unique mission. This song was one of the many forms of propaganda that bombarded individuals to remind them that they were Soviet. Yet efforts to sovietize created great tension driven by unresolvable paradoxes. The structure of the Soviet system constantly underlined nationality as it constantly undermined it. This splicing of identity now serves as a residual factor perpetuating both confusion and apathy toward national re-identification in post-Soviet Ukraine.

Continued identification with the "imagined community" of the Soviet Union is not only evident in everyday practices, it is also reflected in language, in patterns of discourse. This is the criteria upon which many, independent of nationality, recognize themselves to be Soviet. A uniquely post-Soviet distinction has been invented to discern degrees of foreignness. Former Soviet republics turned independent countries are referred to collectively as the "near abroad," whereas countries beyond are called the "far abroad." This distinction suggests that although Russia, Kazakhstan, and all other republics are now technically foreign countries, they are clearly not as foreign as, say, France or China. Going there simply means that one is far from home, but not necessarily abroad. This new distinction between the near and far abroad reflects the disjuncture involved in redefining just where "abroad" is and just who a foreigner is.

Every attempt to create new identities involves reconfiguring the old. I have traveled repeatedly to the Soviet Union since 1980 and only once have I heard someone identify himself as Soviet. In 1984 a young man from Siberia, who could not physically pass for a Russian, identified himself while speaking English as "Soviet."[2] Even though people rarely referred to themselves as Soviet, the tenacity of a Soviet identity should not be underestimated. Many feel Soviet out of recognition of having collectively endured the ill-fated Bolshevik experiment. Soviet culture was, of course, supported by an entire ideological system, a way of life perceived as unique, and the institution of citizenship. Current practices and discursive acts of signification underline the tenacity of Soviet culture and the collective formed by the Soviet state. The pervasiveness and persistence of a Russian-based sovietized culture impinges upon a redesign of Ukrainian society by hampering reform in numerous ways. As we will discuss in this chapter, the enduring practices created by the Soviet system also sustain the social relations they spawned and influence the pace and nature of social change in post-Soviet society.

Canals to Survival

The persistence of Soviet cultural practices is driven largely by incessant shortages of every conceivable item. By 1994, many shortages had been alleviated. Yet the prices for these goods had risen to unaffordable heights making them inaccessible save to a small percentage of the population who had steady hard currency incomes protected from inflation. Widespread economic dislocation, spurred on by rising unemployment and by sporadically paid salaries that fail to keep pace with inflation, creates another type of shortage: a shortage of money. Shortages, be it of goods or money, breed a sustained state of "hustling" (Ukr. *krutytysya*, literally "spinning), which perpetuates Soviet values and a Soviet weltanschauung in spite of massive economic and political change in post-Soviet society.[3]

"Hustling" refers to the machinations involved in working elaborate networks of exchange and constitutes a powerful dynamic influencing social life in post-Soviet society. These networks become vitally important when trying to earn a living, to procure needed goods or services, or to break through the dense morass of bureaucratic regulations that often seem to have been designed to prevent anyone from actually getting anything accomplished. The essence of these networks is trading, trading of favors, connections, and information in an effort to create mutual reliance, trust, and obligation among trading partners. Networks generally include extended and immediate family members, close friends, and colleagues.

Trust is the key factor in deciding with whom one will trade, which is why family members are the preferred trading partners. Because families are small, close friends and reliable colleagues inevitably enter the trading rings.[4] With virtually no recourse to law or the courts, trust between trading partners must be total. Deals are made, money is exchanged, and risks are taken on the basis of trust and goodwill alone, all of which is symbolized by the ritual of drinking together to seal an agreement. Although these networks tend to form along gender and familial lines, they cut across national lines and serve to underline the absurdity of dividing and tagging Russians as distinct from Ukrainians. Allegiances are to one's friends and contacts. In Ukraine, nationality recedes as a meaningless factor in delineating who can be trusted and who cannot. As a young woman who lives in L'viv said, "When you need something, you need it and you'll deal with anyone who can help you get it." Unlike in other former republics, in spite of linguistic and cultural differences, instrumental bonds of mutual cooperation are often forged in Ukraine when they work to the advantages of all parties, regardless of native tongue or nationality.

In addition to trust, another factor in deciding with whom one will trade is an assessment of that person's ability to reciprocate. The offering of "gifts" is often a thinly veiled means of creating a debt, of obliging someone to reciprocate with a similar gift in kind. The compulsion to return favors, gifts, and access to one's own networks further strengthens the relationships that are born in an economy of shortage. Failing to reciprocate or to reciprocate adequately, will quickly lead to expulsion from the network, unless, of course, the offender is a family member or "fictive kin." In these instances, the relationship simply becomes a one-sided venture in giving.

It is important to take a closer look at these networks, at the functions they provide, and at how they have evolved to adapt to new economic conditions. These networks are relevant for our purposes because they forge powerful and meaningful allegiances that cut across national lines. The frantic activity they foster creates an atmosphere of chaos and confusion which impedes cultural and other reforms by diverting attention and time away to fulfilling obligations necessary to ensure a certain standard of living in post-Soviet society.

Essentially, these networks serve three functions: obtaining needed goods and services, cutting through bureaucratic inertia and stonewalling, and locating meaningful employment that pays a living wage. In post-Soviet society, the third function has become the most important, although networks are still immensely helpful in obtaining goods and in dealing with state bureaucracies. Because the Soviet system guaranteed employment to all its citizens, networks were essential not in terms of obtaining a job and a salary per se. Rather they were vitally important to securing a job that gave access to goods in short supply and persons in positions of power. This shift in the function of networks slowly away from connections to persons in positions of authority in the government and away from *access* to goods (which is increasingly determined by ability to pay) to income-generating possibilities, reveals the emergence of money as the new source of power.

These networks emerged in Soviet society to overcome bureaucratic inertia and the perpetual shortage of goods. To obtain something *po blatu*, or with the help of connections, means that one plugs into a vast network of contacts and utilizes the access or leverage they might have to obtain needed goods or services. So extensive are the "canals" linking "*blat* networks" that some scholars have referred to Soviet socialism as a "system of organized shortages" (Verdery 1993: 183; see Hann 1993). There is a famous saying: "Better a hundred friends than a hundred rubles" (Rus., "Luchshe sto druzei chem sto rublei"). The right *blat* connection can produce power, access, and protection—things that money often cannot buy.

These exchange networks remain robust and represent a continuation of practices begun under the Soviet system. The critical difference is one of degree. An ailing Soviet economy and an impoverished consumer sector encouraged people to steal from their workplace, to trade on the black market, and to use their jobs to circumvent standard consumer practices, which usually included lines and waiting lists, to more quickly improve their standard of living. Once the Soviet Union disintegrated and the economy went into free fall, most families began frenetically trading and hustling to put food on the table. As a young man from L'viv with a wife and a child to support who shuttles back and forth to Germany said, "The difference is that now you have to keep hustling and hustling. If you stop, you're already behind, already in debt, already have nothing to eat." The goal of trading for most is no longer to improve their standard of living, but quite simply to live. As pronounced wealth differentials have developed creating a class of "New Ukrainians," as the nouveaux riches are called (they were previously referred to as "New Russians"), their networks aid in solidifying their financial status and privileged station in society by keeping family members employed and by securing enrollment in the best schools and universities. Guaranteed employment exists now only in memory. *Blat* connections have become essential for securing employment and avoiding the bribes that one often has to pay to become employed.

These new functions are handled by the same *blat* networks that originally emerged to soften the difficulties of everyday life under Soviet rule. In the Soviet Union, a multitude of basic foodstuffs were rationed according to residency permits. The list of rationed goods changed seasonally and regionally but constant among the products doled out were cooking oil, butter, sugar, vodka, cigarettes, and matches. The practice of rationing goods bound individuals to their residences or workplaces purely for the purposes of procuring necessary goods (Verdery 1996: 206). Marta Volodymyrivna, a forty-eight-year-old biologist living in Kyiv, claimed the incessant pursuit of goods was a key means by which Soviet authorities created *homo sovieticus*. She says the "Soviet new man is a person who unconsciously doesn't believe in his own strengths. He passively awaits charity from the state like a beggar . . . the shortage of all necessary goods and the allocation of goods by ration cards under the control of the state authorities, whom one had to obey without discussion, led to a system of legalized theft. This made people dependent on the state."

Not all were in agreement with Marta Volodymyrivna's assessment of the central role of shortages in informing the values and character of Soviet citizens. In contrast, Ludmilla Antonovna, a teacher who was born in Donetsk but now lives in Luhansk in eastern Ukraine, had a far more charitable assessment of the effects of the system on character. She said, "If he [a Soviet citizen] is sincere and not hypocritical, he is capable of living and working in a collective environment to the extent that he becomes the collective." This ability to cooperate through "unselfishness," as she termed it, led to "a high level of culture and education." Clearly, she felt the system encouraged such laudable qualities as cooperation and a desire to put consideration of the common good above one's own personal interests. In spite of the fact that she finds such qualities sorely lacking today, she paradoxically maintains with great assurance that "the Soviet way of thinking still exists and it will live for yet a long time to come." Indeed, the collectivism which she applauds is in evidence in every household, as family members and friends pull together in an effort to keep the family stocked with basic necessities.

As of early 1994, there was no longer any rationing. *Blat* networks were no longer necessary to locate needed goods. When prices shot up, for the first time in living memory "deficit" items sat on the shelves in stores. Independent merchants, who haphazardly line the streets of every major city, even in below freezing temperatures, began to compete with state stores by offering wares for sale on card tables or from the backs of trucks. The prices for virtually all goods and food items are considered excruciatingly high by those without access to hard currency. Depending on the degree of disdain or approval one has for this form of "cowboy capitalism," as it is called, these merchants are referred to as "speculators" or "small businessmen." Younger people tend to be grateful for the convenience (usually, the sellers are located at the entrances to metro stations or on main boulevards and rarely are there lines) and for the choice of goods, a refreshing change after years of state stores offering a single variety of any given item wrapped in grainy, brown industrial paper with the price stamped on the package in purple ink. Many others, however, resent traders for reaping a profit from merely buying and selling, an activity that the Soviet system taught does not constitute meaningful, socially productive work.

These traders have also introduced new, unwelcome dynamics to the

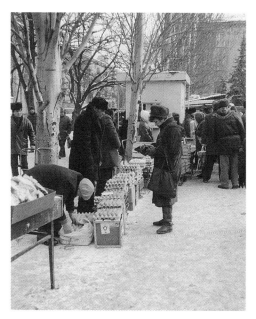

Since the beginning of perestroika in 1985, the inability of state factories and collective farms to satisfy consumer demand for basic food stuffs has been exacerbated. The fall in production reached acute levels following independence. Individual entrepreneurs, however, have attempted to turn a profit in the absence of competition from state enterprises. Here, on the streets of Donetsk, eggs, other foodstuffs, and clothing are offered for sale.

shopping experience. Buyers must beware, given that sellers, who may or may not be there tomorrow, offer no guarantees on any of their goods. Many items are bought abroad second hand and are now offered as "new," and some food items are offered for sale past their expiration date. For many older people unaccustomed to variation in price, the notion of comparison shopping is stressful. When money is in such short supply, the pressure is on to ferret out goods that are cheap, cheaper still, and cheapest of all. Most people are simply very much unaccustomed to the stinging sensation that they have overpaid, been deceived, or otherwise wasted money that has suddenly acquired new relevance for survival. Information on prices, sellers, and on the contents of brightly packaged foreign goods, whose descriptions in the Latin alphabet leave only the pictures to comment on what is inside dominated conversations among neighbors and friends following the lifting of price controls and growing access to foreign goods directly after independence. The constant search for scarce and affordable goods or services remains a very fundamental dynamic shaping social relations to this day. In a multitude of situations, personal networks are the only means by which to get information, locate an item, or alleviate shortages.

A number of quasi-legal or illegal means have also been devised by individuals to procure goods for sale. Often goods are diverted from their intended (state store) destination or clandestinely imported to Ukraine. Here in Donetsk a woman is selling champagne from the back of a truck for a quick profit.

On The Importance of Trust

The designations *svii* (Ukr.), *svoi* (Rus.), literally meaning "one's own," and *chuzhyi* (Ukr.), *chuzhoi* (Rus.), or "alien," have always been important distinctions in the workings of the *blat* networks. The difference in these terms hinges on a perception of cultural and social distance and reflects the degree of trust one invests in the other person. The expression *svoi chelovek* (Rus.) is literally translated as "one's own person" and means someone who can help you navigate through the maze of life in the Soviet system. Interestingly, although one could say this in Ukrainian (*svoia liudyna*), Ukrainian speakers quite simply use the equivalent Russian expression when speaking Ukrainian to underline the close connection between the concept and the Soviet system, which is closely associated with things Russian.

The meaning of *svoi chelovek* is entirely contingent on the Soviet system and the types of social relations it bred. *Svoi chelovek* is a person who can help you get something *po blatu*. The *svoi chelovek* designation indicates that this person can be trusted and is unlikely to betray you. The fundamental underlying principle of this expression is trust and a sense of reciprocal obligation that grows out of this trust. In other regions of the former Soviet Union, such as in the Caucasus, the *svoi/chuzhoi* distinction often mirrors family, clan, or national divisions. In Ukraine, however, the instrumental value of a particular relationship, embodied in the expression *svoi chelovek*, was evaluated largely independent of nationality. Trust and ability to reciprocate were the key factors.[5]

Even though the system per se has disintegrated, the practices that it bred stubbornly persist in post-Soviet society. Not only do the "deficits" structure interpersonal relationships but they also, of course, influence patterns of discourse. Because elaborate personal networks have grown like vines around the perpetual shortages of nearly everything, the verb "to buy" (Ukr. *kupuvaty*) has fallen out of colloquial use. Instead one refers to having "obtained" (Ukr. *distavaty*) a good or service. The pervasive use of "obtained" implies that through connections, the bending of rules, and manipulating the system advantageously, one is able to obtain the otherwise unobtainable.

The comments of Maria, a mother of two living in Kyiv, indicate how dependent one can become on the critical *svoi chelovek* connection. She launched into a long litany of complaints about her husband and his unfaithfulness. Formerly the head of ideology at the Higher Party School (a Communist Party training ground for elites), he now rather successfully represents a variety of diaspora organizations in Kyiv. As her complaints about his behavior became more and more bitter, I finally asked, "Why don't you leave him?" She stared back at me in blank amazement and said, "But who would get me train tickets?" (She is still married and traveling infrequently.)

It is true that obtaining train tickets regardless of destination—as long as the state subsidies were in place—was very nearly impossible without connections. To maintain access to her husband's vast and very powerful networks, which include both the old and new elite (to the extent that there is any difference), Maria was willing to endure his humiliations. The degree to which his connections simplified her life by allowing her to bypass "unpleasantness" in the course of daily life made it worth it for her to stay with him.

Luckily for me, during the period when I conducted fieldwork, from 1992 to 1994, the ex-husband of a good friend of mine had *svoi chelovek* who worked at the train station. Thanks to my friend's willingness to call on her ex-husband, and his willingness to call upon his contact, and this man's willingness to circumvent official channels and sell tickets on the side, I was able to get train tickets without sacrificing literally days in line to buy each ticket. But this meant that my friend was in much more frequent contact with her former husband while I was in town and he, in turn, saw his contact significantly more in order to fulfill my needs.

Obtaining necessary items is not the only sphere in which these connections are important. When an individual attempts to engage state bureaucracies, a network of partners can become essential. To cite an example of how these *blat* networks function within a bureaucratic context, consider this: Nina, a thirty-three-year-old artist living in Kyiv, wanted to establish legal residence at an apartment she obtained by trading her grandmother's one room in a communal apartment near the center of Kyiv for a better one-room noncommunal apartment on the outskirts of town. In essence, Nina traded the central location of her grandmother's apartment for the luxury of not having the neighbors in the kitchen and bathroom first thing in the morning. For the other person, the deal was advantageous because the communal apartment was located within walking distance of the metro and promised to spare the new owner daily rides on overflowing trolleys to and from the metro.

If Nina registers this apartment in her own name, then she will be able to apply for a *propiska*, or residency permit, which everyone must have, claiming this to be her new apartment of residence. A *propiska* at this address will permit her to privatize the apartment, which will allow her to sell the apartment in the future and to leave it to her family when she dies. Without a *propiska* at this address, none of this is possible and the apartment would remain the property of the state.

Procuring registration in the new apartment entails an enormous amount of paperwork at the BTI (Bureau of Technical Inventory [*Biuro Tekhnicheskoi Inventarizatsii*]).[6] Collecting the various documents, signatures, and stamps is enormously time-consuming and complex. Those who work at the BTI have no interest in simplifying the process. Indeed, it is to their advantage to be as uncooperative as possible. The nerve-racking quality of assembling the necessary paperwork in the face of staunch bureaucratic inertia predisposes people to give bribes even if they are morally against it. At one point, an employee of the BTI said in order for her to give the final stamp which Nina needed, Nina would have to help her obtain a foreign passport. (There are internal passports and passports exclusively for travel abroad.) This bureaucrat's only child had immigrated to Canada and she wanted desperately to visit him. She was having difficulties of her own with the bureaucracy at OVIR (Department of Visas and Registration [*Otdel Viz i Registratsii*]), the official police agency that regulates foreign travel and travel of foreigners. She was afraid that her visa might expire before she could ever get her foreign passport and board the plane.

Nina began calling everyone she knew to see if anyone knew someone who worked at OVIR. Finally she found someone who could help speed this woman's application for a foreign passport through the system. For his troubles he wanted to change kupons into hard currency. The kupon, a transitional currency in circulation from 1991 to 1996, was introduced prior to Ukrainian independence to prevent nonresidents of Ukraine from making purchases in Ukraine and maintained thereafter to replace the ruble. Initially after independence, it was forbidden to change money officially without furnishing elaborate documentation of how one obtained the kupons and why it was necessary to have hard currency. (This policy has since been changed.) An acceptable reason would be authorized travel abroad. However, the man at OVIR wasn't going anywhere. He simply wanted a hedge against inflation in the form of hard currency.

Until the advent of official exchange kiosks, it could be both difficult and dangerous to obtain hard currency. Usually, the only ones willing to accept kupons for hard currency were "speculators," who worked the streets illegally, earning a living off currency fluctuations. The more brazen speculators stood on the main boulevards before the Soviet-built department stores wearing dollar signs or copies of $100 bills on their coats to advertise their services. With money in shorter and shorter supply, many resourceful Ukrainians have simply taken to printing their own. Besides the possibility of getting stuck with counterfeit dollars, many speculators are masters at substituting a $1 bill for a $100 bill and, together with the gang members with whom they work, intimidating their customers until the customer becomes nervous, fearful, and distracted and does not notice that he is ninety-nine dollars poorer until he has put a great distance between himself and the moneychangers.

So now Nina set about trying to find someone who would be willing to buy this man's kupons. After several days, she found someone, who was planning to buy a refrigerator from a state factory that had to be paid for in kupons. Quite happily, he did not ask for any favors in return for making the exchange. This meant that the man at OVIR got his dollars, the woman at BTI got her foreign passport, and Nina, after nearly a

A new post-Soviet bank has run out of money. Hyperinflation, especially rampant in 1992–93, made prices soar and actually created a deficit of cash as the government was unable to print bills in the transitional currency in denominations large enough and in quantities sufficient enough to satisfy basic demand. This further encouraged reliance on hard currency as a hedge against inflation.

month of hustling, had one more of the many documents necessary to register herself in this apartment. The irony is that Nina lives with her mother and daughter in her mother's apartment and has no intention of actually moving into the new apartment. She made the trade with the intention of making still another trade. Ultimately, all this effort was expended to create a fictional residency on paper.[7]

This long convoluted story about registering residence at a new apartment demonstrates how the *blat* networks create circles of trusted confidants through a pattern of reciprocity and debt-based social relations that resists easy classification. During the course of these transactions Nina spoke Russian, although her first language is Ukrainian. When asked, she could only state with certainty the nationality of one person with whom she dealt during this whole process. Nationality recedes, especially in the eastern and southern provinces, as a useful factor when evaluating who is *svoi* and who is *chuzhoi*. Nationality is not an element of social identity that can often be manipulated to advantage in the course of *blat* exchanges, since most groups of trusted confidants consist of a mix of Ukrainians, Russians, and Jews.

If it hadn't been for Nina's friends who were willing to call upon their *blat* connections at OVIR for her benefit, she might never have been able to register this apartment. Of course, helping her find someone who will buy kupons is a bit like making a deposit at the bank: her friends know that eventually they will have some difficulty of their own and perhaps at that moment Nina and her *blat* networks might help them. Given how high the stakes are, *blat* networks demand a rigorous and incessant evaluation of who is *svoi* and who is *chuzhoi* to ensure that they continue to deliver the essential goods without arousing the attention of the authorities or, increasingly, without getting ripped off.

Trading Partners

Besides dealing with bureaucracies and obtaining services basic to everyday living, the *blat* networks are essential to anyone who would like to earn more than the salary paid by a state-sector job. At the time I conducted this fieldwork, 1992–94, the average salary was U.S. $20–30 a month and was often haphazardly paid. Although salaries have risen somewhat and hyperinflation has been tamed, they are still frequently delivered as much as six months late. Initially, to ensure a better and more stable standard of living, and now just to survive, many individuals supplement their incomes with informal trading.

Olena is a thirty-eight-year-old Ukrainian woman who lives in L'viv. She told me on repeated occasions that she would like nothing more than to get married and give up working. All of her closest friends are married and they do not work. She looks on enviously as their husbands provide for them. As she sees it, she is forced to engage in the dirty business of trading (Ukr. *torhivlia*) that these wives are spared. She feels that there is something lamentable about a woman who operates in such a shady milieu, almost like a man who is obliged to hand wash clothes. Both activities go against the grain of essentialist conceptions of gender, and such transgressions of established norms are considered shameful.

For many years Olena worked in a toy store on the main thoroughfare in downtown L'viv, recently renamed Freedom Prospect. Because of its location, the store did a brisk business. While in her early twenties, she married a man of Polish nationality from L'viv but this marriage ended several years later in divorce. When she was twenty-eight, a Russian-speaking Ukrainian from Kyiv moved in with her and her parents. He was divorced and his wife had custody of their two children. Her live-in companion (he refused to marry again) was not always gainfully employed, so Olena rapidly became the breadwinner, providing needed financial support for him, her parents, and periodically for his children as well. Five years later he moved out, married a younger woman, and had another child.

This left Olena alone again with her parents, both of whom are retired. However, in 1993 her mother returned to work as a cook in a psychiatric hospital. Pensions at this time barely allowed for the purchase of a loaf of bread a day. Working in the kitchen, her mother has access to foodstuffs, including meat. She could buy, steal, or replace food that was meant for the patients and offer it to her own family or sell it to close friends. This access to food at reduced prices without waiting in line, plus her salary, made the job worthwhile enough so that the seventy-year-old woman left retirement and returned to work, moving from one kitchen to another.

In the late 1980s, as the economic situation deteriorated in the Soviet Union and the restrictions on travel eased up a bit, Olena and her colleagues at the toy store formed an illegal shadow business, composed entirely of women who worked in the store. They began trading toys. In the early years of Gorbachev's rule, Polish traders would come to her store, and Olena, the manager, and several other saleswomen would sell the toys directly to the Poles before they were even put out on the shelves and offered to the public. Shelves empty of all but the toys the Poles had rejected greeted Soviet shoppers. The Soviet toys were produced in state-run factories and the official price tag stamped on each toy (set by some committee of bureaucrats in Moscow) was considerably less than the price it could fetch on the streets of Krakow. Thus, by buying up toys produced at state-run factories at subsidized prices in Ukraine and selling them on the streets of Poland, the Poles did a brisk and profitable business. Olena and her colleagues supplemented their salaries with sales to the Poles, some of which were in hard currency. With fewer wares to sell to Soviet shoppers, their days at the store were easier. Everyone benefited except the Soviet citizens who wanted to buy toys.

Theft from the state at one's workplace for personal benefit was a widespread practice across socialist societies. There is an old saying that dispenses with any sense of guilt for stealing and helps to explain why people felt entitled to take: "Everything around is the people's, everything around is mine" (Rus., "Vse vokrug narodnoe, vse vokrug moie"). State property is public property, which means that it is no one's property. The state was consistently viewed as the enemy, and deceiving the state was hardly considered a sin. On the contrary, individuals encouraged each other to strike a blow at the state by very slowly eroding its ability to function. One's dignity was often offended at work by the inability to make decisions, take responsibility, and achieve an acceptable level of material comfort. As a result, with the encouragement of their families and friends, individuals milked their state-sector jobs for personal benefit.

Eventually, however, the police raided the toy store and caught Olena and her coworkers in the act of illegally diverting Soviet goods to Polish traders in early 1991, before the fall of the Soviet Union. They conducted an elaborate investigation. Much to Olena's disappointment, her manager Paulina, a woman Olena felt very close to in spite of Paulina's alcoholism, decided that someone had to take the fall in order to keep the operation open. Paulina's husband was also an alcoholic and only periodically employed. Her two children and their families essentially depended on Paulina's shadow store for income. Olena, who has no children of her own, was designated to take the blame. All her coworkers testified that Olena organized and masterminded the entire shadow store. Olena was fired and charged with a long list of violations, all of which were inscribed in her official "labor book," a document recording her entire work experience, which would make it difficult for her to get another job with the state.

Stung by the betrayal of her coworkers, she called on other *blat* connections. Her most trusted friends set about to find a solution to her problems. Olena's best friend, a Ukrainian-speaking Ukrainian, is married to a Russian-speaking Ukrainian. He, together with his friend, a Ukrainian-speaking Ukrainian (his Russian-speaking Ukrainian wife from Donetsk is also a good friend of Olena's) took the situation in hand. With each person speaking his or her preferred language, the four of them pooled their contacts and worked out a strategy to Olena's problems.

Before the matter could come to trial, they managed to bribe the appropriate officials, and the case was magically dropped from the court records. No charges were ever made. Olena remained, however, unemployed and blackballed. In repentance for causing Olena's misfortunes when she was no more guilty than the others, Paulina continues to channel Olena toys produced at a state-subsidized factory which she can pay for at the official price and then sell when and where she pleases at market value.

Paulina was then further instrumental in helping Olena make connections with officials in the local education bureaucracy. Thanks to Paulina's contact, starting in 1992, usually about once a month, Olena boards a bus with forty high school students. She is permanently on record as a "chaperone" for high school exchanges between schools in L'viv and Krakow. This provides her with the necessary visa and a means of transportation to Poland. Of course, crossing the border still remains a feat of magic. The wait is merciless as both Polish and Ukrainian officials comb all vehicles for contraband and inspect all documents looking for an excuse to refuse entry or demand a bribe. Olena is somewhat protected when traveling with large groups of children. Forty-five people are on the bus. The Polish border guards select two people who are extensively searched. Both their bags and their persons are inspected. So far Olena has never been picked. The day her luck runs out it will, of course, be very difficult to explain why she is carrying the likes of three dozen children's rattles or forty-six pairs of children's socks. In anticipation of such a moment, she always travels with a $100 bill, ready to forfeit it to an overly curious official.

Olena claims that she sells her wares on the streets of Krakow because she needs a new car, which must, at least in part, be paid for with hard currency. Shuttle trade is the best means she has found so far to raise the money. A car is a luxury item in Ukraine, and gasoline remains very expensive. Although Olena claims she is generally in favor of economic reforms, it does not escape her attention that those very reforms are likely to destroy her livelihood. Her earnings are dependent on two things: the state subsidies which allow goods to be produced below market value and her ability to convert the state's losses into profit for herself through informal, non-tax-paying business activity.[8]

The fear of being caught again, the nerve-wracking process of crossing the border, the humiliation of standing on the street in another country selling meager wares illegally procured, and the dim suspicion that this will all come to an end, slowly bears down on Olena. She sees her salvation in a man who will come along, provide for her and her parents, and relieve her from the relentless pressure of hustling and haggling. Even though Olena is considered a successful black marketer able to provide for her elderly parents and even aim to purchase a big-ticket item such as a car, she still wants out. She would like nothing more than to trade in all the trading for a seat at the kitchen table and a life as a housewife. Over time and across industries, the subsidies that allowed Olena to earn a living have withered and substantially reduced these informal opportunities for profiting from state-sector production. In 1996, much as Olena had hoped, she met a Ukrainian who had immigrated to Canada during World War II. Although he was twenty-five years her senior, she married him and relocated to Canada where she now lives as a housewife.

"Economic tourism" is the term popularly used to refer to the kind of shuttle trade that Olena was engaged in. Profiting from any activity that did not involve socially valuable work, such as actually producing goods, was condemned by a value system based on Soviet ideology. Under the Soviet regime, wealthy individuals were consistently condemned as "unpunished thieves" in the court of popular justice. State salaries were so uniform and so uniformly low that individuals who enjoyed a noticeably higher standard of living were accused of having procured the extra income through one of two questionable means: collaboration with the ruling Communist Party elite in exchange for material privilege or by selling goods on the black market for a profit. This kind of "speculation" was considered shameful because it involved deceiving a buyer into paying more than the purchase price in order to generate a profit and shirk the responsibility of work.

Such a moral code was necessary in the face of state-subsidized goods produced in short supply and sold below market value, which created a situation that predisposed individuals to pay more for goods simply to bypass shortages and lines. Vestiges of this derogatory attitude toward "business" more than just linger. They hinder many people in post-Soviet society from leaving state-sector jobs, even when salaries which do not constitute a living wage are paid with delays of half a year. Because production has fallen so drastically in post-Soviet Ukraine, "business" refers primarily to a middleman function of buying and selling. It is considered by many to be an immoral activity, a license to profit from the desperation and poverty of captive post-Soviet consumers.

Given the dense morass of regulation and a vicious system of taxation, participating in a business inevitably entails lying to officials, bending rules, and cheating on taxes. Olena was the first to recognize this, and it contributed to her conflicted participation in "economic tourism." She wanted and needed money, but the only way she found of procuring it was through illegally taking state-subsidized goods that would otherwise be available to Ukrainians and selling them to foreigners simply for self-enrichment. Others who elect a more modest lifestyle can cast a moral judgment on traders like Olena, robbing them of their dignity by denigrating the work they do.

Under the current tough economic conditions, with factories, stores, and even universities closing, it becomes convenient when so many women, including Olena, want to stay at home. Although it adds a significant burden to the (male) breadwinner in the family, the tendency for women to write themselves a ticket out of the labor force hides unemployment or underemployment and helps the government mask the extent of economic dislocation. Almost inevitably, regimes that support a "return to tradition" ideology, end up shortchanging women. Women lose rights and power in society as they are recast as mystical mother figures, guardians of home and hearth.

The distinctive meaning the home has is another significant factor contributing to the widely shared desire to opt out of the work force. The home serves as a refuge. A hostile, crowded, and tense work environment, combined with little public space, save parks and a few cafés, gives the home a historically and socially specific meaning that is not comparable with Western notions. This heightened importance of the home sharply contrasts with condemnatory attitudes toward new forms of employment available in post-Soviet society which inevitably involve activating the kinds of networks I have described. The glorification of the home and the demonization of "business" conspire to prompt voluntary withdrawal from the labor force. Redefinitions of gender roles and the meaning of home are themes to which we will return when we look at changes in the new state calendar and at how and what is now being commemorated and celebrated in post-Soviet Ukraine.

New Iron Curtains

To understand the full import of these networks, it is necessary to consider the plight of someone who does not have recourse to network-based resources when hard times hit. Anna Grigor'evna is such a woman. I met her, together with her colleague Tamara Antonovna, in July 1993 in

These demonstrators are marching to a town meeting to be held on the central town square of Sevastopol, the home port of the Black Sea Fleet, in support of the Russian Parliament's proclamation of Sevastopol's special status as a "Russian city" in July 1993.

Sevastopol at an event that was billed as a "town meeting" (Rus. *narodnoe veche*), allegedly following the tradition of medieval Novgorod. Earlier that month the Russian Parliament had declared Sevastopol a Russian city and later an "international city," on the grounds that the administrative transfer of Crimea to Ukraine away from Russia in 1954 did not specifically mention this port.[9]

In Sevastopol, this *narodnoe veche* was organized as a widespread popular show of support for reunification with Russia.[10] The police, paid employees of the Ukrainian state, were put in the unenviable position of trying to quell a crowd denouncing Ukraine, celebrating a Soviet past, and agitating for a Russian future. Try as they may, there was no way the police could turn back the thousands of demonstrators carrying Soviet flags, flags of the Soviet Russian Republic, and the Andrevskii flag, the nineteenth-century emblem of the Russian Navy. From a small podium facing a monument to Admiral Nakhimov, a hero of the Crimean War (1853–56) and the man for whom the square was named, one by one the

Some participants in the demonstration carry a banner, written in the style of the Polish Solidarity movement, which reads "Russia is with us!" Alongside this banner are Russian flags, Soviet flags, and the Andreevskii flag, the nineteenth century emblem of the Russian Navy.

speakers, most of whom were local political and naval leaders, voiced support for the aims of the Russian Parliament before a crowd of thousands. In unequivocal terms they condemned the Ukrainian government's intention to turn them into Ukrainians. Portraits of Stalin, the *tryzub* (trident and Ukrainian national symbol) depicted as a noose around Crimea, and banners, written in the lettering of the Polish Solidarity movement logo, proclaiming "Russia is with us," bobbed up and down in the crowd as the speeches continued for nearly two hours. The demonstration was an attempt to reanimate the legacy of Soviet superpower status and the glory it accorded their strategic port city by rekindling the elusive possibility of becoming Soviet once again.

It was in this context that I met two middle-aged women. They had noticed that I was unusually interested in the proceedings of the demonstration and perhaps thought that I would take up their case as well. The urge to have one's unjustifiable suffering acknowledged, a syndrome I had frequently witnessed, prompted them to approach me. When I interviewed them later, they wasted no time and immediately launched into detailed biographies of themselves and their views of the political situation in Sevastopol. Married with two children, Tamara Antonovna is a forty-seven-year-old teacher in a boarding school for retarded children in Sevastopol. Anna Grigor'evna described herself as an unemployed-retired nurse. She had worked together with Tamara Antonovna for twenty-four years. With shrill pleading, Anna Grigor'evna stressed how terribly alone she is. She has no children, no husband, no brothers or sisters and her parents are dead. Indeed, in this society, where the only thing you can count on is that you will need to count on your family, this is a highly vulnerable position to be in.

They began with a litany of complaints. "Ukraine is a swamp!" they said. "Khrushchev was drunk when he gave Crimea away! Our Stalin would have never done this! Earlier we never had any problems with nationalities," Anna Grigor'evna exclaimed with total exasperation. She set the stage for her story by explaining that the communists protected what she called the "simple people" (Rus. *prostye liudi*). There were boards that listened to the complaints of workers, and if a superior was found breaking the rules, she maintained, the authorities would dole out the proper punishment. Superiors, who were inevitably all communists, knew that they were vulnerable, that there were higher Party authorities that the "simple people" could appeal to should they not respect the limits of permissible behavior. She explained that this was hardly the case today:

Today the sky is the limit [Rus. *Sevodnia bezpredel*]. Directors have become masters [Rus. *khoziaeva*]. I worked for twenty-four years in this school but I was fired eight months ago. Do you know why? Well, the food is better at a boarding school than it is at a regular school and our director steals food from the school. I think that this is wrong. The food is there for the children so I told him not to steal. The children get it for free and the teachers pay for their food. But he considers himself to be a baron and this is his fiefdom and he can do whatever he wants. He knows no one will reprimand him. My mother always told me, "Don't speak the truth. You'll die for speaking the truth in this country." But still I complained about our director. I went through official channels. But in Kyiv they said that this must be solved on the local level. So far nothing has happened other than the fact that I've been fired.

"The communists would surely have thrown him out for such behavior!" piped in Tamara Antonovna. "Four of us supported Anna Grigor'evna. We complained too about his stealing and now he wants to fire us. I think his behavior is immoral. This new elite, they are nothing more than masters, than barons. They have disregard and contempt for simple people."

"In Kyiv I don't know who to take my case to. For three months I didn't receive a pension. If it hadn't been for Tamara Antonovna, I might have starved," she confessed.

Here sat two women who had followed the rules and worked hard all their lives and now were entirely disempowered and falling into ever deeper poverty. With no friends or acquaintances in positions of authority, they were virtually powerless to reverse their plight. They had relied all their lives on the ruling Party structure and hierarchy to punish transgressions and with it now absent, they have no recourse of their own, as Olena the trader did, to stave off hardship. As meager as pensions and salaries are, they become indispensable when they are the sole source of income. Once again, these women do not have the networks and the contacts to overcome the logistical obstacles to securing alternative employment. Without the protection of the Soviet state and its roster of cradle-to-grave allotments, in this new social darwinian post-Soviet world without vital *blat* connections they are left highly vulnerable to poverty.

They blame their incomprehensible woes and the elusiveness of a solution on the breakdown of the Soviet state. They recognize that recreating the Soviet Union and the economic and political systems that characterized it is an option that exists only in their dreams. But it is one that exerts tremendous nostalgic appeal. If they can't have the Soviet Union back, as a consolation, at least they want Russia back. They bitterly resent historical events discounting the pride they feel over the Soviet Union's military might, the currents under way pushing them toward total self-reliance, and most of all, they resist being taken from a society characterized by oppression and material hardship and thrust into one which, in their view, is even harsher.

Sevastopol has been a closed city, initially to Soviet and subsequently to Ukrainian citizens. This mid-sized city is largely populated by naval personnel and retired military men. Even though it sustained terrible destruction during World War II, it was quickly rebuilt, and the boulevards are now lined with some of the most aesthetically pleasing examples of Stalinist architecture. To enter the city, a friend of mine who has *svoi chelovek* among the organizers of an international theater festival, the Khersones Games (Rus. *Khersoneskie Igry*), held every July in Sevastopol since 1992, procured a visa for me on the grounds that I was a theater critic from New York and would be a judge in the festival. Without this fiction and the papers to support it, I would have been turned back at the city border. The overall mood among the populace is that this closed-city policy has worked to the advantage of local residents. People from other cities or villages and tourists cannot come into town and raid their stores, a point acknowledged by these two women.[11] They maintain that this practice helps to protect the stocks in stores in spite of the fact that vodka, cigarettes, matches, sugar, oil, and butter were all rationed in Sevastopol until early 1994, when all rationing across Ukraine stopped. Meat at various times was also rationed.

In the "new world order" there is talk of ending this Communist Party practice of closing off cities. In fact, staging an international theater festival (with the exception of one Polish troupe, all other companies were from the former USSR) in this town, where every actor, director, stagehand, and spectator who lives beyond the city limits is potentially obliged to get a Ukrainian and a Sevastopol visa in addition to a ticket to the show, is a step toward cracking the gates open by tiring out the bureaucrats. Both women are against it. The very mention of opening the city prompts them to mourn the passing of Soviet traditions. The Soviet state, with all its bureaucratic rules and regulations, protected its citizens. The closed-city policy assures the residents of Sevastopol a supply of affordable food, these women reason. As these rules wither or are irregularly enforced as the functions of the state change, these women feel vulnerable and insecure, left with only a feeling of emptiness at seeing all they know and value discarded like old shoes.

The anger over watching all that they believed in slip away like sand through their fingers is not easily quelled. Tamara Antonovna, Anna Grigor'evna, and others of their generation, who without the social networks necessary to profit from newfound freedoms, have little to gain and very nearly everything to lose from the breakdown of the Soviet state and the convulsive changes this has wrought in their everyday lives. They tend to see the Ukrainian state as symptomatic of the motor propelling them into uncharted, murky waters. They believed in an ideology, a system, and the goodness of their leaders. They worked hard only to find themselves disempowered, poor, and sitting on a park bench trying to communicate their disillusionment, vulnerability, and fear to a foreigner, who by virtue of her passport and ability to escape the chaos, could never fully understand the depth of their angst.

Wherever We Are Not

There is a line from Russian writer Aleksandr Griboedov's play *Woe from Wit* (Rus. *Gore ot uma*) that, although written over 150 years ago, has enormous resonance today. It has become a popular proverb and is often heard in kitchens across Ukraine today. It sums up in a phrase a seemingly timeless conception of self and society inextricably embedded in and branded by the particularities of a Kafkaesque cultural milieu.

Lamenting the hopeless confinement of a rigid, traditional society, Sofiia asks, "Where is it better?"

"Wherever we are not," Chatsky replies. (Rus., "Gde luchshe? Gde nas net.")

As more and more people dream of emigrating to escape the excruciating experience of a society disintegrating into self-serving anarchy, they long to find a place where "we are not." Much as Ernest Gellner (1983) refers to modern man as "gelded by nationality," many Soviet citizens, more so than any sense of nationality, acknowledge that they have been gelded by the Soviet system. Their patterns of thinking and behavior have been shaped by the structural constraints of Soviet society (shortages, repression, and lack of dignity) and the values that the system bred in Soviet citizens (feeling of inferiority, the "two personalities" syndrome, and sharply honed manipulative abilities).

The Soviet system was brought down by a Brechtian form of struggle: passive noncompliance, subtle sabotage, cynical evasion, and abrasive deception. Open defiance to the system might cost you your life or decades in prison, depending on the period. But passive resistance, the slow and deliberate chiseling away of authority, left little recourse to reaction. For lack of a better solution, it was often grudgingly tolerated by state authorities.

Today the categories, labels, and structure of the Soviet system are fading. But the culture of fraud, the Kafkaesque state regulations, and established conceptions of self and community carry on, all of which give life to the Soviet legacy and persist in the face of attempts at sweeping economic, political, social, and cultural reform. The culture of fraud not only endures but intensifies in post-Soviet Ukraine because of the persistent urge and even need to lie, cheat, and steal when confronting the state and because of decreasing fear of punishment. Siberia is, after all, now in a different country. Meanwhile, state authorities deceive their own constituents in a multitude of ways, ranging from neglect of urgent social problems to active participation in dishonest pyramid schemes which robbed many people of their savings. The pervasive duplicity and frenetic hustling that this confusion breeds is why it has become a common expression to proclaim that it's better "where we are not."

As this struggle continues, the benchmarks for distinguishing the authentic from the fake, the acceptable from the unacceptable, or the enduring from the fleeting have all changed. Exactly how they have changed is not clear. Even though many lament the "sky's the limit" atmosphere that encourages reckless, self-indulgent, self-serving behavior, the consequences of engaging in such lawless social darwinism are also no longer clear.

Amid such chaos, many who live in Ukraine but were socialized into Soviet culture feel themselves to be citizens of a nonexistent state, the products of a system now in free fall. Soviet leaders understood that the state had a vested interest in inculcating individuals with a particular sense of identity precisely because it fosters allegiance to the political order that claims to be its protector. The power of such a strategy lies in the fact that the culture in which one is socialized becomes an inextricable part of an individual's sense of self. But what happens when that very culture is first privately discredited and later publicly lambasted even by Communist Party leaders, its most ardent supporters? Or when networks of power and prestige and sources of income all depend on a strong state, which is at once feared, hated, and perceived to be desperately needed?

Glasnost and independence were meant to pierce the veil of lies and deceit, to dissolve the barricades between private truth and public propaganda. This is neither quickly nor easily accomplished. All ideologies structure and shape social processes and everyday practices that form human subjectivities and a sense of self in the world. When that ideology has informed an entire social system for seventy-four years, a rejection, even if cogently articulated, cannot erase the fact that the ideology has already dramatically informed the thinking, values, and character of those who were subject to it.

This is why the mood is often one of double disillusionment. Oksana Ivanovna, a teacher in the coal-rich Luhansk region said:

> We decided that we would live poorly so that our children would live in a "bright future," as the communists said. We believed them and thought we were building a better society. It all turned out to be lies. One year ago, when Ukraine became independent, we believed life would finally improve for us. This turned out to be a lie too. We were deceived once again. Our political leaders told us that Ukraine was feeding the whole Soviet Union, that Russia could not live without Ukrainian grain. Now we realize that Ukraine fed no one—everyone fed Ukraine.

Although she now distances herself from the Soviet system through harsh criticism of the Soviet way of life, she has nonetheless embraced some of the tenets of Soviet ideology and rhetoric and used them to give her life meaning. Hardships could be glorified and explained away as part of an exchange for a better future for one's children. Now that such ideologies and narratives have been shown to be deceptive, many individuals are left groping for an explanation for their plight within the same framework of ideas and values. How could they have worked hard all their lives and have only growing impoverishment and despair for them and for their families to show for it? How could they have hoped and prayed for Ukrainian independence when all it has brought them so far is poverty and uncertainty? In this period of intense confusion, old dreams are burdensome to remember.

As each one reevaluates, some rely on received Soviet concepts and practices to forge meaning into their lives, and others look to new groups furnishing alternative narratives to explain their collective past in an effort to provide comfort in the present and hope for the future. Personal and collective history informs an individual's sense of self. Under Soviet rule history and historical representations were blatantly ideologically laden for the specific purposes of constructing the "new Soviet man." Yet rival concepts of collective identity born of these representations are likely to be one of the more enduring legacies of Soviet rule. Articulating a revised, re-nationalized sense of self and society inherently mandates the creation of a new set of cultural differences and embues them with new meaning. These new differences are inevitably constructed in terms of the colonial state and a historical experience of socialism. A revised sense of collective identity is therefore inextricably linked to a Soviet identity and dependent on it to define what the new collective identity is not.

Nationalism in post-Soviet Ukrainian society is increasingly conceived of not only as nation-building but also as a project of cultural "normalization," as a means of desovietizing oneself and society. With little cultural capital at their disposal, political and cultural leaders turned to history, first to generate support for Ukrainian independence and now to legitimate it. With russification, sovietization, and sharp regionalization as legacies to overcome and little in the way of broad cultural unifiers, such as common language or religion, how can a fragile state mired in economic chaos forge a collective identity to unify such a highly indifferent, diverse, and disenfranchised population?

Various historical events serve as a site of autonomy, guiding and defining the process of ukrainianization. By reinterpreting them, one can see beyond subordination to a colonial and exploitative regime and reintroduce a sense of agency to one's individual and national historical experience. This historical revisionism has the potential to become the cornerstone of a new national culture. The next part of this book analyzes sites where attempts are made to institutionalize a new historically based national culture. Schools, festivals, the state calendar, and urban space serve as arenas were a post-Soviet national culture can be articulated and, of course, contested as part of an overall project to fortify or challenge the new state.

Part Two

Sites of Nationalizing

Educational Reform

It's the direction given by
education that is likely to
determine all that follows.

—Plato, *The Republic*

Few institutions reflect the complexities and contradictions of cultural
change as poignantly as schools. Whether it is the American debate over
multiculturalism or the Ukrainian debate over language policy, when it
comes to reforming the educational system, a politically informed understanding of nationality demands articulation. Articulation inevitably
prompts contestation and protest, turning the educational system into a
pivotal site of cultural confrontation. Schools also provide a window into
one of the most vibrant and enduringly influential points of contact between individuals and the state. Given the critical importance of education and the near monopoly of control the state wields over it, the school
system was one of the first institutions to undergo rapid and radical reform following independence.

Educational reforms represent a compromise reached among divergent ideological groups wielding zones of influence in the government.

Since independence, educational and cultural policy, as contrasted with economic and industrial policy, have fallen to the "national-democrats," or groups espousing a nationalist ideology. By targeting education for reform, political leaders capitalize on the potential of schools to articulate and instill new norms of cultural and social behavior. The vast state-sponsored effort to ukrainianize public education aims to redefine nationality as based not solely on residency and citizenship but on cultural factors as well. Schools are called upon to naturalize a Ukrainian identity among the first post-Soviet generation by incorporating elements of Ukrainian culture, language, and historical memory into the cultural knowledge that children acquire during the socialization process at school. As an ideological institution, schools acquaint young generations in their formative years with the symbolic meanings of the myths, symbols, and ceremonies of the nation. These efforts to reinterpret nationality through educational reform affect other concepts informing a sense of self, such as gender roles, class membership, and religious sentiment. At this juncture of state and national development, the demands of youth concerning their interpretation of what it means to be Ukrainian reverberate back on to the state and increasingly so with echoes that cannot be ignored.[1]

As Bourdieu (1967) and more recently Ernest Gellner (1983) have pointed out, schools are a critical arena where one learns the cultural currency facilitating communication among members of a group. The structural requirements of a modern industrial economy mandate that workers be mobile and capable of communicating in impersonal situations by trading on common cultural capital. School-transmitted cultural knowledge in the form of values, interests, symbols, and myths, what Bourdieu calls "cultural goods," is a critical factor in formulating a sense of identity by crystallizing membership in a particular generation and in a particular social class (1990: 30). Indeed, many scholars have documented the extent to which schools serve to reproduce the status quo, to reproduce the very class structure in which it is embedded (Bourdieu 1988, Willis 1977, Apple 1990). But what function do schools serve when the status quo is being redefined? Or when the relevance of certain cultural goods is called into question? How do schools bring about the reconceptualization of difference and the recreation of a status quo?

Increasingly, a cultural group is unlikely to reproduce and sustain itself if it does not have its own independent educational system institutionalizing aspects of its culture, delineating cultural boundaries, and providing an institutional site for acculturation to its values.[2] Gellner argues that in the age of the nation-state, one's prime loyalty is no longer to a religion, monarch, or land, but to the medium of one's literacy, the identity-conferring part of education and its political protector. "The monopoly of legitimate education is now more important, more central than is the monopoly of legitimate violence," he asserts (1983: 34). Yet as we will see, the concept of "legitimate education" is often quite elusive.

The educational system, and in particular the strict controls on historical interpretation, played a critical role in the Bolshevik attempt to create *homo sovieticus*. It served as a catalyst for russification and assimilation to the ideal of a "new man."[3] The Soviet educational system's uniformly standard, highly politicized, and Russian-oriented curriculum facilitated communication by imparting shared Soviet cultural values, symbols, and practices among peoples as diverse culturally, linguistically, and geographically as Ukrainians, Yakuts, and Uzbeks. It was also a key means of indoctrinating a multiethnic population to Soviet ideology and of culturally integrating them to form the "Soviet people." The patterns of thinking and behavior, which provided the cultural underpinnings of a Soviet identity, were taught in school.[4]

However, the implementation of "internationalist" policies in an effort to "make Soviets" yielded unintended dividends. The obligatory participation in Soviet institutions and Soviet culture did not preclude the development and even reinforcement of alternative national or localized identities and cultures. The second-class treatment that national and local cultures often received in Soviet curricula triggered alienation, a poignant awareness of otherness, and often a sharp politicization of ethnicity. With glasnost, this reservoir of ethnic resentment, long percolating among certain groups or among certain sectors, such as the intelligentsia, flooded the political scene in the late 1980s once weaknesses in Soviet power were detected. One of the key goals of post-Soviet educational reform, initially articulated by Rukh as the independence movement was building momentum, was to reverse the long-term second-class status accorded to Ukrainian and to Ukrainian history and culture in Soviet schools.

Individuality, Nationality, Morality: New Guiding Principles

An influential post-independence blueprint for education, written by a commission from the Ministry of Education and released one year after independence in December 1992, outlines how the educational system should be reformed to reflect changing political realities. In the process, it also articulates an opinion of the Soviet educational system. The report claims that post-Soviet educational reform intends to eliminate the "authoritarian pedagogy put in place by a totalitarian state which led to the suppression of natural talents and capabilities and interests of all participants in the educational process."[5] The Soviet insistence on uniformity and collectivism are values rejected in harsh language by this commission. In an effort to reverse what they call the "lumpenization" of society produced by Soviet schools, the commission asserts that the educational system must strive to develop "individuality, nationality, and morality" as a top priority among primary and secondary school students. To some degree, these principles were already articulated during perestroika by parents and teachers.[6] To realize a new focus on individuality and morality, the proposed plan goes on to state that educational reform must be based on the national idea, as embodied in such principles "as a national form of education, which is founded on the indivisibility of education from the national soil, the organic unity of national history and traditions, the preservation and enrichment of the culture of the Ukrainian people, the transformation of education into a significant instrument of national development and harmonious relations among nationalities."[7]

The restoration of a Ukrainian cultural identity is seen as part and parcel of the process of fostering individual development. Yet the simultaneous focus on individuality and nationality is inherently contradictory. Even if education is used as a tool for "national development," the choice to be something other than Soviet immediately opens up a multitude of possibilities. In essence, educational policymakers advocate pursuing a nationalist program of education through an individualist approach by cultivating individuality at the same time that it encourages conformity to a national identity and the cultural attributes that characterize it. By mediating between macro- and micro-level dynamics of identity formation, public education does not simply engineer conformity to a redefined national identity. Rather, encouraging renationalization and individuality fuels an awareness of differences in experiences, memories, and identities. There is a persistent tension between the state's articulated goals of encouraging individuality and individual choice at the same time that it aims to impart a collective identity based on an interpretation of Ukrainianness that the state has sanctioned and is attempting to institutionalize in schools.

A school on the outskirts of Kyiv for grades one through eleven. This is one out of two schools in a district of twenty-five that will remain Russian language. Written above the entrance is a banner in Russian proclaiming "Welcome!"

Resistance to state-directed change takes many forms, some of it, as we will see, is overt and direct, as in the move to found private schools that skirt state regulations. Other forms of resistance are more akin to Scott's (1985) "weapons of the weak." They constitute hidden forms of passive-aggressive noncompliance exhibited in everyday life. Let us now look at which reforms have been successfully implemented and which ones have foundered when confronted with resistance.

To foster the principles of individuality, nationality, and morality, the educational system was swiftly reformed following independence. The most significant structural changes have been fundamental and sweeping. They include: (1) a sharp reduction in the number of schools with a Russian language based curriculum; (2) a ceding of total state monopoly on curricular design to allow for measured regional autonomy; and (3) a greater prominence given to the study of humanities over the natural sciences, reversing priorities established in the Soviet era and emphasizing the need to recast notions of morality.

The first reform, switching to Ukrainian, affects the greatest number of people. Ukrainian was declared the state language of Soviet Ukraine in 1989. To change the language of instruction, particularly in urban areas, a two-pronged approach was implemented, targeted at the youngest and oldest students, and thereby affecting all those in between. In 1992, a federal mandate was issued to convert higher education and primary schools, with few exceptions, to a Ukrainian language curriculum. Secondary schools were to be converted gradually, with students initially given the option to complete their studies in Russian. As of 1993, in most regions, Crimea being the notable exception, university entrance exams are conducted in Ukrainian. As a result, many secondary school students have requested to study in Ukrainian in preparation.

Prior to independence, 47.4 percent of the schools taught in Ukrainian but such schools were disproportionately located in rural areas and in the western and central provinces (Magocsi 1996: 669). By the 1993–94 academic year, the percentage of Ukrainian schools in the capital Kyiv had jumped from pre-independence levels of 20 percent to over half the schools (Arel 1995a: 176). Some schools began to offer bilingual English-Ukrainian instruction from the first grade up, testifying to the extent to which English and Ukrainian have replaced Russian as the languages considered to have the greatest potential for social mobility.

Individual directors of schools were given quite a bit of latitude in deciding whether to switch to Ukrainian or retain Russian as the language of instruction. But it was clear that any director, especially in the central provinces, who could speak Ukrainian willingly switched. Such was not the case in the Donbas and in the Crimea where changes were made far more gradually, even though all students had been studying Ukrainian since the third grade (Arel 1995a: 174–75). Almost all of the schools in the western provinces had already switched to Ukrainian. In 1992–94, when the changes in educational policy were most sweeping, there was little visible protest from any of the groups involved, parents, teachers, or students, over the announced plans to change to a Ukrainian language curriculum. For those teachers who had to learn active command of the language before translating their lectures, free courses in "requalification" were readily available. In the eastern and southern provinces, some teachers and administrators coped with the change in language policy, in the grand Soviet tradition of "two personalities," by simply accepting the policy in word and passively resisting it to the extent that they could in deed.[8]

Switching to Ukrainian was but one aspect of curricular reform. The

Inside this school, Soviet era uniforms are still worn by the students, partially due to parental request which stems from a desire to minimize expenses during the economic crisis that followed independence, and partially because the director of the school feels uniforms help create an atmosphere of discipline and order. This young student is standing in front of a billboard announcing the activities of various scholastic clubs at the school.

state-designed core curriculum, which will be a requirement for all schools receiving state funding, has increased the number of hours for Ukrainian literature, language, and history and expanded humanities offerings by including courses on aesthetics, law, ecology, and health. These are all subjects this commission feels were sorely ignored by Soviet authorities. In all schools, instruction in Russian grammar and Russian literature has been reduced to make way for expanded study of Ukrainian and the humanities. Some schools have recategorized Russian as an elective. Russian literature, previously a course taken every year up through graduation, is now incorporated into the new course "World Literature," where only two Russian writers, usually Pushkin and Dostoevsky, are studied. As revealed in interviews, there is near unanimous agreement among parents, teachers, and students that reform was needed. While there is little overt resistance to raising the status and expanding the study of Ukrainian-related subjects, many find it lamentable that this upgrade has come at the price of a downgrade of the Russian language, Russian literature, and Russian history.[9]

More specifically, the commission advocates using the educational system to foster "democracy" by decentralizing the educational bureaucracy in favor of regional boards vested with decision-making powers in an effort to accommodate a plurality of opinions. The commission reports that this is part of the government's plan to break with the "totalizing" effects of state-sponsored, mass, standardized education, as they claim was the Soviet practice. They intend to encourage regional adaptation of a national curriculum and to encourage experimental and private schools, each free to develop their own specializations, pedagogies, and curricula within certain state guidelines, as a means to mark the salient differences between the Soviet and the Ukrainian states.

Recognized diversity is found not only among schools but within them now as well. Some schools have begun to create a tracking system (a four-tiered division of students according to ability). The Soviet practice was to group students regardless of ability. A class remains together not only day after day as students move from subject to subject but year after year until graduation eleven years later. Public humiliation, rather than positive reinforcement, was (and still is) considered the prime motivator and means of disciplining lazy or rebellious students who do not meet the class standard. The division of students by ability makes this disciplinary process of maintaining a class standard less arduous.

In addition to the three fundamental structural changes outlined above—the switch to instruction in Ukrainian, the expansion of humanities offerings, and the possibility for regional or independent adaptation of the national curriculum—there have been numerous changes in educational practices. The formal, structural aspects of Soviet education are easier to reform than the practices instilled by the values of the Soviet system. Aside from a rigorous adherence to a uniform curriculum, Soviet schools were characterized by strict discipline and relatively high standards of learning. The turbulence of post-Soviet society, coupled with extreme material hardship both in school and at home, have prompted a sharp decline in student performance, which all teachers and administrators lament. Students, much like their parents, are increasingly drawn to careers in business because it is one of the few means to earn a living. No great knowledge of physics, literature, or history is required. As a result, commitment to excelling at school has waned when it does not contribute directly to the development of business skills.

As of this writing, Ukrainian schools have yet to embrace the global trend of corporatizing education and using schools as training grounds for students' future participation in the market economy. However, some private, specialized vocational schools have opened and offer training in specific business skills, namely, accounting, finance, advertising, and marketing. Additionally, some large enterprises offer private courses. Graduates, already trained at their own expense in the ways of that particular company, enjoy a slight advantage when applying for a job at the same enterprise. Without a *blat* connection, such an advantage can become the critical decisive factor in obtaining a job or remaining unemployed.

The allure of a university education has rapidly diminished, except in elite circles, since it is no longer a means to more prestigious or lucrative jobs. As belts tighten at research institutes, publishing houses, and cultural institutions, there is little guarantee that a university degree, especially in the humanities, will have any practical application, making it increasingly a luxury that few can afford. Furthermore, much like schools, universities are in the process of undergoing reform. The old ideologically laden departments that were used to socialize students to a communist worldview are undergoing radical reform, often with mixed success. Departments of atheism became departments of religion; departments of political economy transformed themselves into departments of management and marketing; departments of the history of the USSR now focus on the history of Ukraine; former departments of philosophy now call themselves departments of culturology; and so on.

Needless to say, few professors and administrators, nearly all of whom have retained their jobs, are able to "restructure" themselves, their disciplines, their courses, and their work routines from one year to the next. The appeal of higher education is tarnished by the paper-thin facade of reform and the overall poor functioning of universities during this period of transition. The faculty are increasingly disengaged as they search for more lucrative employment or work second jobs to compensate for shrinking salaries paid with tremendous delays. Falling wages, not surprisingly, have led to a sharp increase in the bribes necessary to enroll. The loss of prestige of a university education, caused by a radical shift in the cultural knowledge that is now valued by society, increasingly informs how students approach their studies at school.

Generational Divides

Having taught for nearly forty years, Valentina Maksymivna has seen many changes in the educational system but laments that things had turned for the worse at the school on the outskirts of Kyiv where she teaches English. She taught English for many years at this school before retiring six years ago. Claiming that she is ashamed of her English, she insists that we speak Russian. As business and exchange opportunities with the West steadily increased, many teachers left teaching for better-paying jobs in the budding entrepreneurial sector. The ranks of English teachers were particularly decimated. One year ago, the director of the school where Valentina Maksymivna previously worked asked her to return to ease the growing shortage of English teachers.

She begins to detail how she thinks the atmosphere at school has changed with her husband, a retired customs official at the Kyiv airport, and her daughter, an architect who opened an architectural firm together with her husband in 1991, and her two grandchildren, who dart in and out of the room, ignoring the conversation. She explains that her son, a professor of nineteenth-century Russian history at Kharkiv University, is now teaching at a state university in Maine for one year, having left his wife and two children behind. He hopes to find permanent employment in the United States, send for his family, and eventually settle there. She regrets deeply that he has made this decision but understands only too well why. Indeed, the need for supplemental income to make ends meet was the main reason she returned to teaching.

Until she retired, she had always taught English in Russian. Following independence, her school converted to Ukrainian. Although secondary school students have the option of finishing in Russian, elementary classes are now conducted in Ukrainian. This means that at the time of our interview she was teaching English in Russian to some and in Ukrainian to others. Sometimes she forgets, she says, and begins teaching a Russian class English in Ukrainian, only to be reminded of her mistake as the students break into peals of laughter. Just as she is teaching a foreign language in Ukrainian, a second language to her, many of her students are learning English in a language that is not their mother tongue.

She began her lament about the changes she has seen in the educational system by saying: "Before the level was so high. The students were earnest and they worked so hard."

"If the level was so high, why is this country filled with economists who can't count and politicians who can't govern?" her daughter interjected.

"Never mind," her mother retorted, dismissing the question. "The things that are happening now were unimaginable then. At school, we taught a sense of morality, of right and wrong, of responsibility to others. We had order and discipline. We always used to say, 'If you don't want it, you're getting it. If you don't know how, we'll teach you.' Students showed respect, they behaved, and had a sense of discipline."

"If they learned such respect and discipline, where did so many criminals come from?" her daughter insisted. The generational debate over the merits and flaws of Soviet education continued in an increasingly shrill tone with Anna, the daughter, who issued a blanket condemnation of the rigidity of Soviet schools and the emptiness of an overly ideologized curriculum, while her mother fiercely defended a system that in her opinion had functioned and imparted morality and knowledge. The only point they could agree on was that the decision to improve the standing of the language, literature, and history of Ukraine was a positive step. Valentina Maksymivna is half-Jewish and half-Ukrainian but is registered as Ukrainian. Her Russian husband was born in Siberia but they have lived in Kyiv for the last forty years. Both their children are Ukrainian by nationality but their son identifies himself informally as Russian. They all speak Russian at home and only Valentina Maksymivna has an active command of Ukrainian.

Mother and daughter in unison, they began to stress how much Ukraine has suffered at the hands of Moscow. As we spoke in April 1994, the greatly reduced flow of Russian natural gas to Ukraine due to nonpayment for previous shipments resulted in a winter where the majority of offices were poorly heated, if at all. Heating for homes, hospitals, schools, and other public service facilities was greatly curtailed. The two women continued on about the great wealth of Ukraine and how the Russian government was intent on crushing Ukrainian independence. Withholding fuel was one of the many tactics they were using to bring Ukraine back in to the pan-Slavic fold, they argued.

And with this Sergei Antonovich, who up until now had sat silently in an armchair near the window, bellowed out, "But Russia has always protected Ukraine!"

"The Voice of Siberia has arisen!" Valentina Maksymivna sarcastically responded, alluding to the Voice of America. Generational adversaries became national allies as Valentina Maksymivna and her daughter continued to challenge the benevolence of Russia over the protests of the otherwise silent Siberian. The women, who had been bickering so fiercely a moment ago over the merits, or lack thereof, of the Soviet educational system, now argued together for the ukrainianization of public education over the objections of the Russian half of the family. Educational reform generates such emotional reactions because aspects of change go to the heart of factors that inform identity (generation, gender, nationality, class, profession, and personal experience) and threaten—or at least challenge—a sense of self.

Double Burden

It was quite common during the Soviet era for professionals of all stripes, teachers included, to be obliged periodically to do manual labor or other forms of work far below their qualifications. Obliging teachers to, for example, "volunteer" to pick potatoes at a collective farm was part of the effort to degrade intellectual work and to chisel away at the dignity of individuals. Today, driven by a severe economic crisis and drastic reductions in state spending for education, no longer purely by ideology, this mixing of manual and intellectual labor continues. All students, parents, teachers, and administrators are called upon to perform double duty at all schools, public and private, elite and ordinary.

For example, the children are more than just students. They are the school's janitors and gardeners. They wash walls, scrub floors, and prune bushes. Continuing a Soviet practice, every day two students from each class are "on duty." This means that they are responsible for cleaning the classroom, washing the blackboard, and running errands. On any given day, girls with pom-pom pigtails in white aprons and boys with their sleeves carefully rolled up can be seen dipping tattered rags in steel buckets to scrub down stairwells.

A teacher's job is never-ending as well. Teachers often double as the director's secretary, messenger, or "go-fer." They spend hours not only writing but also typing worksheets, texts, and so on, page by page using carbons. In each instance, those associated with the educational system are frequently called upon to do unwanted, menial tasks well below what they are (or are being) trained for simply to keep the schools functioning.

The brunt of the economic crisis has most greatly affected parents. Each summer before the new school year begins, teams of parents flood the schools to give them a new coat of paint, put up wallpaper, make all possible repairs, and hang posters and plants. Rather than do actual work, some prefer to provide money to purchase supplies to maintain the building and grounds or decorations for the classrooms. Throughout the school year, parents are also expected to contribute money for a variety of causes, including supplementing salaries. The teacher simply announces in class, for example, that three dollars (U.S.) will be collected from each student to purchase new curtains. One parent I spoke to referred to such techniques for collecting money as blackmail. No parent wants their child to suffer scholastically or to incur embarrassment; and therefore, struggle as they may, they feel obliged to contribute.

With all schools running on dwindling state support, the responsibility for basic maintenance falls increasingly on parents, teachers, and administrators. This burden, of course, fuels the system of bribes at all levels of public and private education. When a student wants to enter a particular school, one of the first questions asked of his or her parents is, "What can you help us get?" Parents must state their profession or position. Most directors are savvy enough to evaluate the likelihood of a parent's access to hard currency, deficit goods, or officials in positions of power based on their station in society. Parents have the right to choose their children's schools. Technically, a school is obliged to accept all students in its district, assuring all children of an education. But legal obligation and academic ability are no longer sufficient criteria for admission to any school. In some instances the greed of directors or teachers drives the process of negotiating admission. But often enough directors are simply trying to keep the school equipped with basic supplies such as chalk and furniture. The rule forbidding bribes is turning to utter fiction as fear of reprisal evaporates. Bribery and influence-peddling increase in proportion to decreasing state support. Likewise, inspectors charged with investigating and punishing greedy administrators who blatantly demand outlandish bribes have equally succumbed to corruption. In sum, as educational bureaucracies have become consumed by efforts to redefine their mission, they have ushered in an era of deregulation of the educational system.

Consumerism in the Classroom

The most notable change in the practice of teaching is the intrusion of consumerism into the classroom. Under the Soviet system, all students wore uniforms, suit-like jackets and pants for boys and short black or brown dresses topped with a white or black apron for girls. Makeup, jewelry, and fancy hairstyles were not encouraged. With such rules lifted, most students, boys and girls alike, now try to make a fashion statement by the way they dress. The fetishization of material goods flourishes as each item of clothing or accessory indicates the type of connections one's parents have, whether they have access to hard currency, and the ability to travel abroad. Even during this period of extreme economic hardship, paying for an item is sometimes the easy part. Working one's "canals" to locate it and then create the possibility to actually purchase it, is infinitely more difficult. Hence, the status embodied in consumer goods in post-Soviet Ukraine is power-laden and reveals one's station in society.

Connerton (1991: 12) argues that an individual feature of clothing is actually part of a cluster of meanings. He considers dress as a culturally specific bodily practice and, in fact, one that either serves to maintain or subvert social memories. He argues that new habitual practices of dress can function as a means of breaking definitively with an older social order by precipitating the forgetting of other bodily practices. Indeed, the tight black miniskirts and brash makeup could not be further from the brown long-sleeved dresses and juvenile aprons that teenage girls almost universally wore until 1991. Similarly, the boys who prefer sweatshirts with American logos are expressing a new orientation and issuing an unmitigated rejection of Soviet dress codes.

Some public schools maintain the old policy of requiring uniforms, claiming that they do so at the parents' request. Preempting expression in dress by mandating uniforms saves money and means that children's pleas for the latest fashions fall on deaf ears. Even in schools that allow children to dress as they please, some students continue to wear part or all of their uniforms. The economic straitjacket in which most parents live keeps uniforms in use until they are threadbare, regardless of whether they are required or not.

Literature previously had a highly revered place in society, providing entertainment, social criticism, and, perhaps above all, a refuge from the often harsh realities of daily life as people whiled away the hours buried in books. Today the power and magic of the printed word is withering away, as millions prefer to travel beyond the iron curtain in the only way available to them now: television. After independence, the airwaves were inundated by Americanized mass cultural forms on local commercial TV stations. Meagerly financed Ukrainian state television competed with MTV, Phil Donahue, and Mexican soap operas by showing incessant per-

Students dress up as Cossack warriors to reenact historical myths as part of a holiday pageant at a Kyiv school.

formances of folk dances and folk ensembles reciting poetry and singing folk songs. As one might suspect, much as propaganda slogans were seen but not seen, the folk icon is visibly invisible, passively ignored by older generations and actively so by younger ones. The nineteenth-century peasant, billed as the national essence, is strangely out of place to the TV community in a highly educated and industrialized country such as late twentieth-century Ukraine.[10]

This sharp polarization of Schwarzenegger films on local commercial TV and a peasant takeover of Ukrainian state TV flares up once again in the classroom. Students talk about their favorite rap groups during folk-lore class (*narodoznavstvo*), now a mandatory subject from first grade on. The discussion in English class centers on *Scarlett*, the sequel to *Gone with the Wind*. The simultaneous worldwide release of this book in 1992 was a sensation, less on literary merit and more because the worldwide release allowed Ukraine to join the West on equal terms. After decades of being denied access to Western cultural forms and with so many families and friends divided transnationally because of mounting emigration,

Western mass culture finds a receptive audience among Ukrainians. The mass media's vision of an opulent West becomes yet another "imagined community," an allegiance upon which to stake one's identity to which teenagers are particularly susceptible. This leaves schools trying to ukrainianize the first post-Soviet generation amid mixed vestiges of Soviet structures, ideologies, and habits, and the new values of "cowboy capitalism."

Rewriting History: Soviet versus Post-Soviet Interpretations

Like their Soviet predecessors, post-Soviet public schools take a strictly chronological approach to the teaching of history. Starting in the fifth grade, when the children are approximately eleven years old, they begin with Ancient Greece and Rome and move along a teleological, Eurocentric track to world history, history of the USSR (this aspect has been condensed in post-Soviet Ukraine), history of Soviet Ukraine, until they finish the eleventh grade in contemporary times. Soviet textbooks furnished a macro perspective on institutional and governmental history. Examples of how Union-wide policies played out on the local level or discussion of events that pertained exclusively to Ukraine were largely ignored. Even in the Soviet textbook on the history of Ukraine, there is almost no mention of developments in Ukrainian culture, literature, or the arts (Koval' et al. 1991).

Because of the economic crisis, adequate numbers of new Ukrainian language textbooks have yet to be published, let alone delivered to schools. The first history books to be revised were texts for eleven-year-olds (fifth grade) and for eighteen-year-olds (eleventh grade). But more can be found for sale by black marketers on the street than in school libraries.[11] Even the revised history textbooks, as we will see, still make use of "Soviet language" and concepts. Although revised, the new textbooks fail to make a break with received interpretations of Ukrainian history.[12] Three of the four authors of the last Soviet Ukrainian history textbook penned the first post-Soviet version of the *History of Ukraine* for the eleventh grade.

To explore which historical interpretations were altered to fit the political and ideological shifts of statehood, we will look specifically at how two key moments of twentieth-century Ukrainian history are presented in both versions, the Famine of 1932–33 and Chernobyl. As part of the push to fill in the blank spots of history in the late 1980s, discussion of the Famine was included in the Soviet editions of the textbook. The overall tone is forthright and unapologetic. Amid a discussion of the "collectivization of rural agriculture" and the various decrees that were made and why, there is a page and a half on the Famine. The last paragraph asserts that 3 to 3.5 million Ukrainians died (Koval' et al. 1991: 204). This is about half the Western estimates.[13]

The issue of responsibility for the deaths inflicted by the Famine is key. This difficult issue is resolved by heaping blame on Stalin and exonerating Party cadres because of their powerlessness to challenge his unfair policies. For example, the text states, "Party, Soviet and agricultural workers who stopped storing bread saw the tragedy of the situation with their own eyes. Most of them were no more than a small screw in a state machine without a soul" (Koval' et al. 1991: 202). Indeed, many local party and military officials were aware of spiraling famine conditions in 1932, and some even witnessed the widespread starvation and suffering the following year. Some officials protested the high grain requisitions and even tried to stop grain collection. They were accused of "sabotage" and punished. However, for a famine of this magnitude to occur, it is clear that many local and high-level officials neither intervened nor resisted these harmful policies.

The text states that peasants were forbidden to leave their villages even if all surplus grains, vegetables, and livestock had been depleted. Brigades of workers were assigned to trains and to train stations to check the luggage of peasants traveling into or out of the regions hit by the Famine. They searched for and confiscated any provisions the peasants might have had. Usually, the peasants had bought this food for large sums of money by exchanging their valuables for food in neighboring regions, hoping to delay hunger among their family members (Koval' et al. 1991: 203). In an effort to illustrate the depths of despair brought on by poverty and starvation, some of the more gruesome aspects of the Famine are briefly mentioned without commentary, such as the widespread practice of abandoning children on city streets, the reported cases of cannibalism, and the digging up of dead bodies for food.

The Soviet text tries to show that Stalin was neither innocent nor ignorant of the mass starvation that his policies triggered in Ukraine. Citations are provided to prove that Stalin indeed knew of the suffering of the Ukrainian peasantry and in fact sanctioned it. The text cites a statement he made during a speech to the All-Union Congress of Collective Farm Workers and Stakhanovites on February 19, 1933, during which he said, "In any event the hardships which our workers endured ten to fifteen years ago, compared to those they have today, comrade collective workers, seem like children's toys" (Koval' et al. 1991: 203–4).

Local officials can be exonerated of responsibility because Stalin, who had first been officially discredited following Khrushchev's Secret Speech nearly thirty years earlier, is in the official Soviet textbooks unequivocally held responsible for this tragedy:

> There is no doubt that millions of peasants were brought to death by the cold-blooded decision of Stalin to seize all edible provisions from Ukrainian peasants and then to wrap the starving in a veil of silence, to forbid them any kind of help from either the international or Soviet communities. In order to prevent the arbitrary escape of a huge mass of starving people beyond the boundaries of the republic, a barrage of troops were stationed on the borders. (Koval' et al. 1991: 203)

When Stalin is held solely responsible for the atrocity, there can be no acknowledgment, let alone discussion, of the complicity of numerous individuals involved for a tragedy of this magnitude to occur. Nor can there be an inquiry into the systemic structures and hierarchies that made such starvation possible. Fault is isolated in a particular individual who is no longer alive. And yet the involvement of many institutions and groups is readily apparent from the text, which unambiguously details the vicious policy of grain seizures and blockades.

In contrast, the first post-Soviet textbook written and distributed following the fall of the Soviet system in 1992 includes all of the above verbatim and then some. Following independence, the description of the Famine was extended by one page. Although the authors are almost the same, the revised account of the Famine distinguishes itself from its Soviet predecessor by a somewhat shriller tone and by greater detail on how famine conditions were actually manufactured. For example, the new text cites the Famine as "evidence of the barbarism of a totalitarian state during extreme conditions of economic catastrophe" (Koval' et al. 1992: 281).

The newer narrative attempts to link to a greater extent high grain requisitions to the rapid depletion of peasant herds. In addition, this text details the extent of the confiscations: not only were seeds gathered up from grasses and fields after threshing but livestock, vegetables, fruits, in fact all food provisions deemed supplementary, were taken away from the peasants. "Confiscation was ordered as a punishment for 'kulak sabotage' of grain supplies," the text explains (Koval' et al. 1992: 281).

The most interesting addition to the new textbook is a paragraph on the Soviet practice of erasing history:

> Of that which ended in Ukraine in 1933, not one word made it into official documents. The reason was that Stalin ordered the Famine to be regarded as a nonexistent phenomenon. Even in the stenographic records of the plenary session of the Central Committee of the Communist Party of Ukraine and in the protocols of the Politburo of the Central Committee of the Communist Party of Ukraine the word "famine" was never mentioned during this whole period. (Koval' et al. 1992: 281)

This paragraph, which follows the litany of charges against Stalin's regime, serves as the final nail in the condemnatory coffin. Not only is Stalin indicted for what he did but also for what he did not do. He caused the Famine and then he failed to acknowledge it. In essence, the depiction of the Famine in Soviet versus post-Soviet textbooks varies in that the latter provides a slightly expanded and more animated version, indicting not just Stalin but the entire Soviet system for allowing a tyrant to abuse his power to such a fatal extent.

The Erasure of Chernobyl

The approach to the Famine is in sharp contrast to the coverage of Chernobyl in the two texts. The Soviet textbook addresses the Chernobyl nuclear disaster under a section entitled "Health Protection. Ecological Conditions." After detailing the "catastrophic ecological situation," which was kept "secret from the people," the text responds to the familiar cry of the nineteenth-century intelligentsia, "Who is to blame?" (Koval' et al. 1991: 342–43). The discussion of Chernobyl begins by blaming the "irresponsibility of scholars and specialists who were charged with ensuring the safety of atomic energy" and goes on to indict a number of officials:

> Criminal was the position adopted by the former Minister of Health Protection of the Ukrainian Soviet Socialist Republic, A. Iu. Romanenko, and many other responsible figures who for a prolonged period remained silent regarding the real danger to people's health due to the accident at the Chernobyl AES [Atomic Energy Station].
>
> It is true that there were independent medical teams in Ukraine who immediately and correctly assessed the threat to the health of the people as a result of the Chernobyl catastrophe and did everything possible to provide emergency medical help. These were specialists of the military-medical service of the KGB of the Ukrainian SSR. The top medical leadership in Kyiv and Moscow did not abide by the results of their scientific research and medical training. For years the leadership ignored the successful work of their colleagues and the laws of nature as well. (Koval' et al. 1991: 343)

The indictment of individuals and government ministries for irresponsibility represents a radical break from traditional practices of Soviet historiography where the government was held beyond reproach and "enemies of the people" were consistently blamed for societal ills and failures in policy. This shift of actually laying blame at the doorstep of the regime is a direct result of a wider scope of historical inquiry triggered by glasnost. Indeed the text states that it wasn't until 1989 that the demands of local residents for resettlement were finally heeded.

Although the text acknowledges the inexcusable mishandling of the initial consequences of the disaster, it quickly adds that this does not preclude future actions that can improve the situation. For example, in August 1990 the Supreme Soviet of the Ukrainian SSR passed a special resolution, "On Urgent Measures to Protect the Citizens of Ukraine from the Consequences of the Chernobyl Catastrophe," which, the text claims, accurately assessed the situation in highly contaminated areas as well as throughout Ukraine. The resolution proclaimed Ukraine a "zone of ecological disaster" and demanded the closing of the Chernobyl reactor. The resolution also demanded that "appropriate ministries and departments take concrete measures to develop international cooperation to surmount the consequences of the Chernobyl catastrophe" (Koval' et al. 1991: 344). The text illustrates the magnitude of the damage caused by Chernobyl in no uncertain terms and echoes the popular practice of dividing time into a before and an after in relation to the accident.

> The consequences of the Chernobyl accident, which will not be liquidated within the next few centuries, seem to be catastrophic for the whole planet, a tragedy for the whole world, affecting the fate of millions of people living on vast territories. Rivers, seas, oceans, and outdoor swimming pools of the planet already will never be the same as they were before Chernobyl. (Koval' et al. 1991: 343–44)

Contrast this strong, uncompromising language condemning the Chernobyl disaster—when it was the responsibility of Soviet officials to respond—with the attention the disaster is given only one year later in Ukrainian textbooks. Stunningly, there is only one reference to Chernobyl! In the final section of the textbook, in a section entitled "Ukraine on the Road to Freedom and Independence," there is one sentence which refers to Chernobyl amid an indictment of the whole system:

> The administrative-command system repressed any kind of pro-gressive beginnings. Even when the economic crisis of the country was obvious, the plenary session of the Twenty-Seventh Congress of the Communist Party of Ukraine (1986), the First Secretary of the Central Committee, V. V. Shcherbytsky continued to assert that the economy of Ukraine had made great progress. . . . But one had to respond and support Moscow even when nature sneered during a flowering April, and even during the building of the Chernobyl Atomic Nuclear Station near Kyiv, and even during indecision and even during cowardice as one of its reactors was built, and there was a lot of that. (Koval' et al. 1992: 465)

Chernobyl is given startlingly little attention in the Ukrainian edition of this text compared to its Soviet predecessor. Energy politics have become a sore point of contention because Ukraine does not have the necessary hard currency to purchase energy reserves from other countries. Natural gas and oil supplies from Russia have risen over 1000 times in price compared to Soviet levels. Ukraine has amassed a $2.5 billion debt to Russia for energy supplies to keep its factories, mines, and collective farms running, many of which operate at a loss. In a sense, this plant and the others like it provide a cheap source of energy, independent of the whims and demands of other countries. Although the plant is slated to close, such questions as when, how, and how the energy it produces will be replaced remain acute and entirely unanswered.

As Chernobyl continues to light up Kyiv every night, there is a powerful disincentive for the Ukrainian government to continue the nationalist practice of using Chernobyl to symbolize the victimization of Ukraine. In this instance, much like its predecessor, the new government uses its silence to erase inconvenient episodes of history. The "living memories" of Chernobyl, by virtue of the fact that the event occurred as recently as 1986, are not only fresh but widespread throughout the population. By ignoring them and constructing a narrative that bypasses consideration of an event of such importance, (new) state-sponsored historiography remains discredited. The authors' interpretation of history and a popular counterdiscourse disparaging the state foster the temptation for students to approach the new texts with the same cynicism and dismissal with which they read the old.

The Protective Power of the State

The lack of significant revision of Soviet textbooks is but one indicator of the difficulties the public educational system is having in modifying its curriculum, pedagogy, and practices to fit the new political realities. Given the tremendous shortage of revised textbooks, in essence the public schools are left groping to socialize children to a new political and economic climate with the old cadres using books written in Russian, cluttered with references to the Soviet Union and Lenin. Concerned about the fragility of the new Ukrainian state and the persistent low status of Ukrainian culture in spite of government decrees to the contrary, a small number of individual Ukrainian educators scattered across the country have created a new type of elite, experimental school.[14] An independent Ukrainian state is best secured, they reason, by a strong, culturally unified nation, and a nation cannot exist without a cultural elite. The educators who founded and staff these elite, private schools are often motivated by a conviction that only a state apparatus can protect the Ukrainian language and Ukrainian culture against russificatory trends and the encroachment of an omnipresent American-based mass culture.

Indeed, many argue that without a state, Ukrainian culture would have simply drifted off to the "dustheap of history" as the population silently, steadily russified.

Yet their belief in the protective power of the state is tempered by an entrenched skepticism in the ability of the government to act in the best interests of the Ukrainian people and to advance the Ukrainian cultural revival currently under way. In an effort to bring about changes in the status of Ukrainian and Ukrainian culture more quickly, the founders of these elite schools have circumvented the official educational bureaucracy and created their own storefront schools with state funding. Without the initiative, vision, and unwavering hard work of this handful of individuals, these private schools would not exist. Founding and running these private schools is a highly personal endeavor for faculty and administrators alike. Although government leaders have announced vast and grandiose plans to reform the educational system and to pursue a "ukrainianized" curriculum significantly different from its Soviet predecessor, the founders of these schools are acutely aware of the multitude of obstacles working against the ukrainianization of Ukrainian education.

It is necessary to note at the outset that these elite schools are fledgling enterprises with small student bodies. As of 1997, only about 5 percent of Ukrainian students were enrolled in private schools. The approximately one hundred twenty schools are located primarily in the central, eastern, and southeastern provinces.[15] They are perpetually on the brink of bankruptcy as they search for sponsors to supplement the minimal state funding they receive to expand the very offerings that make their schools both elite and experimental. Their numbers alone do not suggest radical change. Nevertheless, the emergence of this type of school reflects moods in post-Soviet society, particularly among the elite, which, aside from education, find expression in other spheres of public life.

Parents who choose to send their children to such a private school are primarily nouveaux riches and members of the intelligentsia. Most parents are fierce critics of Soviet educational practices and seek a radically different alternative for their own children's upbringing. This is the reason they forgo consideration of reputed elite public schools for their children. Many parents said they were drawn to these schools not necessarily for their nationalized curricula, although they recognize that new political realities mandate new cultural skills to succeed in the nascent nation-state. Rather, they chose these schools because they are elite in the sense that the curricula are more challenging and less rigid and the children enrolled come from more privileged backgrounds.

Only marginally tied to the enormous state bureaucracy, these private schools can introduce far-reaching curricular reform more swiftly than the bureaucratic public schools can, including the most respected public schools. I refer to these private schools as elite because they fulfill the state requirements and a specialized program of study, making for a broader curriculum and a longer school day. Admission is far more competitive, and teachers, nearly all of whom work part-time, are very often recruited from the ranks of university lecturers and tend to design more ambitious classes. In such small settings, students receive a considerable amount of individualized attention. Such schools have also been created in much of Eastern Europe, again largely thanks to the initiative of individual educators. This is arguably part of an overall trend to privatize public services. As socialism both elevated the state and rendered it suspect, the emergence of private schools reins in the influence and power of the state by diminishing its role in everyday life.[16]

There are several factors that distinguish these new private schools from the majority of public schools in post-Soviet Ukraine. The founders and faculty of these elite schools see their mission as the establishment of a non-Soviet-educated Ukrainian national elite. They also seek to reintroduce the social markers based on national, religious, class, and gender distinctions that the Soviet system, in its effort to forge a supracthnic, ideologically based Soviet identity, sought to erase. These elite schools promote both a national revival and allegiances to communities that could potentially compete with a national identity by reinforcing regional, class, gender, and religious distinctions. A third factor is their concern with what can be described as character-building. The collapse of the social contract and a basic understanding of what constitutes moral and appropriate behavior prompts these schools to clearly articulate and foster what they consider to be ethical behavior in an effort to restore some semblance of social order.

This is all very reminiscent of the state commission's recommendations to focus on "individuality, nationality, and morality" when designing educational reform. The essential difference between these private schools and public schools is essentially one of degree. The small size of private schools and the consistently strong personal convictions held by their directors and faculty allow private schools to implement reform swiftly and sweepingly.

By teaching from a Ukrainocentric point of view, they are moving beyond the state program to desovietize their curricula and are derussifying them as well. They examine historical events in terms of how they affected Ukraine and how Ukrainians affected them and seek to underline Ukraine's status as a European country by highlighting its tradition of statehood, peaceful coexistence with neighboring countries, and its history of democratic institutions.

A derussifying orientation to Ukrainian history often adds up to a large dose of Said's Orientalism for the Big Brother, as Russia is recast as an Asiatic empire built on oppression and subjugation. Of course, it is easiest to identify something by stating what it is not. In this vein, many of the most unattractive, sinister qualities are heaped on the Russians in order to paint a tableau of Ukrainians as "civilized, peace-loving, and European." The characterization of Ukraine as victimized by statelessness and colonialism is used to explain the chaotic and "uncivilized" state in which Ukrainian society finds itself today. Ironically, the effects of statelessness on Ukrainian culture are studied in conjunction with Ukraine's "tradition of statehood."

To give an example of this new Ukrainocentric orientation, one of the most basic historic myths learned in Soviet schools was that the principality of Kievan Rus' was "the mother of Russian culture," the forerunner to the Russian state. Such an interpretation served to legitimate and neutralize Russian imperial aspirations and colonial practices, which culminated in the unification of "fraternal Slavs" and "peoples' friendship" in the Soviet Union. These elite schools are issuing a corrective to this historical myth by reclaiming Kievan Rus' as a proto-Ukrainian state and by maintaining that Ukrainians and Russians have anthropologically distinct origins.[17] The Kievan Rus' period is held up as the genesis of the "thousand-year tradition of state-building in Ukraine," a direct quotation from the Ukrainian declaration of independence.

Myths of national genesis and national grandeur are a critical ideological battleground for the definition of national identity. Such myths tease apart the cultural and historic differences between Russians and Ukrainians to advance a national essence in order to justify political independence and a separate state apparatus. Myths are never held accountable to the facts. The key function of myths is to provide meaning to experience by furnishing a glorious interpretation of the past and, by extension, a promising glimpse into the future.

History is not the only realm, although it is one of the more notable, in which teaching differs significantly from elite to standard public schools. Religion and religious education have emerged as another distinguishing factor. In some public schools, where the teachers almost universally claim to be atheists, a class on the history of religion is offered on an optional basis and, generally centers on the study of Roman and Greek mythology. In these elite schools, however, religious study is quite often integrated into the curricula and includes such themes as ancient Ukrainian mythology, the history of religious practice, including pagan rituals in Ukraine, and, perhaps most important, lessons on the array of religious holidays that are replacing Soviet holidays. Such classes do not propagate a particular faith or promote one denomination over another. They simply seek to encourage the religious revival currently under way. In a curious twist, however, whereas Soviet teachers were often required to stand outside churches on religious holidays to ensure that children did not attend holiday services, some teachers from these private schools take the children to church on holidays to ensure that they do attend.[18]

Fueling an interest in religion often creates sharp generational conflicts at home. During decades of Soviet rule, many parents went to church as they would go to an art museum—an excursion to see beautiful paintings and architecture. Their children, curious and even anxious to embrace the teachings of the church as a means to shed the poisonous values of Soviet atheism, are troubled by their parents' skepticism of organized religion, which remains highly politicized and marred by interconfessional conflict and corruption. Deep mistrust of the church and memories of the Russian Orthodox Church's collaboration with the KGB keep older generations at bay. Undeterred, many children agree among themselves which service they will attend and go to church together. Regardless of whether they attend a private or public school, the reversal of religious atheism among the young is occurring, in spite of parental disdain.

Within the Monastery

In January 1994 a small school opened on the second floor of a very old building on the grounds of the Kyiv Pecherska Monastery on the banks of the Dnipro River in central Kyiv.[19] Surrounded by the golden cupolas of churches, monks walking about in black robes, and many strolling tourists, sixteen students, nine girls and seven boys, began studying at one of Kyiv's newest experimental schools. The rector and founder of the school is a small, overworked, middle-aged man with a bushy mustache. He originally taught history in a Soviet school and more recently worked at one of the monastery's museums before opening his three-room school. From the thirty applicants the school received, they accepted sixteen, ranging in ages from eleven to fifteen, from the sixth to the eighth grades. Sixteen part-time teachers, all on one-year renewable contracts, and two administrators are employed at this school.

During Soviet rule, the Kyiv Pecherska Monastery was largely converted into a museum complex. Although several churches and residencies have recently been restored and are functioning again, the museum esplanade remains largely intact. This, combined with the rector's personal experience as a museum employee, led him to bill his school as the "first Ukrainian national museum school" and to forge a relationship with the Institute of Ukrainian Studies at Kyiv University. This school aims to train Ukraine's future curators, the preservers and catalogers of Ukrainian culture.

Tuition at the this school as of spring 1994 was 200,000 kupons a month (ca. $3). Given that the average monthly salary at this time was approximately $20, this made education here a luxury for almost all save the old and new monied classes. Tuition pays teachers' salaries. The main sponsor, a financial services company, contributes student lunches and material support for the school and, of course, the Orthodox church provides the three rooms, two of which are classrooms and the other is a teachers' room. At the time I was visiting this school (April 1994), ecclesiastical access to the monastery was under dispute. The building that housed the school was under the jurisdiction of the Russian Orthodox Church or, as it increasingly calls itself, the Ukrainian Orthodox Church–Moscow Patriarchate. The rector made no secret of the church's periodic critical comments of the overtly nationalist slant to the curriculum he has designed and his steadfast refusal to honor the church's request to teach Old Church Slavonic, a liturgical language. As a final source of income, the school runs a kiosk on the grounds of the monastery that sells artwork to tourists. This combination of sources has thus far allowed the school to refuse state funding, thereby freeing its curriculum of state requirements. Raising funds to keep the school doors open is, of course, the biggest challenge. High levels of taxation on contributions encourage sponsors to give aid in the form of goods and services. Although such contributions are welcome, this practice leaves the school cash poor—making the payment of salaries and other bills problematic.

According to the rector, the biggest obstacle to the school's success is the very entity he wishes to protect: the state. He laments the "colonial psychology" of bureaucrats resistant to educational reform who "do nothing but open sabotage." He notes how the harsh economic conditions in Ukraine have prompted many bureaucrats to defend their jobs first and foremost over Ukraine. "They will never fight for Ukraine," he sighs, "Their job is their trough [kormushka] and they can't tear themselves away." The rector complains that the very same bureaucrats who fulfilled Soviet orders to institute a highly ideologically laden, russified curriculum, which relegated aspects of Ukrainian studies to the margins, are today incapable of creating and institutionalizing reforms to desovietize the curricula and give Ukrainian, as the new state language and national culture, its proper prominent place in post-Soviet curricula. He says:

> As long as the old cadres still wield power and are still resistant to any kind of educational reform, there won't be any normal Ukrainian language schools in Kyiv. These bureaucrats sabotage efforts at every level. . . . When important people in the administration couldn't stand khakholi [a pejorative term for Ukrainians] yesterday, then they can't fall in love with them today. They'll stand on the barricades to defend their positions but they won't let people like me in. . . . Why are there so many new unnecessary structures? Because you have to "give" to the bureaucrats. (He makes a gesture with his fingers to indicate paying a bribe.) And there are too many of them! They control and keep everything under their control. It's ridiculous!

In spite of endless problems and what one teacher referred to as the rector's "bulldozer approach" to solving them, he seems undaunted by the challenge of launching this school to create a new generation "that is not psychologically twisted like my own."

To achieve such a goal, the rector has designed a curriculum with several distinctive courses: theater, oratory skills (enunciation, pronunciation, gestures, and so on, taught by an actress), fine arts, music, religious studies, and karate. Standard subjects include Ukrainian material and spiritual culture (*krayoznavstvo*), the Ukrainian language, Ukrainian history, world literature, foreign languages (English and French), geography, math, country studies (*zemliaznavstvo*), chemistry, physics, and nature studies. The students not only receive a grade for each of the aforementioned subjects, but receive a series of grades for how well they get along with the "collective." They are graded on such personal attributes as creative initiative, moral behavior, discipline, ability to pay attention, and emotional expression. Initially, grades are delivered to each student orally at a meeting between a group of teachers and the student. Then they are posted for all to see.

The rector has to explain and defend his curriculum over and over—especially for sponsors. He remains adamantly devoted to the curriculum he has made and resists accommodating the specific requests of his would-be sponsors. Recently, the rector turned away a contribution from a bank because it was not in keeping with the "national idea of the collegium." The bank stipulated that the aid be used for a Russian culture class, since Russia remains a formidable trading partner for Ukrainian businesses. Such logic was untenable to the rector and he did not accept the contribution.

> These wouldn't be big compromises to make but if we make one after the other then at the end, God only knows what will be left of our Collegium and our national idea. Whenever a sponsor begins to ask for even small changes in our program, already we're very cautious with them. These banks have their own interests. The banks say, "Why culture? Why don't you have commercial or business classes? What Ukrainian culture? Ukrainian culture is on its last legs! Ukrainian culture is dead, like Latin!"
>
> I explain to them that when Israel created its government, Hebrew was even deader than Latin. They should have their own language and they were able to do it. Our Ukrainian language is alive. We created a new Ukrainian state but you want to bury Ukrainian. That's our tragedy.
>
> We have to create a new generation which wasn't enslaved. It doesn't just appear. Because we want to create this new generation, people in power, in government offices, middle level bureaucrats, the Moscow Patriarch, they are all against our Collegium.

This feeling of being besieged, of fighting a very much uphill battle, was common to others attempting educational reform. In spite of the rector's steadfast dedication and determination to reform the psyche through education, the Soviet past fades quite slowly. I understood to what extent this is true when I showed up on the third day to observe at this school. It was a brisk Saturday morning and the children were scheduled to have a three-hour English lesson from nine o'clock until noon. I came fifteen minutes before the class began to find a group of students in the teachers' room. With no teachers or administrators in sight, I asked the children how they got in. One explained that all students know where the key is. The first student to arrive simply unlocks the door. Several students had come early to type up a script for a play they were performing in theater class as part of their Easter celebrations. At five to nine the rector's assistant arrived. At nine o'clock the English teacher telephoned to say that she was not coming in. (I suspect she was intimidated at the prospect of having a native speaker observe her class.) The kids squealed with fleeting delight as the assistant turned to me and asked if I could take over the three-hour English class. Sure, I said.

The class began with the students reminding me that today was Lenin's birthday (April 22). Although his birthday had not been celebrated in schools for three years, which meant that most of these students could have partaken only once or twice in a school celebration of Lenin's birthday, three years after Ukrainian independence these children paused nonetheless to note the anniversary of Lenin's birth and to tell a visiting American of all the school festivities associated with this day and how much they missed them. Socialization at Soviet schools to the icons of Soviet culture, once again, had proven itself to be devilishly tenacious.

Aesthetic Sensitizing

Another elite, private school on the outskirts of Kyiv opened in October 1992 in a renovated daycare center. It offers a specialized program of study in aesthetics taught entirely in Ukrainian. Financially speaking, this school began much like the one previously discussed. The administration found three banks to provide 91.5 percent of the necessary funding to run the school. An additional 2.5 percent of their funding came from individual donations, 2 percent from special gifts, only 2 percent from tuition, and an additional 2 percent from "revenue from scientific workshops and products" derived from marketing the philosophy of the school. This independent funding allowed the school to forgo state funding and all the curricular regulations that come with it. When the school opened, five children whose parents work at the banks sponsoring the school applied for admission. Two were accepted and a third began attending in January. The administrators were quite proud of this fact. In a society where connections are seemingly everything, they prided themselves on prioritizing academic standards over according privileges to sponsors.

The director, a folklorist, author, and former school inspector, developed and implemented his vision of an ideal curriculum specifically designed to foster creativity, individuality, and nationality. The director explains the philosophy behind his school, "Our focus here is on national originalities. Through the study of distinctly Ukrainian art forms, we are trying to help these kids fulfill their creative potential. You only need a few talented people with creative ideas to have an influence on many. We want these kids to remember that they are Ukrainian wherever they are and to become committed to solving the problems in Ukraine."

This vision is shared by the other administrators, two vice directors, both of whom teach, and one full-time fund-raiser. All are male and all are under forty years of age. The school's tuition in 1992–93 was 10,000 kupons for the entire year. (Just to illustrate what hyperinflation really is, as of the beginning of the next school year, annual tuition in dollar terms had shrunk from ca. $335 to about 63 cents.) Funding the school is an ongoing colossal undertaking. Initially, the director of development advocated forming a joint-stock company to be run by a board of trustees to support the school. The board would print and sell shares to the school. The administration would maintain a "packet of shares," ensuring ultimate control over the curriculum and other critical matters. This, he felt, was the best solution to insure the financial solvency of the school, given that there is no point in developing an endowment because of hyperinflation.

Under financial pressure, two years after the school opened, the director reversed all plans and decided to accept state funding to ease the burden and uncertainty of fund-raising and to stabilize tuition levels. During the 1994–95 school year, 30 percent of their funding came from the state. The following year, they expected this to rise to 60 percent, although they would like to receive 80 percent. Eventually, they were forced to modify their curriculum to accommodate state requirements by eliminating several of their specialized classes.

In its first year of operation, the school accepted twenty-six eleven-year-olds to the fifth grade. Each year the administration plans to add two new fifth grade classes, one for boys and one for girls. Here, as at other elite schools, the director personally selected the teachers, most of whom are young and former public school teachers or university lecturers. All teachers are on one-year renewable contracts, providing the needed economic incentive to do a good job, which, he claims, is sorely missing in the public schools. Job security, a staple of the Soviet labor market, he feels is a crutch and encourages mediocrity among teachers. The school has an affiliation with the Kyiv Mohyla Academy, a private university whose highly nationalistic, elite program of study has earned it the nickname "new higher party school" after the old "higher party schools," which trained the elite of the Communist Party.[20]

Admission is selective and based primarily on three criteria: an assessment of the psychological condition of the child, verbal skill, which is tested by a dictation in Ukrainian, and an analysis of the child's character. The emphasis on the child's personality reflects the administration's commitment not simply to educate but to develop individuality. As the director explained, they see their project as diametrically opposed to the Soviet system of education, which "sought to eradicate individuality and cultivate a herd or slave mentality" through uniform standards and public humiliation. Paradoxically, much like the assertions of the post-Soviet Ukrainian state, they wish to encourage individuality as long as it falls within certain national perimeters. They argue that embracing a Ukrainian nationality and feeling national pride is a means of shedding Soviet values and practices.

To cultivate consciousness of a particular cultural heritage and to promote individual creativity, this school offers an extensive array of courses designed to develop aesthetic sensibilities. In reaction to the aesthetic desensitizing fostered by the seemingly omnipresent gray drabness of Soviet architecture, the director has used his background in folklore to pioneer a curriculum featuring folk traditions, folk songs, folk crafts, folk theater, and folk dancing. A reduction of instruction in natural sciences, a strength of Soviet schools and a requirement in Ukrainian schools today, has cleared the way to expand this aspect of the school's curriculum.

Folklore is meant to be a vehicle by which to inculcate the national component of the curriculum and the means by which individuality is strengthened. The students perform folk tales in a class on folklore theater and sing Ukrainian folk melodies, which are legendary for their mel-

Table 1 Weekly Plan for the Fifth Grade

Day of the week		Number of periods
Monday	Ukrainian literature	1
	Ukrainian language	2
	Math	1
	Gym	1
	Lunch	1
	Psycho-training	2
	English	2
Tuesday	English	2
	Nature studies	1
	Math	1
	Gym	1
	Lunch	1
	Musical culture	2
	Fine arts	2
Wednesday	Math	1
	Chess	1
	Ancient history	1
	Nature studies	1
	Gym	1
	Lunch	1
	Folklore theater	1
	Arts and crafts	1
Thursday	English	2
	Math	1
	Language studies	1
	Gym	1
	Lunch	1
	Nature studies	1
	Choir	2
	Instrumental music	1
Friday	Ancient history	2
	Fine arts	2
	Folklore theater	2
	Lunch	1
	Karate	1
	Musical culture	2

ancholy and beauty, in choir and music classes. All children study art in addition to drawing and calligraphy. By incorporating a folk-based interpretation of Ukrainian national culture into performance at school, the folk songs, folk costumes, folk traditions, and so on, become part of the experience and memory of youth for these children. Such a pronounced emphasis on folk culture and folk art is far in excess of the folklore component in the state-designed curriculum. However, it is precisely this emphasis on folkloric training which distinguishes this private school from all others.

Recapturing the Essence

While public schools remain coed, almost all of these elite schools advocate single-sex education.[21] Several members of the faculty expressed the conviction that Soviet society contaminated and vulgarized the essence of masculinity and femininity in the course of pursuing gender equality. They believe the system empowered and masculinized women, particularly in the workplace, at the expense of men, who were correspondingly disempowered, denied the role of provider, and encouraged to take refuge in drink. The Soviet project to create gender equality deformed the inherent psychological subtleties that differentiate men from women, they argue. Albeit far from equal, women did achieve measured advances in the public sphere, through education and professional development, and assumed positions of some authority and power. Yet in spite of these gains, on the home front gender roles have remained very traditional. Basic household duties, including child care, are routinely considered women's work.

To counterbalance this inherited legacy, the director hired a psychologist who has designed a course called "psycho-training," which tries to peel back the corrupting influence of the Soviet system on the psyche. The goal of this class is to reformulate gender-based conceptions of self instilled by the Soviet system and to restore the "natural" roles of the sexes, which, it is believed, will contribute to the strengthening of the nation and the state. The policies of socialism and the particulars of life in the Soviet Union led to exceptionally high levels of divorce, frequent abortions, and a birthrate so low that the population is declining. Nationalist-driven pro-natalism is a reaction to socialist policies that were seen as having threatened the nation's very existence. Manifestations of retraditionalizing gender roles are visible throughout the former Soviet bloc (see Funk and Mueller 1993). Rubchak (1996) argues that reformulating gender roles based on essentialist notions is a project widely embraced in post-Soviet Ukraine and even one espoused by the leaders of women's groups and women's associations.

Marta Bohdanivna, the psycho-training teacher, has designed classes tailored to advance these goals. She traces the general anomie, indifference, and brutality of contemporary Ukrainian society to the absence of a mother at home. She thinks working mothers and daycare are aberrations. (She is a working mother herself!) As she sees it, the mission of her female students is to have children, care for them, and educate them in a patriotic spirit. Patriotism, she argues, comes from mother's milk.[22] Through discussion of astrological signs, the correlation between emotions and colors, and collective nurturing, the teacher hopes to "sharpen the students' intuition, raise their energy levels, and deflect any intention to aspire to positions of power." At the beginning of each class, which is held once a week, each girl chooses a color which she feels represents her mood at that moment. As the children sit in a circle on the floor, they explain their choice of color and why they are feeling the way they do. Sometimes they use pantomime to act out their moods and the reasons for them. Although the goals are quite lofty, the problems expressed by the girls were quite mundane and usually centered around little brothers who won't leave them alone, stubborn parents who refuse to buy a dog, or fights with siblings over which television program to watch. Given the tense situation in the country, which often spills over into a stressful home life, the teacher argues that such therapeutic moments are necessary for the psychological well-being of each child.

As was quite fashionable following independence in Ukraine, Marta Bohdanivna believes in the powers and insights provided by astrology. By examining the personality strengths and weaknesses associated with each girl's sign, they discuss how one can best overcome weaknesses in character. Psycho-training aims to enhance the genteel side of girls, to preempt any chances of them joining the army of screaming salesladies already running rampant in Ukrainian society. They also play games designed to foster self-esteem by allowing individual students to express admiration and affection for each other. For example, they play a game whereby one girl stands in front and turns her back to the group. The other students form two lines. Girls who want to be friends with the girl in front stand in the first line closest to her and the others stand in the second line. The girl in front has to guess who stood where. The idea is that this is a nonverbal form of expressing friendship, desired or actual. Birthday celebrations also allow the group to periodically shower each individual girl with attention and expressions of good will.

The emphasis on developing self-awareness, relationships, and nurturing skills is greatly softened in the boys' class. As part of their preparation tion to become the post-Soviet elite, rather than stimulating communication and sensitivity, the boys are encouraged to be decisive, self-confident, and committed to serving Ukraine through proactive problem-solving. With rates of emigration soaring and the romanticization of life in the West, especially among youth, continuing unabated, the director considers it a top priority to instill in his male students a commitment to solving Ukraine's problems. He is not interested in training sharp minds who will then immigrate to America and use their Ukrainian-learned skills to benefit Western society. This is a familiar pattern which Ukrainian teachers have seen all too often over the past fifteen years.

By reinforcing the importance of and dependence upon nature, the teacher hopes not only to cultivate in these boys a love of their native land but also to encourage them to dedicate themselves to repairing the massive ecological damage left in the wake of the Soviet military-industrial buildup. With mounting ecological damage everywhere apparent, the teacher encourages her male students to tackle the daunting task of rectifying such environmental havoc. Marta Bohdanivna also tries to foster self-confidence by engaging the boys in role-playing, sometimes relying solely on nonverbal communication. They keep a journal, which she reads and discusses periodically with each student. If the emphasis of the girls' class is on relationships and emotion, here it is on developing the morals and values necessary to lead.

The conviction that boys and girls have different innate abilities and psychologies is also operative in other classes. The teaching of literature and creative writing is used to further enhance gender distinctions by re-masculinizing boys and re-feminizing girls. The choice of readings in literature class and the choice of topics assigned in creative writing class are guided by the conviction that girls and boys have different capabilities, divergent patterns of learning, and are destined for different roles in society. The tendencies to institutionalize newly defined and highly traditional gender roles are in part a reaction to the reformulation of gender roles pioneered by socialism. Additionally, redirecting gender roles and strengthening the nation are primary to the hegemonic project of modern state-building. A prime site to strengthen the interconnection between gender and the nation is via the family, and it is schools that socialize children to new realities and the new values that this new era has ushered in.

Prerevolutionary Traditions

Another means of gender revision and of strengthening national consciousness is the resurrection of the nineteenth-century tradition of "Boys Humanitarian Gymnasiums." In 1990 one opened in Zaporizhzhia, an industrial center in eastern Ukraine, and a second in 1992 in L'viv, the largest city in western Ukraine. With forty-five students in two grades, the L'viv school is a hypernationalist enclave ironically located within an ordinary Russian language, Soviet-styled school. After independence, the Russian language school had excess class space as students in increasing numbers transferred to Ukrainian language schools. Part of the government funding this school receives is five classrooms, one of which serves as a teachers' room.

Indicative of the skills that the director believes are needed, this school offers a choice of two specializations, one in law and ethics and the other in foreign languages (Table 2). The emphasis on developing competency in foreign (Western) languages throughout Eastern Europe is testimony to the widespread efforts to disassociate from the Soviet experience and reorient toward Europe and another zone of influence. As Ukraine aims to reposition itself as a European state, a goal held particularly dear in Halychyna, given its historical heritage as part of the Austro-Hungarian empire and Poland before it was annexed to Soviet Ukraine, developing foreign language abilities is considered essential. The motivation to create a school specializing in law and ethics was born after the director's first trip abroad to Germany in 1991. Impressed by the smooth functioning of German society, by the punctuality of Germans, and the notion that they make and fulfill commitments, he returned to Ukraine with a mission. To explain why he chose a nineteenth-century aristocratic tradition as a model for post-Soviet education, the director, a former history teacher, said, "Without a cultural elite, the nation cannot exist. This elite will, of course, be male as it has always been. With the limited resources that we have today, we must focus our efforts exclusively on a select group of boys."

The director shares the widespread concern over the contaminated nature of gender relations, identities, and roles left in the wake of socialism. He is particularly concerned about the increasing contempt men and women have for each other as evidenced by a high divorce rate and the multitude of women who choose to forgo marriage and simply raise a child on their own. Single-sex education, he argues, encourages boys to develop respect for girls. He abhors the current fashion of miniskirts, makeup, and garish jewelry, which suddenly appeared among sixteen-year-olds when the requirement for uniforms was dropped in many public schools. In today's post-Soviet consumer euphoria, single-sex education, he argues, curbs the cult of materialism and Madonna-inspired sexual display through bodily ornamentation. The fifteen- and sixteen-year-old boys at this school are required to wear a suit and tie to school every day, another sort of uniform, if you will. Interestingly, the students claim that it sets a tone of professionalism and that they happily wear their suits and ties surrounded by a sea of students in jeans. Clothing, once again, functions as a signifier. It is a sign of their conviction of their impending elite status.

The director and several teachers of the Gymnasium advance many arguments to support single-sex education and their decision to exclude girls. They argue that peer pressure in coed classrooms creates a hierarchy based on looks and access to status goods, such as Western clothing. In contrast, they argue, student leaders at this school are chosen by their peers based on ability and demonstrated intelligence. A single-sex environment promotes a different type of competition and sets a tone of discipline and order sorely needed in post-Soviet Ukrainian society. The director further buttresses his decision to exclude girls by arguing that his school demands more class hours, an additional two-and-a-half hours a day, to fulfill the state curriculum plus the school's specialized courses in law, ethics, and foreign languages. The discipline and physical strength needed to keep up with an intense, challenging, and elite program of study is just something girls don't have, he argues. This attitude is not unique. The director of a coed private school near L'viv cited the same reason when he explained why his school automatically gives extra points to boys in the admissions process. The school's official policy is to accept as many boys as possible. Girls are admitted when they are exceptionally

Table 2   Plans of Study—Ninth Grade*

Foreign Languages Program		Social-Humanities Program	
Subject	Hours/week	Subject	Hours/week
Ukrainian language	2	Ukrainian language	2
Ukrainian literature	3	Ukrainian literature	3
First foreign language (English, German)	8	Law	2
Second foreign language (Arabic,** Japanese)	2	World history	2/3
World literature	2	Ukrainian history	3/2
World history	2	Foreign language (English)	4
Ukrainian history	1	World literature	2
Math	4	Math	4
Physics	2	Physics	2
Chemistry	2	Chemistry	2
Biology	2	Biology	2
Geography	2	Geography	2
Principles of statehood and law	1	Gym	2
Specialized course	1	Specialized course	2
Electives***	2	Electives***	3
Gym	2	Individual or group consultation	1
Self-defense	2	Elective	1
Total	39		39

Note: In terms of hours per week of instruction, the state school program is the same in five areas: Ukrainian language, Ukrainian literature, Ukrainian history, world history, and world literature. The state program has an additional hour of math and two additional years of chemistry and biology. This school offers study in a second foreign language, which few public schools do.

*The eighth grade in the foreign language program has two hours less of foreign language and does not have the Statehood and Law class. The eighth grade in the other program has one hour less of specialized study.
**The Arabic class was dropped when the teacher insisted that part of his compensation be taxi fare to and from school. Swedish will be the new offering, making this the only school in Ukraine to offer this language.
***Electives include chess, additional self-defense, which is taught by two police officers, and a class called Country Studies (*Krayoznavstvo*), where the architecture of L'viv is studied.

talented and likely to help maintain high standards or if their parents can be particularly instrumental in procuring goods and services.

Revived traditionalism often places a burden on the female half of the population. Casting women as birthing machines, bearers of tradition, and creators of patriotism disempowers them as it firmly sequesters them at home. Returning women to the hearth also conveniently hides rising unemployment and underemployment as they retreat into the home, "voluntarily" dropping out of the workforce. The combined effects of a national and religious revival have created moods that have left women in a severely disadvantaged position. A look at these private schools, most of whom unashamedly grant advantages to boys does little to suggest that the situation for women in post-Soviet society will improve anytime soon.

Perhaps even more notable than efforts to redefine gender and gendered relations, the teachers at this school strive to teach inner discipline. Unlike a Western economic system, the director argues, which provides financially driven motivation to learn and succeed, the swirling, spinning out of control impression that post-Soviet Ukrainian society creates does not inspire young men to set goals and strive for them. Most students argue that there are really only two ways to make a decent living: by "speculation," or traveling abroad to buy discount, second-hand, or defective goods, and selling them for several times the price at one of the massive flea markets that have sprung to life in every major Ukrainian city, or by joining a criminal organization and probably working those same markets in a different capacity. Going against the tide, the director of this school strives to show that there are other possibilities. Instilling order in the face of disorder for these young boys, the future elite of Ukraine, is the goal of this school.

Attitudes Toward the State

Although these elite schools represent a fragile enterprise riddled with paradoxes and plagued with incessant problems, I believe we can expect more of these storefront schools to open their doors for business in the upcoming years. The state in post-Soviet society has been revered for its ability to protect Ukrainian cultural interests, and yet the government has simultaneously been discredited for its lack of will or ability to do anything good for society or for the Ukrainian people. This conflicting dynamic has produced profound skepticism among the intelligentsia about whether state-designed public education is up to the task of socializing children to the values and skills needed to ride out this excruciatingly difficult period of transition. The founders and faculty of these private schools are both committed to an independent Ukrainian state and dubious of its abilities to govern. It is because of their own initiative, personal convictions, and national pride that they have taken it upon themselves to reclaim and remake post-Soviet Ukrainian society via educational reform.

Children who attend these elite schools actually enjoy the experience and claim they look forward to coming to school. Rekindling a curiosity for learning and a respect for knowledge amid economic chaos and enormous social tension is a remarkable achievement. This eagerness and optimism is in sharp contrast to the dread that permeates the attitude of students in public schools. Aside from stolen moments with friends during breaks, students in public schools claim they detest being there, have little respect for the teachers, and assert that most of what they know they learned in spite of the system. It is with mixed emotions that parents turn their children over to the public schools, cognizant of the damage to self-esteem that the system is notorious for inflicting on young vulnerable minds.

Although these new elite schools share a common ideological agenda with public schools of fostering national consciousness, their elite orientation and their firm emphasis on national culture and gender essentialism create a traditionalism that sets them apart from public schools in Ukraine. Perhaps most important, they are much more actively engaging issues of character and morality in an effort to rescue the Soviet-tainted psyche of their students. To the extent that the nationalized curricula which the private schools offer is seen by the new monied class as a means of desovietizing young minds, placing their children in a milieu of privilege, and securing their children's place among a new post-Soviet elite, these private schools could continue to grow in number, despite the fact that they often offer a plan of study focusing on subjects, such as folklore and museum studies, marginal to new business climates, but perhaps increasingly central in a political arena.

The public school system is colored by its Soviet predecessor and is unable to deliver the same kind of (nationalized) cultural knowledge. The monolithic educational bureaucracy and the structures and practices of Soviet schools remain virtually in place despite decrees and announced reforms that suggest otherwise. As regional cultural differences have contributed to an uneven implementation of various changes, some diversity now exists among public schools. The goodwill of directors has also become more critical in implementing reform. With revised textbooks either in short supply or nonexistent, the initiative and motivation of individual teachers greatly affects the quality of learning. Each of these levels, regional, administrative, and classroom, has de facto gained measured autonomy, and this has infused new ideas and standards into the educational process.

Through the lens of schools and education we see divergent attitudes toward the state. The government's announced plans to address issues of "individuality, nationality, and morality" and the private schools' actual efforts to restructure these concepts bespeak agreement that a new social order must be accompanied by a new social contract. Yet how that social order should be redefined is sharply debated when it comes to educational reform.

Although an independent state has the power to institutionalize aspects of Ukrainian culture so that it no longer needs to be in perpetual "revival," those involved in private education are acutely aware of the fragility of the state and of the wavering commitment of government leaders to strengthening Ukrainian culture for fear of alienating the large russified constituencies. They see education in general, and their private schools in particular, as a means of ensuring the survival of the Ukrainian state. The state to such educators has almost a mythical, sacred status because of its potential to enshrine and protect Ukrainian culture. At once reverent and protective of the state, they are totally disparaging of the government. Precisely because they have little confidence in state ministries and bureaucrats to reform the inherited Soviet educational system and institute changes, they have taken the task upon themselves. Reverence, distrust, and hope motivates the staff of the schools educating the first generation of post-Soviet Ukrainian elite. Caught in the crossfire of optimism and fear in post-Soviet society are the children, who, above all else, are perhaps learning a guarded cynicism toward the state and an indifference toward the government.

5

Festivals

Exactly eight days before the failed coup of 1991, which brought down the Soviet regime and unraveled the Soviet empire, a Ukrainian nationalist song festival opened in a highly russified region of Ukraine.[1] Through the medium of music and the intercultural connections it provides, the Chervona Ruta Music Festival showcased aspects of the Ukrainian historical experience that had been suppressed, marginalized, or discredited by the Soviet regime. In this russified area of Ukraine, a Ukrainian music festival became the site of transmission of an unofficial past, a past which glorified Ukraine and its suffering under Soviet rule. By portraying an alternative historical interpretation not sanctioned by the Soviet state, the festival cultivated the potential to raise Ukrainian national consciousness among a primarily Russian-speaking population with the hopes of challenging Soviet power by recruiting converts to the nationalist cause. The festival was building on a successful precedent.

In 1989 the first Chervona Ruta Music Festival was held in Chernivtsi in western Ukraine. Chernivtsi is the historic capital of Bukovyna, a territory that passed from Austro-Hungarian hands to the Romanian state during the interwar period before it was occupied by Soviet troops in March 1944. Although highly heterogeneous, Chernivtsi was known as the most easterly German cultural center because of its large German and German-speaking Jewish populations. The city also had large numbers of Romanians, Poles, Hungarians, and Ukrainians. Because Bukovyna was annexed to Soviet Ukraine by Stalin's Red Army only during World War II, Soviet culture was imported much later to this region. The ability to externalize socialism and to conceive of Soviet rule as a foreign imposition is a critical cultural difference between the western provinces, such as Bukovyna, and other regions of Ukraine. In general, Ukrainians throughout western Ukraine have managed to keep alive national histories and to continue using the Ukrainian language to a far greater degree than in other regions of Ukraine, in spite of the fact that these provinces were also subject to russificatory policies following annexation.

"Chervona Ruta" (Red Rue) was the name of an immensely popular love song written by Volodymyr Ivasiuk, a pop-culture icon who has often been compared to Vladimir Vysotskii in Russia. Ivasiuk was born in 1949 and is credited with writing over fifty songs. His songs became renown for their blend of Ukrainian folk music and a contemporary pop music beat. "Chervona Ruta" was a top hit played throughout the former Soviet Union and was widely known by Russians and Ukrainians alike. Ivasiuk was frequently persecuted and in 1979 he was found hanged in Chernivtsi. The authorities claimed that he committed suicide but it was widely believed that he was murdered by the KGB. As testimony to his vast popularity, his funeral was attended by over 10,000 people. Holding the festival in Chernivtsi, near where Ivasiuk was born and died, and naming the festival after his most renowned song created much emotionally charged symbolic capital.

The initial festival was the brainchild of Taras Melnyk, a professor of music at Kyiv's Tchaikovsky Conservatory, who went on to become the chief organizer. The festival followed on the heels of the inaugural congress of Rukh, held on September 8–10, 1989, in Kyiv. The festival was designed to perpetuate and intensify the momentum the congress had generated among independence supporters. Just one year later, Rukh emerged as a burgeoning opposition movement effectively uniting a variety of national, ecological, gender, and religious-based anti-Soviet groups under the banner of Ukrainian independence and plans were under way to institutionalize the Chervona Ruta Music Festival as a biannual event.

Although the festival featured a variety of music styles, it was organized expressly around the theme of promoting the Ukrainian national revival already under way. A rendition of the song "Chervona Ruta" opened the festival, with many members of the audience singing along. Kyrylo Stetsenko, the director of media for the festival and author of the festival program notes, explained why a music festival was the chosen vehicle to generate support for Ukrainian independence, "The strength of popular songs lies in the fact that these songs can bring back those who have lost their nationality. The strength of these songs is to be able to uncover in the souls of these people sources of national existence which have been destroyed by foreign influences" (cited in Bahry 1994: 251). In other words, by "uncovering" a "destroyed" sense of national consciousness, the festival organizers hoped to revive a sense of self as Ukrainian by purging the Soviet influences. In the age of the nation-state, "uncovering" a sense of Ukrainian identity was part of the strategy to challenge the legitimacy of Soviet rule and a music festival was seen as an effective means to do so.

Featuring traditional folk balladeers and Ukrainian rock, the festival was straightforwardly a celebration of Ukrainian culture. All songs were sung in Ukrainian. This condition was set by one of the main sponsors, Kobza, a Ukrainian-Canadian joint-venture company. Many of the performers sang openly pro-Ukrainian songs condemning the Soviet system and russification.[2] The recurring theme of the festival was one of revival, recovery, and remembering. For example, Taras Kurchyk sang a song entitled "We have forgotten everything" ("My zabuly vse"):

> We have forgotten everything
> We have forgotten our native language
> For which our grandfathers spilled their blood.
> No. Do not judge me.
> I have forgotten that which is native, which is close to me.[3]

Stressing the hurtful effects of cultural and historic amnesia collectively experienced by Ukrainians, this song tried to encourage the process of publicly remembering the horrors inflicted on Ukrainians by the Soviet system. The process of collectively remembering was greatly facilitated by the liminal, and hence protected, atmosphere of the festival. Such songs also served to remind the audience that the disillusionment and disappointment that engulfs them today is not characteristic of the way Ukraine and Ukrainians have lived in the past. Recalling a more dignified, more honorable pre-Soviet past serves as a springboard to imagining a better future. The subtext, of course, is that the means to turn such a vision into reality is to unshackle Ukraine from the Soviet Union.

Another song, sung by a group from Zaporizhzhia called Advance (*Avans*) lambasted the incessant shortages of all imaginable goods and bitterly complained of the system's inability to meet the basic needs of the people of Ukraine. The song, entitled "My Mother Washed Me" ("Myla Mene Maty") began slowly and gently in the style of a Ukrainian folk song and then broke into a harsh rock rhythm with the following biting lyrics:

> Where is the soap?
> Where is the meat?
> Where is the bacon?
> Everything, everything is only available
> with ration coupons.
> Why? Because—
> We're sick of everything.
> You can't find anything anywhere.
> There's a shortage of food
> What can one do?
> The theory arises
> that the ration coupons are
> as useless as the system.[4]

Such bitter critiques of the Soviet way of life were enthusiastically received by a public intoxicated with newly won freedom of expression under glasnost. The embracing response of the audience reflected a nagging thirst for a genuine depiction of the drudgery and hardships of their daily lives.

The very occurrence of the festival was widely seen as a historic event, given the Soviet state's official aversion to rock music and "bourgeois nationalism." This festival was considered a raging success, drawing huge crowds and generating considerable media attention. Technology gave the inroads achieved by the first Chervona Ruta Music Festival a multiple and long-lasting life. Kobza, the festival's sponsor, had the performances videotaped and recorded. In addition to being sold in Ukraine, the audio and video recordings were widely marketed in the west to the Ukrainian community. From the comfort of their living rooms, through the medium of music, diaspora Ukrainians took part in the struggle for Ukrainian independence and thereby reaffirmed their Ukrainian origins and commitment to an independent Ukrainian state. In 1990 Kobza sponsored a Canadian tour of the Chervona Ruta Festival winners, bringing ever greater exposure to contemporary Ukrainian music and the plight of Ukrainians under Soviet rule. The success of the initial festival contributed momentum to Rukh's struggle for independence. It coincided with an increasing vulnerability of the Soviet leadership brought on by an unforeseen barrage of heated criticism of the Soviet system triggered by glasnost.

This combination of factors influenced the decision to move the next festival to eastern Ukraine. Still under the guise of trying to generate support for Ukrainian independence, in 1991 Chervona Ruta was held in Zaporizhzhia, a provincial, industrial, highly russified, Communist Party stronghold. Zaporizhzhia, the sixth-largest city in Ukraine, lies along the Dnipro River and forms an industrial triangle with Donets'k and Dnipropetrovs'k. Throughout the Soviet era this region was heralded as the "cradle of the proletariat" because of its dense concentration of heavy Soviet-style industry.

Although the political and cultural realities of this region seemed inhospitable to a Ukrainian nationalist song festival (especially when compared with Chernivtsi), Zaporizhzhia nonetheless provided a rich site of historical myth and legend. Choosing Zaporizhzhia, the historic "homeland" of the Cossacks, as the second location of the festival held out the promise of softening local antagonism to a nationalist agenda by evoking the appeal of historical mythology and nostalgia symbolized by Cossack warriors through the medium of music.

By capitalizing on the allure of music, the festival created the possibility of extending membership in a redefined nation to Russians, Jews, and russified Ukrainians, all of whom knew by heart the words to the famous song, "Chervona Ruta." The "We" it posited was an inclusivist one, which largely hinged on the intercultural connection of music. Ironically, the second Ukrainian nationalist song festival closed in a highly russified region of Ukraine the day before the coup attempt on August 19, 1991. Thus, the Chervona Ruta festival was the last event orchestrated by nationalist groups in an oppositional mode to Soviet rule before the entire

An outdoor flea market in Zaporizhzhia. These markets offer shoppers a plethora of goods that traders engaged in "economic tourism" have been able to obtain (usually abroad), bring home, and offer for sale. Here a couple shops for a wedding gown.

empire and the system that had sustained it crumbled. For this reason, I dwell on the themes that informed this festival and on how they were received. Elements of Ukrainian culture, which here were used to revise historical consciousness and create a new sense of Ukrainian identity in a spirit of anti-Soviet agitation, later became the foundation and forum for producing a national culture in a post-Soviet Ukrainian state.

Public Liminality

The opening performance of the 1991 Chervona Ruta festival presented a kaleidoscope of symbols, derived from both a reinterpretation of the past and a reassessment of the present, in a highly charged political context. By presenting multivocal symbols of what an independent Ukrainian state would stand for, in contrast to its nemesis the Soviet Union, nationalist supporters hoped to generate enthusiasm for Ukrainian independence among an alienated, russified population. The performers throughout the evening tried to steer the anti-Soviet feelings of anger, deception, and disillusion, which they had purposefully evoked, into a strategy of empowerment by advocating Ukrainian independence as a cure-all strategy for the ills currently plaguing their society.

The festival's opening performance was distinctive in many respects. Riding the wave of newfound popular interest in the spiritual world and emphasizing the symbiotic relationship between religion and nationalism, the organizers wanted to begin the opening ceremony of the festival with a mass. Paradoxically, Zaporizhzhia had only Russian Orthodox churches. Nonetheless, the organizers insisted that priests participate from one of the two historically national churches, either the Ukrainian Catholic Church or the Ukrainian Autocephalous Orthodox Church. Yet as an enduring sign of the tenacity of Tsar Nicholas I's proclamation of the indissoluble unity of autocracy-orthodoxy-nationality, local Communist Party officials refused to allow the local Orthodox church to be left out. With the notable exception that the Ukrainian Catholic Church submits to papal authority, there is great similarity in the rituals, symbols, and architecture of the three churches because of their common Orthodox origins. The critical distinction following the fall of the Soviet Union became their different political visions. Previously, the decision to practice religion was a political statement regardless of faith. Today in Ukraine the church with which one chooses to affiliate often carries political overtones.

The dispute proved unresolvable, and the plan to launch the music festival with a mass was dropped. The organizers opted instead for clerical participation in the opening ceremonies. Thus the rock concert began with a religious procession. A stream of priests solemnly entered the soccer stadium walking along the track in black robes, graced by long hair and beards, carrying candles and crosses. In this way, twenty chanting priests introduced, so to speak, the first rock band. Subsequent songs were interspersed with prayers and speeches from priests of both churches emphasizing the necessity of a Ukrainian cultural revival as an antidote to sovietization.

Beginning the music festival on this sacred note challenged the "naturalness" of the historic links between a pan-Slavic identity and Orthodoxy. By undermining the authority of a pan-Slavic organization such as the Russian Orthodox Church, the organizers extended a parallel challenge to the legitimacy of the Soviet empire in the age of the nation-state. By insisting that the national churches participate, Rukh lent its support to nationalizing religious institutions, inverting and at the same time perpetuating the historic link between identity and religious affiliation in this part of the world.

Following the priests, a lineup of rock bands mixed with folk singers was the featured entertainment for the opening-night ceremonies of Chervona Ruta. Rock music helped to combat the prevailing stereotype that contemporary Ukrainian culture is marginal, on the brink of extinction, and interminably locked into its peasant origins. The Soviet acknowledgment of national differences over time often meant no more than caricatures of nineteenth-century peasants performing in folkloric dance troops, theaters, and choral groups around the Soviet Union. By confining Ukrainian culture to the realm of folklore, Ukrainian musical groups were left with little appeal beyond evoking nostalgia for innocent days past.

The heavy metal music of long-haired rebel guitarists participating in the festival was obviously meant to debunk this stereotype and to appeal to eastern Ukrainian youth. Featuring rock groups also showed that contemporary Ukrainian music had kept pace with the West. The ability to mimic the Western pop music tradition had the potential to lend some credence to nationalists' claim that Ukraine is an Eastern European country and does not belong in an "Asiatic empire," as many independence supporters referred to the Soviet Union. These rock musicians sported the same long hair, passion for black clothing, and rebel attitude that characterizes their Western counterparts. Yet even while mimicking the Western rock music tradition, these rock groups emphasized their Ukrainianness in lyrics. Indigenous characteristics were integrated into a Western musical style, forging a blend that could be embraced by a broad audience including ethnic Ukrainians, russified Ukrainians, Russians, diaspora Ukrainians, and other Westerners. Much as at the first festival, at every step of the way the musicians, through their critical lyrics and irreverent comments about Soviet life, were testing the limits of official tolerance before a multitude of uniformed police officers who stood around the track lining the bleachers.

As the feeling of solidarity with the performers and euphoria among the audience accelerated, during the third song of the opening ceremony of the festival most of the audience poured down from their seats in the bleachers, through the line of policemen, and onto the soccer field to dance. They broke traditional patterns of segregation of performer and audience and joined hands or elbows in a human chain, encircling the singers on stage and each other. Some formed spinning circles of twenty or more people all holding hands. Others formed swirling chains connected by interlocking elbows and traveled up and down the length of the soccer field. The musicians were warmly received as children of the nation, proof of their collective talent. The soccer stadium became the central town square as the "imagined community" of Ukrainians, at least for one night, was reified and celebrated in music and dance.

The cosmopolitan appeal of Western-styled rock music provided an inclusivist mode in which to present the often fiercely nationalistic and exclusivist lyrics of the performers. For example, one of the best-received rock bands, the Snake Brothers (*Brati Hadiukini*), who integrate an anarchy symbol into the written name of the band, sang a song, "Peace and Order in Ukraine," criticizing the russification and sovietization of the Ukrainian people. The lyrics told of a people whose spirit had been broken:

> The oppressed and the hungry have gone to sleep
> Whoever was no one has become nothing
> That's the way it will be tomorrow and today
> If you don't want to go to sleep, lie down and be quiet
> Peace and order in Ukraine
> The nightingale is chirping
> The Party and God are with us.[5]

Many members of the audience who had long feared being accused of espousing nationalist ideals, a crime often punishable by years in prison, began shouting nationalist slogans and denunciations of the Soviet regime as the police stood idly about. It appeared that the familiar Soviet-imposed taboos on social and political criticism in the public sphere were suspended. As the musicians sang, all the while encouraging members of the audience to disassociate themselves from the Soviet regime and from the Soviet experience, more and more blue and yellow Ukrainian flags popped up. Some members of the audience began waving them from the bleachers while others danced around on the playing field with the flags blowing in the wind behind them.

In another of their songs, the Snake Brothers confronted one of the most controversial and inflammatory moments in the history of Ukrainian nationalism by performing their song, "We're the boys from Banderstadt" ("My Khloptsi z Bandershtadtu") referring to L'viv, the cultural center of Ukrainian-speaking Ukraine. Reference in public to the legendary nationalist leader, Stepan Bandera, who masterminded Ukrainian nationalist collaboration with the Nazis against the Soviet Red Army during World War II, was forbidden for decades. Additionally, the Snake Brothers used the German word *Stadt*, meaning "city," to underline the links and heighten the connections among Bandera, Ukrainians, and the Nazis. Once the singers had cracked this taboo wide open with their song, a half-dozen members of the audience began to wave the forbidden black and red flags of Bandera's outlawed organization.

> We're the boys from Banderstadt
> We go to church
> We respect our parents
> No one can party like us
> Til the bugles don't play
> Til the drum doesn't beat
> Some say we're bandits, hooligans
> From this swamp
> There won't be human beings.[6]

The fiercely critical lyrics and the highly vocal reaction they prompted from the audience provided a forum in which to reject the Soviet definition of what it means to be Ukrainian. No longer marginalized subjects of a suppressed history, the band's songs tried to reposition Ukrainians as agents participating in their own historical experience and embracing it all, good and bad.

In contrast to contemporary rock performers, folk music was also part of the featured entertainment. Folk music catered to an age-old tradition of singing minstrels immortalized in the work of the national poet Taras Shevchenko and harked back to an "authentic" and unique Ukrainian cultural tradition. These folk performers, who ironically carried forward, and in doing so endorsed, the Soviet image of a Ukrainian "peasant" culture, were dressed in traditional folk costumes. They performed a round of peasant ballads using traditional string instruments, such as the *bandura*. But here too, there was evocation of the West. The four groups of folk performers, all dressed in nineteenth-century Ukrainian peasant costumes, were from the diaspora community. With cries of "Slava Ukraini!" (Glory to Ukraine!), they brought greetings and signs of solidarity from the Ukrainian communities in Canada, the United States, France, and Australia. Their performance suggested that the "real" and "authentic" Ukrainian culture, protected from the ravages of the Soviet experience, was viable and thriving in the West. The appearance of Ukrainian-speaking diaspora folk performers also showcased the breadth and strength of the Ukrainian nation outside Soviet borders, suggesting the existence of a worldwide network of Ukrainian independence supporters safeguarding the Ukrainian cultural heritage. Save the group from France, each ensemble introduced themselves and addressed the audience in Ukrainian. The French group, a highly accomplished four-piece instrumental band of guitars, bandura, and percussion, called themselves "Les Banderistes."

The decision to mix folk ballads with rock music is a critical one. It is important for nationalist leaders to keep the peasant motif alive. Among other things, it supports nationalist claims that since the Ukrainians were a peasant people, Stalin's brutal policies of collectivization which triggered the Famine of 1932–33, amounted to genocide. As discussed earlier, the Famine, like Chernobyl, is submitted in a multitude of forms as evidence of the victimization of Ukraine at the hands of a Moscow-based government.

Rukh chose the city of Zaporizhzhia to host the festival because it is the historic "homeland" of the Cossacks. Many scholars have noted that nationalists inevitably refer to a glorious past to evoke images of future grandeur via national liberation. For Ukrainian nationalists, this glorious past is Cossack. From this warring group, nationalists have created a myth of a fiercely independent people who successfully resisted subjugation and lived autonomously. Save the three years following the Revolution after which the nascent Ukrainian state government succumbed to Bolshevik pressure during the Civil War—there is no real period of independent statehood to point to in the modern era as inspiration to make the break from Russia. Nationalist leaders nonetheless try to illustrate a spirit of independence and self-sufficiency. The resurrection of a particular historical consciousness fueled by a myth of Cossack heroism was also a goal of the festival and a key reason Zaporizhzhia was chosen as its location. In commemoration of Cossack warriors, many young men in the audience, as well as the performers, wore baggy pants belted over a white embroidered shirt and had their heads shaven the way Cossacks supposedly did, leaving only a forelock (*oseledets'*).

The myth of Cossack bravery burst onto the scene during the festival in the form of crowd-pleasing improvisation. In spite of the fact that Zaporizhzhia produces vast amounts of electricity, twice during the first song and periodically thereafter, the entire sound system collapsed be-

For the purposes of political protest and holiday festivities, some men will dress in the style of the legendary Cossack warriors, as seen here.

cause of a power failure. During these moments of technical difficulty, Cossack horsemen charged into the arena at a full gallop and performed gravity-defying, life-threatening stunts to the delight of the crowd as they encircled the hordes of Polish technicians desperately trying to restore the sound system. A financial backer of the festival, an Englishman, had brought in technicians from Poland as a hedge against anticipated party sabotage. One by one the horses galloped around the track at a full speed as the Cossack horsemen dismounted, remounted backwards, dismounted in somersault, and remounted again on their hands. As the horsemen raced around the stadium track for the third time, the crowd began to shout "Ukraine without Moscow!" Little did they know that this would soon become reality.

As jubilant as those dancing on the soccer field were, it quickly became apparent that not everyone in attendance was so euphoric. The notion that the vitality and vibrance of Ukrainian music was directly correlated to the vitality of the Ukrainian nation and an independent Ukrainian state failed to carry some members of the audience into the dancing, celebrating crowds. For those who remained in the bleachers and did not dance along with the others on the playing field, equally intense feelings and forms of consciousness were generated as they were excluded from the feeling of euphoria. Made aware of their Russianness at a Ukrainian nationalist festival, they understood themselves to be trapped in an amorphous colonial space. Suddenly, these people were unsure as to whether they were the colonizers or the colonized.

I had gone to the festival with a Ukrainian woman from Kyiv who worked as a nurse at the Higher Party School, a training ground for Communist Party elites in Kyiv. At the outset of the festival she was buoyant in spirit, curious, and ever so slightly beaming with pride that she was at a Ukrainian nationalist festival. Her family speaks Ukrainian at home and she was educated in Ukrainian through high school. Yet she claims that although she understands Ukrainian, she does not speak it. For others sitting nearby in the audience who did not understand Ukrainian, she translated the speeches and announcements and words of welcome written on the electronic scoreboard, which here doubled as a message board. Letters unique to Ukrainian and not found in Russian were represented by numerals, adding a sense of displacement and foreignness to finding things Ukrainian in eastern Ukraine. It became undeniably clear at this festival that although Ukrainian by nationality, Natasha was socialized in russified Kyivan society and this is where her allegiances lay. It didn't take long before she felt uncomfortable.

During the third sound system collapse when the Cossack horsemen raced around the stadium and the crowd chanted "Ukraine without Moscow!" Natasha instantly began explaining that it was unwise for these nationalist hotheads to be advocating such a cavalier policy. She made an emphatic distinction between her unrelenting criticism of the failures of the Soviet system and exonerating Russians from blame. She countered that perhaps Ukraine needed economic independence but she was certain that the historic link between Ukraine and Russia would never be, in fact *could* never be, broken by political independence. When asked whether she thought it was feasible to have real economic independence (an end to a centrally planned economy) and still remain tied to Moscow politically, she said, "I hope it is possible because it would be impossible to completely split from Russia. We've lived so long together. It would be like cutting off one side of my body." Ultimately, she was arguing for independence from the Soviet Union, but not from Russia. Twelve days later Ukraine was to declare independence.

Also with us was Vitalii and his wife Galina. Vitalii is Ukrainian by nationality but was born in Vladivostok in the far eastern reaches of Siberia where his parents were exiled in the 1930s for no apparent reason.

Except for university studies in Latvia, Vitalii has lived his whole life in Russia. As national revivals sprung up around the Soviet Union, he became very interested in exploring his Ukrainian roots. He joined a recently formed Ukrainian club in his hometown, developed an interest in Ukrainian folk music, and began studying the Ukrainian language with his wife. His newfound enthusiasm for his ethnic origins prompted him and his wife to spend the summer in Ukraine. They were delegates from their hometown club to a Ukrainian-language summer program in Kyiv. It was through the auspices of this language program that they came to the festival.

His wife, an ethnic Russian, never lived in Russia until she married Vitalii. She was born and raised in Riga, Latvia. She was clearly aghast by the anti-Moscow chants that erupted when the sound system broke down. She and Vitalii blamed it on the incompetence of the Polish technicians, whose inability to master the technical difficulties caused a lull in the entertainment in the first place and created the possibility of provoking even more shrill, in their opinion, reactions from the crowd. In a moment of extreme discomfort, Galina claimed that she had always suspected, but now she was certain, that Rukh was "an instrument of the KGB." She argued that the KGB staged this festival and was behind the other Rukh events as well. The KGB used Rukh, she explained, to stir up nationalist sentiment in order to have an excuse to send in the army and crush Ukrainian separatism. Vitalii told her that she was very naive and glared at her in such an uncharacteristically aggressive way that she knew not to voice other opinions on Ukrainian politics that night.

Each of the three wanted so much to feel the euphoria of celebrating Ukraine, but they just couldn't. Condemning Russia was too mixed up in the process. This heightened consciousness of being Other at Home, triggered by the performers' lyrics and use of historic imagery to illustrate the oppression of Ukrainians at the hands of a foreign government, gives insight into why the abundant pleasure the music was bringing to others failed to carry these three, and others like them, into the performance space. For most of the concert they sat stone-faced, their empty eyes following the intertwining chains of dancers circling the performers on the field, as they sat, feeling excluded, far up in the bleachers.

Illusion of Belonging

The multiple and fluid qualities of nationality in the Soviet Union begin to explain the ambivalence Natasha, Vitalii, and Galina felt at the Chervona Ruta Festival. Why couldn't they and the others who remained in the bleachers celebrate Ukraine? The nationalist reinterpretation of the Ukrainian historical experience and redefinition of what it means to be Ukrainian provided for some a point of orientation to understand present predicaments and future aspirations in a rapidly changing society. Yet after decades of Soviet discourse which divided the world into "socialist" and "capitalist," to form an experiential "We" in terms of "us" (Ukrainians, the colonized and the oppressed) and "them" (Russians, the colonizers and chauvinists) rang hollow to many Ukrainians. Decades of assimilation, coerced and noncoerced, have produced comparatively little cultural and linguistic difference among some Russians and Ukrainians. This means that some cannot dislodge the weight of their past in favor of a new identity quite so easily. The redefinition of the political and historic relationship between Ukraine and Russia, and by extension of Ukrainian culture, for some became yet another destabilizing factor in late Soviet society.

Why did advocates of Ukrainian independence turn to music to recast the critical relationship between Russia and Ukraine? The demarcations between musical styles, genres, and performances, while nonetheless reflective of a cultural tradition, are infinitely more porous than other avenues of culture that also inform identity. For analytic purposes Chervona Ruta could best be conceived of as a cultural performance, since it united a multitude of cultural elements in a mass performative setting. As we will see in the next chapter, many of the same dynamics are also at work during commemorations and ceremonies. The term "cultural performance" was first used by Milton Singer (1955). He expanded the concept of performance to include social drama as well. Singer argued that performative genres (concerts, plays, rites, ceremonies, festivals, and so on) were often orchestrations of various nonlinguistic modes of communication and provided a window on how "cultural themes and values were communicated as well as on the processes of social and cultural change" (1972: 77).

Building on Singer's initial cultural performance concept, Victor Turner (1987) argued that cultural performances create a space of public liminality. Liminality is the "betwixt and between" antistructural stage of the tripartite ritual process and the point at which new forms of consciousness can be created and a change of status can occur. The entire audience, by virtue of its attendance at the festival, is thrown into public liminality.[7] Rukh's use of cultural performance to challenge the legitimacy of Soviet rule was distinguished from that of Soviet authorities by its voluntary, interactive, and improvisational nature. In contrast, the highly predictable and prescribed nature of Soviet parades and rituals was designed to reinforce the established social order and rearticulate Soviet authority by eliminating the possibility of change.

Victor Turner argued that cultural performances were a form of performative reflexivity: they do not merely "reflect" or "express" a given social order or cultural configuration, rather they are "active agencies of change." In particular, Turner identified the dialectical and reflexive qualities embodied in the critiques they deliver of the way society handles history (1987: 22). The liminality created by the festival and the euphoric reaction of the crowd (communitas) provided a forum in which individuals could publicly reject the Soviet definition of what it means to be Ukrainian and articulate an alternative version. The performers accelerated this process by encouraging members of the audience to dissociate themselves from the Soviet regime and from the Soviet experience, prompting for some a change in historical and national consciousness, as they imagined themselves belonging to a different community. Ceasing to be a participant and becoming a performer yields a different perspective and heightens reflexivity, facilitating the process of dissociation.

The audience at the Chervona Ruta Music Festival on the eve of the breakdown of the Soviet Union was primarily made up of diaspora Ukrainians, supporters of Rukh from the western provinces who arrived specially for the festival, and some Ukrainians from the area. But judging by the fact that only a third of the stadium was full on opening night and successive performances were even more sparsely attended, it is safe to conclude that the festival had minimal appeal for russified Ukrainians. I am quick to note, however, that unexpected delays, some of which mandated that a performance began up to nine hours later than its advertised time, last minute on-the-spot schedule changes, such as performances starting in the evening, breaking for the night, and finishing up the following morning, and overall poor communication of time and location of events, also diminished local interest in the festival.

Attendance at formal events, however, is but one avenue of exposure to nationalist ideas. Such cultural performances derive their power through their ability to communicate multiple messages in a variety of expressive forms. For the residents of Zaporizhzhia, the festival most likely represented the first time in their lives that they had seen their city draped in the Ukrainian national flag. From flag-toting pedestrians, to bumper stickers, to makeshift fliers, to buttons (*znachky*), the *tryzub*, the national symbol of Ukraine, and the blue-and-yellow Ukrainian flag were apparent everywhere.

In addition, a half-dozen disgruntled residents decided to capitalize on the influx of foreigners attending the music festival to launch a group hunger strike in protest of the abominable environmental conditions produced by the sea of Zaporizhzhian smokestacks belching gray air. Indeed, in Zaporizhzhia one can literally see what one is breathing. The pitiful sight of disempowered people sleeping in makeshift tents and literally starving in the center of Great October Revolution Square underlined the failures of the Soviet system and heightened consciousness of the environmental devastation it has wrought on Ukraine. In a very real sense then, the festival, its very occurrence a voice of opposition, opened wide the gates enclosing discontent.

The former Soviet Union is a land of ironies and paradoxes. One of the greatest ironies surrounding the Chervona Ruta Music Festival is that it provided a rare public forum in which to express spontaneous support for Ukrainian culture in the modest hope of advancing the struggle for an independent Ukrainian state. As I stated earlier, the festival achieved mixed results, alienating some Ukrainians and appealing to others. Yet the festival promoted alternative visions of Ukrainian culture and history up until the night before the putsch occurred. On the morning of August 19, 1991, as the news of the coup became public, those who were involved in the staging and promotion of the festival went underground, fearing retroactive punishment and a return to the pre-glasnost policies forbidding public expression of anti-Soviet agitation. Within three days, however, the coup had failed and the irreversible process of dismantling the Soviet Union and its social system had begun. Ironically, the end of this modest Ukrainian music festival coincided with the end of the Soviet era.

The Past in the Present

This festival, like the other anti-Soviet pro-Ukrainian commemorations and spectacles realized before Ukrainian independence, was an instance where unofficial histories and alternative remembrances were represented and reexperienced. It gave a physicality to alternative historical representations and provided a site of voiced opposition to Soviet rule. Now that an independent Ukrainian state has been established and the Soviet Union recedes into memory, these unofficial histories and unsanctioned recollections of the Ukrainian experience of Soviet rule are becoming institutionalized. No longer presented as spectacle, the unsanctioned, unofficial perspective of the Soviet period has now become standard rhetoric of the new Ukrainian state. The historical representations seen at the Chervona Ruta Festival, such as Cossack mastery, religious devotion, and folklore, were essentially mythic images that ignored chronology and historical accuracy. These elements, however, are being integrated into new national historical narratives and national charters. Formerly unsanctioned historical representations whose very expression risked incurring the wrath of the Soviet state police, now find a home in a Ukrainian state-sponsored biannual music festival.

Opposition events in the late Soviet period, such as the Chervona Ruta Music Festival, merit our attention because in some instances they have become "traditions" perpetuated in the post-Soviet period. The festival has since been held in several other highly russified regions in an effort to bring Russians and russified Ukrainians closer to Ukrainian culture through music. In 1993 the festival was held in Donets'k, a city similar to Zaporizhzhia in its ethnic and economic profile. Donets'k is the center of the Donbas region of eastern Ukraine. Since independence, this region has been particularly hard hit economically because of its reliance on unprofitable coal production. Incessant talk of shutting down expired mines fuels fears of unemployment and deprivation, especially among multigenerational mining families.

Amid such social tension, not surprisingly, the 1993 festival was plagued with organizational problems of all kinds from the start. The festival became quite controversial when organizers decided to bar Russian-speaking groups from performing. This was seen by the overwhelmingly Russian-speaking local population as a strong indicator of the loss of status of Russian language and of its eroding place in the public sphere thanks to Ukrainian statehood. Up until a month before the festival was scheduled to begin, it was unknown whether local opposition and financial and organizational difficulties would prevent it from occurring at all. Although it generated comparatively minimal impact, in the end, the show did go on.

Just two years later, in 1995, the festival was held in Sevastopol, the home of the disputed Black Sea Fleet and a large contingent of Russian and Ukrainian navy personnel. Located on the southwestern side of the Crimean peninsula, Sevastopol, much like Donets'k and Zaporizhzhia before it, was chosen as a festival site because of its highly russified population.

"European" music was once again chosen as a means to expose an alienated, youthful population to Ukrainian culture. Now expanded to a nineteen-day event, over 250,000 spectators came to hear 310 performers from each of the twenty-five oblasts singing songs in Ukrainian. Speaking of Crimean youth, the founder and director of the festival, Taras Melnyk, said, "After hundreds of years of Russian domination, they are psychologically opposed to anything Ukrainian. And pushing it on them, whether it be language or literature, is a step backward. A young person wants to feel modern, contemporary. They were isolated from Ukraine, and everything Ukrainian was foreign to them. But now we have the opportunity to acquaint them with the Ukrainian language and the culture" (Kolomayets 1995: 10).

This festival was more successful than either of its two most recent predecessors in a number of respects. Not only was attendance up but a greater number of musical categories enhanced the competition aspect of the festival and this combined to encourage participation of musicians from a wider geographic spectrum and to broaden its overall appeal. For example, when the festival was held in Donets'k, only a handful of local musicians participated. In contrast, just two years later in 1995, forty performers from the city of Donets'k entertained large crowds with songs performed in Ukrainian. In spite of its success, the festival remains in debt. Although the Ministry of Culture has supported the festival since its inception, in 1995 the Ministry of Finance provided only half of the 46 billion karbovantsi (ca. U.S. $300,000) needed to stage the festival.

Financial woes have left the organizers undaunted. Each year they have seen improvement in attendance, press coverage, the number and quality of the musicians participating, and in the impact winning a festival prize has on the individual careers of performers. In 1997, the festival was staged over a two-week period in Kharkiv, another industrialized, russified city in eastern Ukraine, and continued to draw record crowds. The Cabinet of Ministers contributed 400,000 hryvnia, the new Ukrainian currency, and undisclosed sums were provided by two sponsors, Coca-Cola Amatil and Korona Chocolates.

Although still in debt and struggling each year to find adequate sponsorship, the festival continues to become more elaborate. The closing acts, held on the immense Freedom Square in the center of the city, drew nearly half a million people. The performances were enhanced by deejays and dance leaders, whose job it was to encourage the crowd to partake in the festive spirit. The deejays led the crowds in collective chants but at one point their efforts yielded unintended results and served as a reminder of why the festival was created in the first place. The deejays stirred the crowds into exclamations of "Kharkiv! Kharkiv!" only to hear them respond in Russian with "Kharkov! Kharkov!" (Panchyshyn 1997: 7; Woronowycz 1997: 10–11).

No matter how mixed the reaction is to certain festivals or to certain performances within festivals, the overall consensus among organizers is that a music festival is an effective site for articulating and imparting aspects of Ukrainian culture to the younger members of its nation. Music provides a vitally important intercultural connection that can viscerally link an individual to a group. Clearly, state leaders agree. Although still struggling to fund basic medical care and education, government leaders have proven themselves committed to funding Chervona Ruta.

Cognizant of the fact that as a site for the transmission of a post-Soviet national culture, the Chervona Ruta music festival through its celebratory crowd setting and ensuing solidarity offers the potential of facilitating reorientation of individuals to a nationalized collective. To ensure that this reorientation, should it occur, is lasting and not fleeting, Chervona Ruta has been institutionalized with state funding that has been steadily forthcoming. Festivals are but one performative genre categorized under the rubric of cultural performance. We now turn to an analysis of commemorations, both state sponsored and popular, to analyze how they too have the potential to prompt a change in consciousness.

6

Commemoration and the State Calendar

State structures play a key role in shaping and maintaining a nation's narrative of collective historical experience. One fundamental way states organize and articulate this narrative is through the state-designed calendar of official holidays, commemorations, and celebrations. The institutionalization of this narrative in the calendar provides a temporal framework that brings pivotal events in a nation's history into popular practice and consciousness in a ritualized, cyclical fashion. Because of the enormous symbolic significance of the state calendar and its capacity to reorient a group, the calendar is a powerful means by which to mark discontinuity between the past and the present, between a former regime and a new one. Through cyclical repetition, the calendar can later serve to reinforce and naturalize an established social order—that is, as we shall see, if it withstands the challenges from groups in disagreement with the historical narrative upon which the calendar is based.[1]

Much like the flag or a national anthem, the calendar symbolizes the distinctiveness and uniqueness of the nation. The calendar of annual commemorations creates a distinct rhythm of social life that unifies a group through collective action. By virtue of the fact that such collective action engages only the members of the group, the calendar sets them apart from others by functioning as an intergroup boundary, uniquely marking time and salient moments in the group's history.

Once institutionalized as part of the state apparatus, the calendar becomes a vital link between the state and individuals as the life cycles and everyday practices of individuals are gradually grafted onto state-designed commemorations. By connecting individuals to a group through a shared calendar of celebrations and commemorations, a sense of belonging is created. State-sponsored commemoration, therefore, can be viewed not only as the practice of history but the practice of belonging as well.[2]

The stability of the calendar is tightly linked to the stability of the state. Therefore, calendrical change is not lightly undertaken. Rather, it usually occurs during a period of immense social upheaval. The calendrical reforms that followed on the heels of the French Revolution constitute one of the most formidable attempts in modern history to reorganize units and frameworks of time by which a nation categorizes, classifies, and dates events.[3] Taking inspiration from the sweeping calendrical reforms of the French Revolution, Lenin attempted a similar redefinition of temporality following the Russian Revolution. Less than three months after taking power, on February 1, 1918, Lenin dropped the Julian calendar in favor of the Gregorian, the latter having become a symbol of modernization and westernization. (The thirteen-day shift this mandated explains why the "Great October Revolution" is commemorated on November 7.) Calendrical reform served a twofold purpose. First, coordinating calendars with other Western countries could facilitate the internationalization of the Revolution. Second, the Bolshevik regime also sought to make a break with the temporal framework of its imperial predecessor whose celebratory calendar melded notions of the sacred and the profane. By changing to the Gregorian calendar and eventually eliminating the religious calendar as a means of organizing social life, the Bolshevik regime reduced the status and influence of the Orthodox Church and heightened the importance of its own calendar of Soviet and internationalist commemorations of secular events.

Following the Russian Revolution of 1917, intellectuals combed the historical record for events and heroes that could be showcased in commemoration to legitimize the new Soviet state's authority in the face of economic hardship. Then, as now, symbolic forms demonstrating belonging, legitimacy, and common history assumed great importance in the absence of material or cultural incentives for endorsing the state. The repetitive nature of commemoration implies a continuity with the past and indeed even claims a direct link to the past—even when it has been freshly invented—and this can serve as an effective source of solidarity among those who participate in the commemoration.[4] The dimensions of the group acknowledged in commemoration usually reach mythic proportions, often including the living, dead ancestors, and those still to be born. Such grandeur serves the ritualistic atmosphere of the commemoration and lends authenticity to it.

In this chapter we will look at how the process of remaking the state calendar unfolds while noting the resistance of large segments of the population to such statist projects. By examining not only the state's efforts to institutionalize a revised calendar of commemorations but also popular indifference and resistance to it, we discover that individuals often have a clear vision of what they would like their national culture to be and what they would like their nationality to mean. Before exploring exactly which forms calendrical revision has taken, it is essential to examine the legacy of Soviet commemorations inherited by the new Ukrainian state for this legacy impinges on all efforts to recast national history in commemorative ceremonies.

Commemoration in the USSR

In 1918, five days marking key events in revolutionary history were proclaimed nonworking days: Memorial Day for Bloody Sunday (January 22), Overthrow of the Autocracy Day (March 12), Paris Commune Day (March 18), May Day (May 1), and Great October Revolution Day (November 7). New Year's Day (January 1) was also a nonworking day. Two of these dates had been part of the Marxist calendar for decades. International Day of Working Women (March 8) was also noted but was not considered a rest day.

In addition to the aforementioned holidays, on the local level a weekly rest day was established. Local authorities were granted the autonomy to select initially ten, later eight, religious festivals, albeit not festivals directly connected with tsarism, which were to be considered official holidays. Gradually, the Bolsheviks shifted the locus of social time away from the Orthodox calendar to its own.

At the urging of Trotsky and Lunacharsky, the Commissar of Enlightenment, to complement the calendar of commemorations, the Bolsheviks staged a number of mass spectacles following the Revolution to forge a mythic past out of a few years of revolutionary activity (von Geldern: 1993; Stites 1985: 1–24). The pomp and majesty of the Romanov dynasty rites and the supreme beauty of Orthodox services had accustomed much of the population to lavish spectacle. Bolshevik leaders recognized the importance of the visual and the tactile when trying to impart political and social visions to a largely illiterate population.

The mass spectacles, which were largely improvised reenactments of the past, allowed citizens of the new Soviet state to experience and celebrate the values of the new society in ways that other forms of discourse could not. Much like the Jacobins, the Bolsheviks saw mass spectacles as a "school of citizenship." These popular extravaganzas served to make socialist ideology accessible to the masses, to create legitimizing myths of the goals of the Revolution, and to shroud the myths in an aura of sacred mission (Binns 1979: 585–606; Stites 1985). However, spectacles lack the scripted and rehearsed qualities of other genres of cultural performance such as commemoration and even festival. It was only a matter of time before, in the spirit of spectacle, revolutionary fervor gave way to wit and satire. A number of mass spectacles took on a sarcastic tone as the mass participation escalated beyond the control of leaders of Narkompros and Proletkult, two bureaucracies responsible for shaping aspects of culture, and became political carnival.[5] In a parody of "The Storming of the Winter Palace," noted animal trainer Vladimir Durov staged a children's performance during which he led an "army" of live rabbits in storming the Winter Palace. Once the palace was captured, they mounted a banner proclaiming "Rabbits of the World Unite!" (Ehrenburg 1962: 388).[6]

As it became more difficult for Lunacharsky and the other cultural leaders to control the political content of mass spectacles, their staging grew more infrequent. Artists, too, grew resentful of the growing number of directives that dictated more and more both the content and the form of the spectacles and began to avoid such projects. The vibrancy, spontaneity, and popular participation of these early spectacles peaked by 1920. Having garnered enough support to see the new state through its initial years of existence, the goal became educating the populace, not simply generating enthusiasm, and as a result, mass spectacles were replaced by formal commemorations.

Official Soviet commemorations became "demonstrations," as they were called, which took over city centers and town squares. They inevitably involved soldiers, veterans, and the members of the local Communist Party leadership. The first anniversary of the Great October Revolution in 1918 was portrayed as a national triumph of the proletariat and was held up as evidence of the Soviet Union's messianic mission. In contrast, May Day, established in 1889 at the Paris Congress of the Second International, was decisively international in character, celebrating the international unification of proletarians. Originally, the celebration of May Day stressed the hope for revolution in Western Europe and the proletariat's critical role as revolutionary agent. When it became increasingly apparent that the Russian Revolution was not to trigger a worldwide revolution, Stalin countered with his "Socialism in One Country" slogan and the international component of the May Day festivities subsided.

Although the orchestrated aspects of these commemorations became more and more solemn, they were never entirely serious events. In 1929, some participants carried "enemy masks" in a satirical jab at Stalin's growing list of "enemies of the people," which now included kulaks, or prosperous peasants, any remaining capitalists, and soldiers of the White Army. Additionally, amateur actors poked fun at Soviet policies by agitating for a continuous work week by portraying Saturday as an old woman, backward and religious, and Sunday as an old drunken man (Lane 1992: 175).[7]

Over the years, these two demonstrations of state power and party grandeur grew more similar as they became professionalized and formulaic mass exhibits of Party prowess. Local initiatives and spontaneous participation were severely discouraged as Stalin's regime tried to rein in public celebrations that deviated from a standard program dictated by Moscow. Under Stalin, demonstrations became routine. Spectators were no longer invited into the performance space but obliged to attend and watch from the sidelines. Every factory, farm, and office was obliged to send representatives to participate. Processions showcasing military and economic might emerged as the centerpiece of the commemorations and, to varying degrees, ceremonial decorations of towns. Red, the traditional symbol of beauty (hence, Red Square), was the preferred color, with white and green used sparingly.

During commemorations of the October Revolution marchers carried red Soviet flags, red banners with Soviet propaganda slogans, giant portraits of Marx, Lenin, the current leader of the country, and members of the Politburo. This was followed by a vast parade of military might, which featured soldiers marching in close formation and a display of the latest weaponry. The local Communist Party leadership was always standing by to oversee the display. The row of standing, solemn men formally dressed earned them the popular term "red iconostasis." The Moscow version of the commemoration was broadcast in the evening across the Soviet Union, showing the elite of the Communist Party leadership standing atop Lenin's Mausoleum, with the Kremlin in the distance, reviewing the scores of troops paraded before them. The pomp and force of the Moscow demonstration was not matched in any provincial city. These broadcasts were often followed by reruns of speeches made by Lenin.[8]

The sheer grandiosity of the November 7th commemoration remained enough to hold the interest of some spectators. Over time, however, people increasingly preferred to spend a quiet day at home instead. Individual and local resistance, often simply in the form of passive compliance or indifference to these commemorations, were among the few visible indicators of deviance from state mandates tolerated.

Ivan, a middle-aged historian from Kharkiv I interviewed, explained, "When I was a child and a student, I used to go to the demonstrations but later I always found a pretext not to go. It was cold. The ceremonies last forever. There are crowds. It's really an unbearable situation. The only ones who enjoyed it were some factory workers. They were given flags and banners to carry. When they handed them in at the end—only when they gave them back—they got ten rubles. About two bottles of vodka. In the old days, I mean. I think they earned it." According to Ivan, and numerous others whom I interviewed, this holiday came to mean little more than two days off and an excuse for a meal with plenty of vodka toasts. (Those two days off had to be compensated for by working over the next weekend so that there was no actual reduction in the number of working hours.) Some personalized the commemorations and added a consumerist dimension by exchanging cards and offering flowers and small presents to family members or friends.

In other words, the central, most important commemoration of the Soviet regime, which was designed to generate legitimacy and support for the regime and its ideology, came to be seen as spectacle and held little appeal for the majority of Soviet citizens because of its formulaic and tightly orchestrated nature. Using commemorations of the Revolution to generate enthusiasm and support for Marxist-Leninist ideology failed miserably. Other overtly political holidays, such as Constitution Day (October 9) and Soviet Army Day (February 23), were even less successful.

Of course, it is important to note that July 4th parades in the United States frequently draw only the mothers of the marchers as spectators. Memorial Day to many means little more than a rained-out barbecue. This suggests that the state does not have to be delegitimized, as the Soviet Union increasingly became, in order for the national holidays expressing national histories to become virtually meaningless to vast sectors of the population. The key difference is that the Soviet Union with its mighty propaganda machine relied to a greater degree on such commemorations to generate legitimacy and allegiance in the face of extensive restrictions on public speech and behavior and in the absence of consumer prosperity. Therefore, when commemorations failed to generate a meaningful reaction among spectators, the ramifications were greater. Over time the resentment toward the state and its growing list of shortcomings ironically triggered disdain for the commemorations that were supposed to celebrate its grandeur. Perceptions of the state as deceptive and untrustworthy served to cultivate, not just active disdain for Soviet commemorations, but a deep-seated view of state-designed commemorations as self-serving and inauthentic.

Yet a paradox remains: if the ceremonies were so meaningless, why did they become ever more institutionalized and why did the initial six holidays give birth to a roster of secular rituals?[9] Binns cogently argues that individuals and groups managed to wrest control of these events away from the state and appropriate them for their own purposes (1979: 183). Ultimately, state commemorative ceremonies and secular rituals were used to forge meaning into individual rites of passage and to reinforce group solidarity (1979 and 1980). Furthermore, he asserts that because these commemorations precluded meaningful spectator participation, once appropriated they indirectly encouraged pluralism, individualism, and consumerism. Out of rigid uniformity, diversity was born. Once individuals and groups began sculpting state-designed commemorations to suit their own needs, they became meaningful once again, but in a highly tailored way and certainly not in the way that state authorities intended. Indeed, in the face of commemorations designed to further assimilation to Soviet culture, a nationalized sense of self was kept alive through local appropriation and facilitated the eventual nationally based challenges to Soviet rule that emerged in the late 1980s. The key point I am trying to make is that Soviet state-designed commemorations have left a legacy of discredited displays of state power and a public accustomed to disdaining them or remaking them in favor of refashioned, atomized events celebrated at home. State-sponsored collective commemorations in the Soviet Union became unable to generate solidarity, community, and identity with respect to the state itself.

Glasnost and Commemorating Alternative Histories

In the late 1980s, the leaders of Rukh used commemoration as an effective weapon against the Soviet state, chiseling away at its legitimacy by commemorating alternative histories or staging protest demonstrations of Soviet commemorations. The increasing number of people who were dissatisfied with the Soviet system often banded together on key commemorative occasions to note their opposition to the regime in a collective and highly public way. Under the Soviet system historical events were commemorated at several levels: federal, republican, and local. Nationalist opposition leaders especially challenged the validity of the narratives and representations communicated during republican-level commemorations. Efforts to wrest Shevchenko from Soviet iconography and restore him to his proper place in Ukrainian history as the father of the nation and its most gifted poet were ongoing at anniversary celebrations of his birth and death.[10] I noted earlier unofficial popularly staged anniversary commemorations of the independent Ukrainian state, which existed from 1917 to 1920, and efforts to emphasize the commemoration of the Millennium of Christianity in Kyiv over Moscow.

In addition, other counterdemonstrations of Soviet commemorations were also staged. For example, Rukh and other groups opposed the official Soviet commemorations of the anniversary of the Battle of Poltava on July 6–9, 1989. This was a momentous battle in which Peter the Great's armies defeated those of the Swedish king Charles XII and Mazepa's Ukrainian Cossacks and paved the way for the "reunification" of eastern Slavs under one (Russian) state. Rukh wished to celebrate the heroism of the Cossacks and to reclaim the battle as a nationalist uprising that in spite of bravery and military acumen, was unfortunately defeated.

A group of Ukrainian Insurgent Army veterans from western Ukraine gathered in 1995 before the entrance to St. Volodymyr Cathedral, a Ukrainian Orthodox Church in Kyiv.

Similarly, Soviet efforts to commemorate the fiftieth anniversary of the "reunification" of the western Ukrainian provinces, which were part of other Eastern European countries, with Soviet Ukraine during World War II were met with nationalist resistance. The official commemorations, not surprisingly, were celebratory in mood and silent on the issue of the repression and deportations that followed Soviet occupation. Rukh activists sought to highlight the alternative to Soviet rule posed by the Organization of Ukrainian Nationalists (OUN), a forbidden topic of historical inquiry in the halls of the Soviet academic establishment.[11] These commemorations of suppressed historical events were clearly held in an anti-Soviet spirit that inherently made them meaningful to participants.

Yet the entrenched indifference associated with state-sponsored commemoration remains a legacy to be overcome by the new Ukrainian state. In revising the state calendar, the leaders of post-Soviet Ukraine face a formidable challenge: creating inclusive commemorations that will resonate with individuals as authentic and meaningful in a public space that has long been discredited as a forum for lies. The emotional and experiential bankruptcy of Soviet holidays leave in their wake a reluctance to partake in refashioned post-Soviet state commemorations. This has perpetuated the tendency to retreat out of the public sphere to the home front where commemorations, if they occur at all, are atomized, not collectively shared. Even in such a context of fragmentation and lack of consensus, commemorations nonetheless retain the potential to become a broad avenue of collective representation, a vital means of sculpting history into a national culture.

Revising the Calendar

Beginning in early 1992, one month after the referendum that provided a popular mandate for Ukrainian independence, the new annual calendar of official Ukrainian state holidays was introduced. Absent after seventy-four years were the Anniversary of the Great October Socialist Revolution (November 7), Constitution Day (October 9), and Soviet Army Day (February 23). Some holidays celebrated during Soviet rule, such as New Year's (January 1), Women's Day (March 8), May Day (May 1), and Victory Day (May 9), were preserved. Two new days, marking critical historical events contributing to Ukrainian independence, were commemorated with festivities of their own. Ukrainian Independence Day (August 24) marks the end of the Soviet era, and Referendum Day (December 1) celebrates the demonstration of a popular mandate for Ukrainian independence. In 1993, the Day of National Mourning (September 12) was added to commemorate the sixtieth anniversary of the Famine of 1932–33. Debates continue over whether several other commemorative holidays should be added to the state calendar: January 22, Ukrainian Unity Day; March 9, Day of National Spirituality and Taras Shevchenko's birthday; and March 8, Mother's Day or Day of Respect for Women.

Establishing the state calendar constitutes a focal point where the state is obliged to articulate a particular interpretation of which events are pivotal to the Ukrainian historical experience. Such an articulation emerges as a compromise among the visions articulated by various groups within the government espousing national, Soviet, local, and religious priorities. Those with an interpretation of the national experience and national essence that departs from the interpretation articulated by the state capitalize on the symbolic significance of the day to air their discontent with the hopes of institutionalizing the commemoration of other events or other

Table 3   A Comparison of the Official Calendars of the Soviet Union and Ukraine

The Soviet calendar		The Ukrainian calendar (as of 1997)	
New Year	January 1	New Year	January 1
		Christmas	January 7–8
Soviet Army Day	February 23		
Women's Day	March 8	Women's Day	March 8
		Easter	March/April
May Day	May 1–2	May Day	May 1–2
Victory Day	May 9	Victory Day	May 9
		Mother's Day*	2nd Sunday in May
		Independence Day	August 24
		Day of National Mourning	September 12
Constitution Day	October 7		
Great October Revolution Day	November 7–8	Great October Revolution Day**	November 7–8
		Referendum Day	December 1

*Only celebrated in western regions of Ukraine
**Reintroduced after having been eliminated in 1992

aspects of the same events. Regardless of the specifics of the dynamics of interaction, which, of course, are always changing in tandem with current power relations, the key point is that commemoration triggers a dialogue of sorts that can be quite confrontational. The state is forced to grapple with the collective memories of its citizenry when it commemorates an event in an unacceptable manner. As such, calendrical reform provides a window to diverse visions of the nation and political allegiances.

Enemy of the People: Popular Commemoration of Chernobyl

Perhaps the most stunning aspect of the new calendar is the omission of any kind of recognition of the Chernobyl nuclear disaster, much like its removal from the first post-Soviet textbooks. The new Ukrainian state has thus far not acknowledged the disaster with a day of commemoration in spite of its relevance for galvanizing support for the new Ukrainian state. Yet Chernobyl is no longer Moscow's problem. It is no longer Mos-

A popular rally held in Kyiv in 1991 to mark the fifth anniversary of the Chernobyl nuclear accident. The event was used as an occasion to denounce the "Soviet Empire" and the legitimacy of Soviet rule on Ukrainian lands and to vocalize demands for Ukrainian independence.

cow's responsibility to compensate victims of the accident.[12] The new Ukrainian state is straddled with this daunting task. Although the state is forced to acknowledge the tragedy in various arenas, overall acknowledgment remains muted because of continued dependence on Chernobyl as a less expensive (in a purely monetary sense) form of energy. Yesterday's symbol of Moscow's dominance and exploitation became a post-independence symbol of Ukrainian self-sufficiency and economic potential.[13] In response to the state's silence, many groups, organizations, and individuals have taken it upon themselves to keep the memory of the accident alive in the minds of today's Ukrainians.

For example, on April 26, 1993, a crowd gathered on a grassy knoll in a park in downtown L'viv, just beyond the jungle gym and the green wooden benches. There were no announcements, no signs, no advance notices that this gathering would occur. But it was clear to all why they were there. Exactly seven years after the Chernobyl accident, the religious leaders of the Ukrainian Autocephalous Orthodox Church in L'viv took it upon themselves to commemorate the anniversary of one of the greatest tragedies to befall Ukraine in the twentieth century.

The Ukrainian Autocephalous Orthodox Church pursues the mission that propelled it into existence after the fall of the Russian empire: it aims to strengthen the Ukrainian nation and its national culture through a nationally based church, as is in keeping with the Orthodox tradition. It comes, therefore, as no surprise that the clergy of this church would deem it appropriate to commemorate an event that many feel was inextricably linked to Ukraine's colonial status. Furthermore, in this region of the country where historical experience has produced a strong national consciousness, there is a predisposition to see national tragedies as personal tragedies. This encourages individuals to participate in such improvised commemorations, and such participation, in turn, reinforces the consciousness and convictions that prompted the commemorations in the first place.

The sound of chanting priests and the glimmer of icon-banners beckoned would-be spectators to come closer. With chants imploring "Lord! Have Mercy!" sung in unison, a religious service of sorts was held. The crowd was made up of many older people, often grandparents with grandchildren in tow, and others of mixed ages and genders who most likely stumbled upon the commemoration on their way home, to the tram, or to the store. With about three hundred in attendance, approximately twenty bearded priests in glittering golden robes, recited, and sang prayers to remember those who still suffer the effects of radiation sickness. They also acknowledged the firefighters who gave their lives to minimize the extent of the danger for others in the initial phases of the accident.

Some members of the crowd carried banners with icons of different saints framed by traditional Ukrainian folk embroidery patterns, reminiscent of the *rushniki*, or embroidered white runners, which adorn icons in western Ukrainian churches. Other participants held the yellow and blue Ukrainian national flag. Other banners paid tribute to the Brotherhood of the Ukrainian Autocephalous Orthodox Church. Through collective prayer, efforts were made to atone for the massive environmental damage that the system ravaged on Ukrainian lands and to ask for forgiveness. The ceremony rekindled the collective angst, the so-called "radiophobia," at the same time that it was an expression of it. The combination of collective guilt and collective goodwill toward other (unknown) Ukrainians became an expression of solidarity based purely on perceptions of common heritage and experience. Lasting well over an hour, this gathering in downtown L'viv fused the nation with the Autocephalous Church, its spiritual protector.

This tribute to unknown heroes, the firefighters and soldiers who died of radiation exposure while containing the accident, is akin to the immortalization Benedict Anderson describes nations bestowing on unknown soldiers (1991: 9–10). Indeed, Soviet authorities also celebrated the bravery of the "liquidators." The message on this seventh anniversary was that they died so that other Ukrainians could live. In response, the firefighters are granted a form of immortality through commemoration. These types of improvised commemorations awaken the national imagination to rethink concepts of community by repositioning Ukraine and its relationship to the Soviet Union. It also stirs the historical imagination to conceive of new forms of agency. Rather than an accident which happened *in* Ukraine, it becomes an accident which happened *to* Ukraine.

Even if the state recognizes the tragedy only tepidly, continued popular and artistic commemorations of the event by organizations such as the Ukrainian Autocephalous Orthodox Church, which have a stake in strengthening the state and closely aligning themselves with the nation, will keep it alive in collective memory. Unlike under Soviet rule, individuals and groups now take to the streets and commemorate events they feel the state has overlooked. The iconic use of Chernobyl as emblematic of Ukrainian suffering at the hands of foreign rulers and the angst it inspires generate legitimacy for the new Ukrainian state, even as it teeters on the brink of economic chaos and even as Chernobyl continues to light up the homes of Ukrainians.

Day of Mourning

Although the Famine of 1932–33 had been swept down the Orwellian "memory hole" by Soviet authorities, by the end of the 1980s, such taboo events became legitimate topics of historical inquiry. With estimates of the number of Ukrainians who died varying between six and ten million, or one in five Ukrainians, the Famine was labeled the "Ukrainian genocide." Several factors combine to give the Famine a more cerebral appeal than the visceral reaction, that, say, Chernobyl or World War II prompts. Although massive in scale, the Famine affected the central and eastern regions of Ukraine—as well as several regions in Russia and Kazakhstan.

The remaining survivors of the Famine are quite elderly, which means that the last "living memories" of the Famine are dying out.[14]

In September 1993, nearly two years after Ukrainian independence had been secured by referendum, the first official commemorative ceremonies ever in Ukraine were organized to mark the sixtieth anniversary of the Famine. The purpose was to revive those memories and raise consciousness of yet another tragedy that befell Ukraine under the yoke of a Moscow-based government.

"Only an independent Ukraine can guarantee that such a tragedy will never repeat itself," said former historian and deputy prime minister Mykola Zhulynsky as he opened a scholarly conference titled "The Great Famine of 1932–33: Its Causes and Consequences." Zhulynsky went on to say, "This is perhaps the most tragic page in the history of our ancient state, and in the history of mankind the worst crime of a government against its own people. . . . One's blood chills when one realizes the dimensions of this Great Famine, which has been rightfully called a mass murder of people, a genocide, and a Ukrainian 'holocaust'" (Kolomayets 1993: 1). The two-day scholarly conference drew speakers from around the world and was part of the memorial activities scheduled in Kyiv in 1993 to mark the commemoration of the sixtieth anniversary of the Famine.

Ivan Drach, a poet turned politician, leader of Rukh, and chairman of the World Ukrainian Coordinating Council, also gave a speech in Kyiv to commemorate the Famine on September 9, 1993. His speech was remarkable in several respects. Drach demanded the "repentance" of Russia for her "sins" and suggested that Russia should follow the example of German acknowledgment of guilt before the Jewish people. Borrowing much of the language of the Holocaust, he refers to the Famine as the "Famine-Genocide." He held up the example of the Jews, who "forced the whole world to admit its guilt before them" and who are vigilant to this day in their search for the "ravagers of their nation."[15]

Remarkably, Drach does not exonerate Ukrainians from responsibility for the Famine. He states quite boldly: "But first let us be forthright about ourselves. Bolshevik marauders in Ukraine mobilized Ukrainians as well" (1993: 357). This is, of course, true. Orders came from Moscow but the soldiers and the local Communist Party officials carrying them out were often Ukrainians.[16] Having made the point, he rapidly warns Ukrainians against ignoring the lessons of history and succumbing to the dangers of the Soviet-created "memory hole." He assures his fellow countrymen that "forgetting is a bequest to the descendants of torturers. Eternal remembrance is a sacred lesson for the descendants of the innocently martyred"(1993: 358). And with this he repositioned, and even absolved, the Ukrainians of responsibility for the Famine and at the same time recast Russia as the enemy. Drach goes on to state:

> The first lesson which is becoming an integral component of Ukrainian national consciousness is that Russia has never had and never will have any other interest in Ukraine beyond the total destruction of the Ukrainian nation. In many Russians, from the most sophisticated philosopher to the most primitive drunk, we see an almost pathological Ukrainophobia. This Ukrainophobia constitutes a critical feature of the "Russian idea." It foments a truly animalistic hatred of Ukraine in the Russian Parliament. It is engraved on walls throughout the cities of the Crimea: " 'A good Khakhol is a dead khakhol!' " . . . . Ukraine's 750 years of statelessness have proved before all of humanity that our nation is immortal. Perhaps, herein lies our cosmic essence: the cycles of our history spiraling from the tragic state of half-dead existence forced periodically upon Ukrainians by foreigners, to the inevitable resurrection—the mighty eruptions of the nation's will to exist. (1993: 359–60)

Russia becomes the dreaded Other who threatens the nation. The defense Drach proposes is for Ukrainians to maintain their "cosmic essence" and mount another Ukrainian cultural revival to acknowledge the dead and preserve their memory. This, he argues, is a vitally important means to ensure the continued greatness and eternity of the nation (1993: 360).

Commemoration of this important anniversary of the Famine was not limited, however, to the academy and to elites lecturing the populace on how they should preserve the memory of the dead. It assumed a popular and didactic dimension as well. All along Khreshchatyk, Kyiv's main boulevard, three stations were set up with the intention of educating the populace about the Famine. Documents and eyewitness accounts were put on display to try to communicate the gravity of the event. Most moving of all were the photos of starving peasants pinned on the billboards. These photos humanized the tragedy by attaching faces to the scores of victims. Visitors to these stations placed flowers, fruits, and bread at an altar set up in the middle of the boulevard to honor the victims of the Famine.

The blue and yellow flags that stand above government buildings were draped with black streamers and lowered to half-mast. The main event of the day was a service near St. Sofiia Cathedral, around the monument to Hetman Bohdan Khmelnytsky (who ironically forged an alliance with the Russian tsar in 1654 to gain protection against Polish landlords and thereby secured the unification of Eastern Ukraine with Russia). With all of the top government leadership and approximately 5,000 spectators present, President Leonid Kravchuk began the ceremony with a moment of silence. There were representatives from all of the major faiths in Ukraine, including the Ukrainian Orthodox Church–Kyiv Patriarchate, the Ukrainian Autocephalous Orthodox Church, the Ukrainian Catholic Church, the Ukrainian Orthodox Church–Moscow Patriarchate (who was not asked to offer words of prayer), the Roman Catholic Church, a rabbi, and, testifying to the active recruiting of Western missionaries, representatives from the Seventh Day Adventist, Baptist, and Evangelical churches.

After the ceremony around the monument, the crowd formed a procession, called the "Way of the Cross," to St. Michael's Square where a new monument was installed to commemorate the sixtieth anniversary. The monument consists of a large stone slab, from which a large cross has been carved out and a metal cross inserted on which a mother with her hands outstretched has been placed. Inside her is a child, its arms outstretched once again in the shape of another cross.

Representatives from almost every oblast in Ukraine placed wreaths at the monument. Some individuals from the central and eastern provinces, the area affected most by the Famine, brought soil from the mass graves of famine victims. Others brought clay pots and steel capsules filled with black earth, a symbol of fertility and abundance of food. Representatives from the western provinces brought documents to show the efforts they made at the time to lessen the suffering in the stricken areas. This ceremony and monument constitute the first official commemoration of the Famine in Ukraine and the post-Soviet state's initial attempt to make this commemoration an ongoing annual event.

Commemorating the Revolution in Postrevolutionary Society

Once the Soviet regime had fallen, some of its celebrations, commemorations, and ritual parades were "carted off to the dustheap of history," seen as no more than painful reminders of a fallen and misguided system. Commemorations were a key site where historical knowledge—as dictated by the Soviet state—was represented and enacted. Initially after independence, as I stated above, key Soviet holidays defining the national and ideological charter of the Soviet Union were officially eliminated from the state calendar. However, just because the state dispensed with official recognition of these commemorations does not mean that they were entirely ignored by the population.

In 1992, some people, still stinging from the sweeping changes and new borders that had unexpectedly reorganized their lives, took it upon themselves to commemorate the essential moments of Soviet history.

Ivan, the historian from Kharkiv who commented earlier on Great October Revolution Day, describes how November 7th was commemorated in Kharkiv in 1992. In a flat, rather disinterested tone, almost bored by the question, he said that "out of custom a small group of old people gathered next to Lenin [the central monument in Dzerzhinsky Square renamed Independence Square] for about one hour and then left."

Alla Alexandrovna, a retired biologist living in Kyiv, describes the spontaneously staged popular commemorative activities on November 7 in Kyiv far more harshly, "A bunch of old people marched down the street making fools of themselves. There were more police than there were demonstrators. What idiots!" She does not share their nostalgia and cannot conceive of actually wanting to commemorate this discredited system after its demise.

Such harsh condemnation of the Soviet system was far from universal in the early years of Ukrainian independence. The estimated 3,000 to 5,000 marchers in Kyiv on November 7, 1992, most of whom were pensioners, carried placards with such slogans as "Stop the Americanization of the People!" and "Down with the Banderite trident and the yellow and blue Petliurite flag!"[17] As the demonstrators paraded down Khreshchatyk toward the Lenin monument to place flowers in homage, rows of policemen protected them from the jeering spectators.

During the initial years of independence as the new Ukrainian state decided against commemorating this important Soviet holiday, small spontaneous and improvised demonstrations were staged in cities around Ukraine by those who perceived a lacuna on November 7th. Interestingly, however, when Leonid Kuchma was elected president in 1994, after having espoused a more pro-Eurasian, pro-Russian language policy platform (from which he retreated somewhat after being elected), key Soviet holidays were gradually and often haphazardly reintroduced. This is less attributable to nostalgia for the Soviet period than it is to sheer pragmatism. As the economic crisis wore on following the breakdown of the Soviet system, numerous factories, farms, and offices were functioning well below capacity. Enterprises, as well as a multitude of other state-sector jobs in health care and education, began to delay the payment of salaries for months. As a sort of compensation for loss of job security, greatly diminished income, and rapidly shrinking buying power, the government began to increase the number of nonworking holidays.

So after several years of state dismissal of the key historical event the Soviet state commemorated as defining of its national and ideological charter, the anniversary of the Great October Socialist Revolution has been reinstated to suit new political realities. Regionally varied popular efforts to publicly commemorate this day are carried out by those still loyal to Soviet Union. In post-Soviet society the November 7th commemoration retains its symbolic significance. Every year it becomes a focal point of power relations, an opportunity to express opposition or support for the current regime in terms of the past, and more specifically, in terms of the Soviet state. In 1994 and 1995 national democrats, led by the founders and leaders of Rukh (Vyacheslav Chornovil, Les Taniuk, Ivan Drach, Slava Stetsko, and others), and socialists, led by Parliament chairman and Socialist Party leader, Oleksander Moroz, used the occasion to agitate for support and to reinforce their claims as the legitimate inheritors of power in Ukraine. In a show of strength, both camps organized processions through the center of Kyiv. In 1995 the socialists were prohibited on this day from marching down Khreshchatyk, Kyiv's main boulevard, for the first time since the Nazi occupation of Kyiv. As we will see in the next chapter, not only does the date for commemoration have symbolic significance but the site does too.

In short, with or without the new Ukrainian state's efforts, the commemoration of the Revolution provides a repetitive and ritualized articulation of the ideology upon which the Soviet state rested by those who are strongly supportive of it and those who are resolutely against it. Popular commentary on the Revolution is visible either in the form of improvised demonstrations in the streets or indifferently by savoring another day off. This dynamic interaction of opposing viewpoints forces a negotiated change of the nature of the commemoration and by extension of the ideology in which it is embedded.

The Cult of the Dead: Commemorating Victory Day

In 1992–94, the overwhelming majority of people I interviewed voiced the opinion that nearly all Soviet holidays should be eliminated. Regardless of gender, nationality, generation, and region, the uniformity of responses emphatically rejecting Soviet holidays as meaningless was stunning. The one exception, however, was May 9. Unlike the anniversary of the Great October Socialist Revolution, Victory Day commemorations on May 9 have traditionally been more modest in scale and more locally tailored, and have a solemn meaning for most citizens of Ukraine. Victory Day was introduced in 1945 following the close of the Great Patriotic War, as World War II was officially known in the Soviet Union. However, factories, offices, and schools only began to close on Victory Day in 1965.

The Red Army's victory over powerful fascist armies and the massive devastation and suffering inflicted on the Soviet people during World War II became a grand myth of patriotism, sacrifice, and heroism validating the Soviet system. Out of such mythic meanings came a "cult of the dead," which commemorates dead heroes, fallen soldiers, and national victimization. Given the extent to which lives were shattered as a result of the war in Ukraine (and elsewhere in the former Soviet Union), there is a readiness to embrace this myth. In spite of all the system's shortcomings, there was no denying the fact that millions were willing to fight to protect the Soviet Union and that the system, its factories and its armies, had equipped them to win. To the extent that the Revolution founded the Soviet Union, the Soviet Red Army victory during World War II sustained it for almost another five decades in spite of widespread passive sabotage in the form of indifference to propaganda, noncompliance with official practices, and theft from state organizations. Yet for some, especially the veterans of the war, the victory validated the sacrifices they had made to construct the system and increased their patience with its inadequacies and failures. This kind of sincere, heartfelt recognition of a tragedy that is at once personal and Soviet created an identification with the state, manifesting itself as loyalty and allegiance.

Under Soviet rule and continuing today, the Victory Day commemorations have been devoted to keeping alive the memory of the war, of the suffering, heroism, and solidarity that led to the Soviet victory. The day is a time for private remembering of suffering and deprivation, one's own or one's parents' or grandparents'. Although the state-sponsored festivities are more modest today, the individual and localized commemorations of Victory Day have not changed radically since independence.

Private pilgrimages to the graves of family members are the essence of the day. Families place flowers and often certain kinds of food on the

A military parade down Khreshchatyk, the central boulevard of Kyiv, to commemorate the fiftieth anniversary of the end of World War II.

graves of fallen friends and relatives. The creation of war memorials was a veritable industry in the Soviet Union. There are over 27,000 of them in Ukraine alone. Actual sites of destruction, battlefields, command posts, and graves (the immense Babyi Yar mass grave in Kyiv being the most notable),[18] were turned into war memorials. Other commemorative sites were created in the form of obelisks, monuments to soldiers and officers, and displays of war machinery. Much as every village had a church in tsarist times, after World War II villages across Ukraine had memorial shrines to mark the bravery, triumph, and suffering experienced during the war. These war memorials were "guarded" by Pioneers, the children's unit of the Communist Party, and it was considered an honor, especially on Victory Day, to be the memorial guard. These monuments usually serve as the sites of the Victory Day memorial ceremonies. In Kyiv, for example, the festivities are held at the Unknown Soldier Monument in the Park of Glory or at the Museum of the Great Patriotic War, which is part of the Mother Motherland monument. (The monument is usually referred to by its Russian name *Mat' Rodina*; *Mat' Bat'kivschyna* would be the Ukrainian and it translates literally as Mother Fatherland.)

In other cities, the festivities are held at an eternal flame or at the grave of an unknown soldier.[19]

Although there is variation regionally, nearly all ceremonies include short memorial speeches by local officials, stories about heroic deeds, a moment of silence for those who died, and the laying of wreaths. Under Soviet rule some towns included a military parade or a march of the town's veterans. In areas particularly affected by the war, such as Kyiv, there was an artillery salute and fireworks.

Reverence for Victory Day remains in post-Soviet society. As Anya, a forty-year-old housewife from L'viv, said, "This holiday means a lot to me, mostly because it means a lot to my father. He fought in the war. His brother died fighting and so did many of the men of his generation. It was really a tremendous loss for him. He takes this day very seriously and out of respect for him and all the others who sacrificed and suffered, I would keep this holiday."

She does, nonetheless, make a significant suggestion: "I think that we should celebrate this holiday at the same time that they do in Europe. After all we met victory together. But as usual, we in the Soviet Union had to do things differently. As it is, our religious calendar is different. We don't celebrate Easter or Christmas together with other Europeans. At least I think we should commemorate the end of this tragic war together." Indeed, the end of the war is commemorated in Europe on May 8 and one day later in the former Soviet Union on May 9. Here is an attempt to use the calendar of commemorations as a means of collective re-definition, a means of joining an "imagined community" far larger than the nation. Her desire for simultaneous commemoration with Europe bespeaks her perceptions of the war as a collective, European—no longer Soviet—experience. After nearly five decades of being cut off behind the iron curtain, Anya is anxious to turn the meaning of being Ukrainian away from the Soviet Union toward Europe by redefining the meaning of "collective suffering" to be a European experience, not an exclusively Soviet one. Transcarpathia, where she grew up, is truly the borderland of the borderland to Europe. It was originally part of the Austro-Hungarian empire, and Anya's father completed all his schooling in Hungarian at a Hungarian school. In her mind, Transcarpathia's abrupt cleavage from Europe and unwanted annexation by the Soviet Union can be, symbolically at least, reversed to some degree by commemorating the tragedy of the war with other Europeans.

Post-Soviet efforts to trumpet the strength of an independent Ukrai-

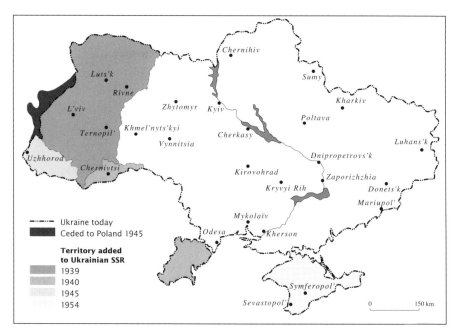

Chernihiv

Luts'k

Sumy

Rivne

Kharkiv

L'viv   *Zhytomyr*   *Kyiv*

Poltava

Ternopil'   *Khmel'nyts'kyi*

Cherkasy

Vynnitsia

Luhans'k

Uzhhorod

Chernivtsi

Dnipropetrovs'k

Kirovohrad

Zaporizhzhia

Kryvyi Rih

Donets'k

Mariupol'

Mykolaïv

---- Ukraine today

█ Ceded to Poland 1945

Territory added to Ukrainian SSR

1939
1940
1945
1954

Odesa   *Kherson*

Symferopol'

Sevastopol'

0   150 km

Map of Soviet Ukraine showing border changes, 1939–54

nian state by capitalizing on the patriotism and bravery exhibited by Ukrainians during the World War II are inevitably haunted by the ghosts of the Banderites. The Banderites were supporters of Stepan Bandera (1909–59), the leader of the Organization of Ukrainian Nationalists (OUN). On June 30, 1941, surrounded by German armies, the OUN declared Ukraine an independent state. Although some pro-Ukrainian historians claim that OUN "immediately met the ruthless repressions of Nazi Germany" and began "an open anti-German resistance," OUN actually forged a military alliance with Nazi Germany as a strategic move to secure Ukrainian independence.[20] The nazis rapidly repressed the OUN by arresting its leader, Stepan Bandera, imprisoning him in the Sachsenhausen concentration camp, and driving the organization underground. In the fall of 1942, OUN reemerged as the Ukrainian Insurgent Army (Ukrainska Povstanska Armia, or UPA) and fought against the Germans and the Red Army under a somewhat less authoritarian and exclusionary program. At one point, the UPA had 200,000 guerrilla fighters, intelligence, and medical personnel. Although they briefly controlled large areas of Halychyna, they were no match for the Soviet Red Army. The UPA waged a guerrilla war for Ukrainian independence until 1953 when the organization was finally eradicated by Soviet authorities. The Soviet propaganda machine demonized Bandera and his supporters and forbade public mention of his name and this chapter of Ukrainian history. UPA was condemned as a bourgeois nationalist organization and laden with mythic proportions of evil and danger.

However, this prior struggle for independence is currently enjoying a revival, especially in western Ukraine, as UPA's dedication, discipline, and military acumen are celebrated as forerunners to the Ukrainian state. The glorification of UPA is often resented in the eastern provinces where eastern Ukrainians perceive themselves as the "enemy" against whom Bandera and the guerrilla army fought. Toward the end of 1993 the presidium of Ukraine's parliament announced its intention to study the activities of the OUN-UPA, and, at the urging of diaspora groups, to consider rehabilitation. At this time, there are no state-wide commemorations of OUN-UPA's role in the struggle for Ukrainian independence. However, in those regions where Bandera's organization enjoys popular support, primarily in the western provinces, localized commemorations of the various fiftieth anniversary celebrations of the ending of World War II noted the contribution of UPA, providing an example of local divergence from the standard post-Soviet nation-wide commemoration of Victory Day.

Reorienting

In a reversal of the Soviet glorification of labor, in 1997 the first ten days of May effectively became holidays in Ukraine. Official commemoration of May Day (May 1) was followed in short order by Orthodox Easter (May 5), which was exceptionally late this year, and May 9 marked Victory Day, another government holiday. The three days from May 6 to May 8 effectively became nonworking days for most, although state-sector employees were officially obliged to compensate for the time off by working over the previous weekend. However, with shrinking salaries paid after months of delay, strict discipline is difficult to enforce. Tax officials were quick to project vast sums of lost government revenue (ca. $191 million) as a result of the string of holidays. Some parliamentarians quoted verse from Shevchenko in protest ("It's terrible to lie in chains /

And rot in dungy deep / But still it's worse, when you are free / to sleep, and sleep, and sleep"). And yet the country's state sector economy slowed dramatically, some parts even grinding to a full halt, for ten days in May as the nation celebrated. During this period some have suggested that the "shadow" economy demonstrated the extent to which it is the "real" economy as informal businesses continued to operate and serve the populace.[21]

Binns notes that increasing the number of holidays and nonworking days serves to multiply the landmarks in social time and create the illusion that a period of time is longer than it truly is (1979: 592). In this case, the "holiday marathon," as it was called in the news, is motivated in part by an attempt to garner support in the face of economic decline from different contingencies by granting recognition to a greater number of national, Soviet, religious, and gratuitous holidays within the state calendar.

The symbolism evoked in commemoration forms a "quasi-textual representation," to use Connerton's phrase, which narrates a particular interpretation of events (1991: 49). We generally think of commemorations as a traditionalizing instrument used to reinforce the status quo by ritually enacting it. During a period of such intense change, revision of the state calendar can even set the group apart from itself by marking a discontinuity in its history. Even though the purpose of calendrical change and commemorative revision is to try to forge a new, single, shared vision of the past, they nonetheless emerge as sites of discussion and contestation. By focusing on commemorations as a site for a potential change of consciousness and as a public forum for dialogue about the past, we see how conceptions of self and others change, develop, or are reinvented.

Save for the final years of Gorbachev's rule, it was virtually unthinkable for a group of people to bypass the state and spontaneously organize a commemoration on the central town square of, say, the Famine of 1932–33 or any other event ignored by Soviet historiography. Individuals might have noted such events in the privacy of their homes, but organized, public commemoration without state involvement was strictly forbidden.

In post-Soviet society, when the state elects not to commemorate a certain event, and some citizens think it should have, they now organize a commemoration themselves as compensation and agitate to make the state reform the calendar and conform to their visions of the past. Pro-Soviet pensioners challenged the Ukrainian state when they demonstrated on November 7th as the new state ignored old traditions. Correspondingly, ardent supporters of Ukraine commemorate the tragedy of Chernobyl to fill the gap left by the state's decision to avoid reminding its citizens of the dangers of nuclear power. This more open dialogue between the state and its citizens over history, commemoration, and the choice to acknowledge certain events or not gives far greater public voice to the *narod*, or people, to influence the institutionalization of memory. By contesting state-sanctioned interpretations of the meaning of certain historical events, individuals and groups create the possibility to articulate alternative interpretations on a symbolically charged day. Furthermore, commemorations are increasingly tailored to regional experiences and provide a window to understanding regional variation in Ukraine. Regionally based cultures and localized historical experiences are collectively represented during commemoration and reflect differences in political orientations to the new Ukrainian state. I already alluded to commemorations of the role of UPA-OUN in western Ukraine. In this region, the proclamation of the Western Ukrainian National Republic on November 1, 1918, referred to as the "Flame of Statehood in the hearts of Ukrainians," is also commemorated. The many spontaneous, popular commemorations and regionally organized ceremonies mean that the post-Soviet state is forced to respond to its citizens and their views of their historical experiences in a way that the Soviet regime clearly was not.

Yet the legacy of bankrupt Soviet holidays remains a large hurdle that new state holidays will have to overcome in order to become meaningful. A key component in assessing the authenticity of the new histories presented in commemoration in post-Soviet Ukraine is the extent to which they coincide with life experience narratives, which are based, in essence, on memories. However, memories are not fixed entities. They are constructions evolving over time within a field of power relations. As John Gillis writes, "Identities and memories are not things we think about, but things we think with. As such they have no existence beyond our politics, our social relations, and our histories" (1994: 5). When a group of people assume they hold certain memories in common because of shared experiences, this provides the underpinnings that give an imagined national community an existential reality. During commemorations, states deliberately and self-consciously define categories of meaning to influence collective memories, which in turn, will sharply influence self-definition and the options for self-identification. Thus commemoration becomes a means by which particular ideologies infiltrate memories and individual self-conceptions. This constitutes the foundation upon which a meaningful "ethnic" part of the self is constituted and individual citizens of a particular state are transformed into ideological subjects who regard themselves as national.

In the Soviet Union, the intersection of official historiography and life-course narratives created a contradictory dynamic that often impeded individuals from seeing themselves as national, or Soviet, during commemorations. When individual memories recall an account of events radically different from that advanced by the state in commemoration or recognize the occurrence of events that are denied by the state, the legitimacy of the state is undermined. Some commemorations actually served to inhibit the cultivation of a sense of Soviet nationhood and instead produced alienation, suspicion, and disdain for the Soviet state.

There were some exceptions, however. Victory Day commemorations had powerful components that were at once personal and national in the Soviet sense. Victory Day commemorations kept alive a mythology of Soviet grandeur, of solidarity among the *sovetskii narod*, and of a sense of self as citizen of a superpower state. Commemoration of the tragedy and suffering incurred during the war made an effective connection among nationalized, localized, and personalized experiences and thus served to prop up the legitimacy of the state.

However, commemorations of historical events in the public sphere only partly define the celebratory calendar that articulates what it means to be Ukrainian in post-Soviet society. A formidable religious revival has whisked back into consciousness and practice the major Christian holidays.[22] The state's calendar of commemorations has had to accommodate a full array of religious-based celebration. Even the many nonbelievers I interviewed, who often had uncharitable words for organized religion, consistently endorsed the reinstatement of religious holidays, such as Easter and Christmas, as part of the national heritage. The new Ukrainian state has responded by recognizing the major religious holidays as national holidays. But religious festivities are not celebrated in the same collective, inclusive, and public way that state commemorations are.[23] Religious holidays are celebrated in church and at home, and their festivities do not often enter the public sphere. In a culture that has grown up around public spectacle—even inauthentic ones—this private, atomized quality of religious celebration complicates the process of institutionalizing a broad, inclusivist national culture.[24]

Furthermore, religious and secular holidays belong to two different modalities of temporality. Secular commemorations are based on history and are constantly modified to incorporate new interpretations. Although commemorations are by nature repetitive, the attachment to history places them in a larger linear framework of a teleological progression of time.[25] In contrast, the religious calendar operates in an ahistorical, cyclical fashion and is far more fixed. Time in the liturgical calendar focuses on a self-contained, closed circle that endlessly repeats itself, even as it progresses forward. Therefore, the reintroduction of the religious calendar eliminates the exclusive dominance of a secular sense of temporality, which the Soviet state institutionalized, and reintroduces multidimensional temporal patterns that inform definitions of the self.

The enhanced status of religion, an increasing interest among many to learn more about the language, history, and traditions of Ukraine, and a faltering economy have combined to give new validity to religious worship and celebration. The renewed interest in religion has given the various competing churches a new status as centers of power and influence. As the churches vie for parishioners, power, and the designation "the national church," their relationship to the state and to one another grows more complicated.

This shift away from public sphere secular celebration and commemoration to religiously based celebration in the home also has strong implications for gender roles and identities. Although commemoration in the public sphere is still primarily a male-dominated activity, festivities at home give a far more central role to women as wives and mothers. As the home, not the town square or the workplace, becomes a more significant site of commemoration, this transfers some of the more traditional responsibilities of keeping alive personal and historical memory formally away from the state and back to women and begins to dismantle the gender roles and practices established under Soviet rule.

As we saw in the schools, a nationalist redesign of society includes a gender-based traditionalism that links the strength of the nation to motherhood and increases the importance of the home. The coincidence of a national and religious revival means that socialization to entirely redefined cultural values is occurring. Revised, re-gendered commemorations serve to shatter Soviet-created notions of gender and create a forum to enact newly redefined gender identities, roles, and relations in a cyclical fashion.

The state calendar in this process emerges as a site where an ideology of the present, used to fortify the state, is articulated in terms of a nation's historical experience. As the sites, practices, and objects of commemoration shift during this period of reestablishing the state calendar, the purpose of commemoration remains the same: to create a sense of belonging, commonality, and mutual obligation among citizens of a particular state by imagining or remembering commonly experienced events. In post-Soviet society, the responsibility for commemorating the national heritage and for preserving (new) old traditions has shifted somewhat away from the state and out of the public sphere to women and into the home. Once established, the state calendar serves to express an interpretation of the national charter and dominant national culture in terms of the defining moments of history using myth and symbol in ritualized commemorations. Those who participate in and watch commemorations will reinterpret their collective experience, all the while maintaining that the undying, continuous past of the nation is what is being celebrated.

Urban Landscape

Following the Revolution of 1917, Bolshevik leaders were faced with the formidable challenge of establishing legitimacy for the Soviet state and imparting new values and beliefs suited to the revolutionary social and economic order they sought to establish. They were surrounded by an imperial urban landscape filled with monuments to tsars, churches, and other signs that were anathema to their desired revolutionary vision of society. In the same vein, amid monuments to Lenin, "people's friendship," and signs of the evaporated superpower status of the Soviet Union, Ukrainian elites are trying to promote a national culture based on an alternative historical interpretation that repositions the historic relationship with Russia and sets the parameters of a new independent, European-oriented, Ukrainian nation-state. Although the process of manipulating monumental propaganda to construct forms of consciousness and identity differs today from that following the Revolution of 1917, the

Bolshevik-created cult of the monument continues to impose itself on efforts to desovietize post-Soviet Ukraine.

In 1918 at Lenin's behest, Bolshevik leaders removed selected tsarist monuments and replaced them with ones that communicated a new worldview and represented the new Soviet state. Cognizant of the fact that to have a history and a historical memory is to have power, authority, and a base of resistance, the Bolsheviks launched a campaign of organized forgetting, spearheaded, among other tactics, by the destruction of cultural, architectural, and monumental landmarks likely to prompt recollection of prerevolutionary values and practices. The Bolshevik redesign of the urban landscape erased sites that had the power to evoke memories of a prerevolutionary way of life. New visual symbols were installed and used to generate popular enthusiasm for the revolutionary mission and stimulate loyalty among an overwhelmingly rural and illiterate population accustomed to the glittering icons of the Orthodox church and the pomp of the tsarist regime. Recognizing the symbolic, didactic, and mnemonic powers of monuments, Lenin harnessed the power of visual representation to acclimate the populace to a radically new political culture.

In time an iconography of the Revolution could be found across the Soviet Union in every village, town, and city. New monuments, visual representations of the official state-sponsored historical narrative, were built and rebuilt throughout the Soviet period, reflecting shifts in historical interpretation to suit political concerns. The monuments projected the official historical interpretation of the Soviet mission to its citizens and to the world beyond in a highly visible summary form. As such, these monuments became one of the most distinguishing and indelible features of the Soviet urban landscape.

Now that the Soviet system has collapsed, these monuments have become contested political terrain, the sites of shifting conceptions and emotions about the past. As omnipresent and as consistently uniform as these monuments are, they mask multiple interpretations and experiences of the Soviet regime. They are prime targets of a state-sponsored effort to recast interpretation of the Soviet period to support the legitimacy of the nascent Ukrainian state. As representations of a vanishing social order and the way of life it supported, the monuments have become a focal point of discontent, a site of popular protest, unleashing a barrage of pro-Soviet lament in some circles and anti-Soviet celebration in others. The monuments assume critical importance because, as Michael Herzfeld (1991: 5) writes in his study of historic preservation in a Cretan town,

"The battle is over the future of the past." By examining the transformations of Soviet monuments in post-Soviet society, we will analyze the implications of the urban landscape for the social production of memories, historical consciousness, and identity. I depart from the assumption that a particular monument functions as a sign, as something more directly representational than a symbol, and as such triggers certain associations. The maintenance, alteration, or removal of monuments affects the interpretative frameworks and categories individuals use to understand the past and current predicaments. This, in turn, has the potential to spark the development of particular forms of historical and national consciousness capable of prompting the negotiation of new forms of identity.

Empire of Signs

Throughout the USSR urban public space was used to showcase an "empire of signs."[1] A particular reading of these signs contributed to the fiction of enduring Soviet power. Signs contained in public space, much like Geertz (1973) argues on behalf of symbols, provide a window to cultural analysis. To be sure, there was a tremendous gap between the image conveyed through signs of a progressive cradle-to-grave welfare state and the grim reality of Soviet life. But at times the image of the state proved to be so powerful and commanding that it eclipsed appreciation of the harshness of everyday life, especially for outsiders.

The latest shift to a post-Soviet perspective on historical interpretation has triggered sharply conflicting reactions among sectors of the population concerning what should be done with Soviet signs in the post-Soviet urban landscape. Each new author, or rather new political leader, is saddled with the text of his predecessors, a representation of collective experience that no longer validates present predicaments and patterns of authority. Indeed, as the following discussion of debates in Luhansk show, urban signs are fictions that are incessantly rewritten with each new perspective on the past, the emergence of which is largely driven by historically engaged political struggle.

In downtown Luhansk, a coal-mining city on the border between eastern Ukraine and Russia, there stands a beautiful monument which Stalin ordered erected on the banks of the Luhan' River to commemorate the achievements of Marshal Voroshilov (1881–1969), a celebrated Party and military hero. A member of the Communist Party from 1903 until his death in 1969 and a staunch Stalinist, K. E. Voroshilov received a multitude of awards and orders, including eight Orders of Lenin, six Orders of the Red Banner, and the greatest honor of all, a burial plot in Moscow on Red Square alongside the other heroes of the Soviet Union. In 1935 when Voroshilov was the People's Commissar for Defense of the USSR and awarded the title marshal, Lugansk (as it was then called) was renamed Voroshilovgrad to honor him.

During the Khrushchevian thaw, however, a more critical reassessment of Stalinism and of the Soviet military concluded that among the stunning number of casualties incurred during World War II, many could have been avoided. Voroshilov served as commander in chief of the troops on the Leningrad Front, on the northwest axis of operation, and for the partisan movement. High military commanders, such as Voroshilov, who were previously unambiguously hailed for their patriotism, military acumen, and greatness, were now accused of having made unpardonable mistakes in defending the Soviet Union. In response to a revised historical interpretation of the performance of the Soviet military command, Khrushchev changed the name of the city in 1958 back to its prerevolutionary name Lugansk but left the monument standing. One year after Voroshilov's death in 1969, Brezhnev restored his honor by changing the name of the city back to Voroshilovgrad.

Another sea change came with glasnost. A franker assessment of the Soviet past led to renewed criticism of Soviet leaders, such as Voroshilov, whose Stalinist views led him to resist Khrushchevian reforms when he was a member of the Politburo. This, combined with a renewed interest and nostalgia for a prerevolutionary way of life, prompted the renaming of the city once again back to Lugansk. But this was not to be the end of the story. Following Ukrainian independence in 1991, President Kravchuk ordered all place-names to be rendered in Ukrainian. Lugansk became Luhansk.[2]

The incessant renaming of the city only confuses the issue of what should be done with the bronze marshal himself. Nearly all the residents of Luhansk with whom I spoke felt that the monument should remain as it is. As a history teacher and mother of three said, "Part of being a citizen is to protect the culture, nature, and monuments of the nation. We should keep all of these horrible monuments as a reminder of our history." "Rather, as a reminder of our stupidity," her colleague interjected.

Political leaders seem to feel otherwise. By February 1993 the issue was not whether the monument should be removed or changed but how.

The main options under consideration were (1) dynamite; (2) removing the plaque identifying the man as Voroshilov and claim that the monument represents an unknown soldier; or (3) removing Voroshilov's head and replace it with the head of a military figure who is more acceptable to Ukrainians and more compatible with post-Soviet historical interpretation of the Soviet army.

The controversy surrounding the monument to Voroshilov remains unresolved and the marshal, as of this writing, still overlooks the Luhan' River. The lack of closure reflects the need for public remembering. This results from seven decades during which the Soviet regime attempted to create and control a single historical narrative and shape private recollections to coincide with it by denying access in the public sphere to alternative interpretations. Dissident or alternative voices of historical experience were sequestered in individual memory while the public sphere was uniquely reserved for showcasing an unambiguous and glorious past. Building on the work of Maurice Halbwachs, the Popular Memory Group at the Centre for Contemporary Cultural Studies at the University of Birmingham has argued that given the relational nature of memory, memories must have some manifestation in the public sphere to ensure their persistence (Johnson et al. 1982). Just as the residents of Luhansk today rely on the monument to Marshal Voroshilov to remember their Soviet past, some officials seem intent on erasing it.

In the Soviet Union, official historical narrative was intended to forge a single collective identity based on a "common" historical experience. Creating it was problematic since numerous cultural differences testify to a plethora of historical experiences. The significance of monuments lies not only in their ability to reflect a particular historical interpretation but also in their capacity to structure consciousness by denying recognition of certain historical events or interpretations. By erasing public recognition of certain events, memories wither. Soviet leaders used monuments as signs containing both an absence and a presence of historical representation to forge a consciousness that was to become part of the cultural underpinnings of a Soviet identity.

Monumental Propaganda

As part of the Soviet regime's overall project to create a "new man," which envisioned an entirely new relationship between the citizen and the state, Lenin authored the "Plan for Monumental Propaganda" in 1918. The Plan reflected Lenin's vision of artist as agitator and of art as instrument, transmitting socialist ideals. He was committed to infusing artistic creation with the spirit of the Revolution and its progress on the path to a "bright future." Stites argues that Lenin envisioned Soviet cities adorned with monumental propaganda that would directly deliver "the artifacts of a museum, the teachings of a school, and the reverent milieu of a church" to an impoverished and illiterate population (1989: 90).

On April 14, 1918, Lenin signed a decree that was published in *Pravda*, the main Party newspaper, under the title "On the Dismantling of Monuments Erected in Honor of the Tsars and Their Servants and on the Formulation of Projects of Monuments to the Russian Socialist Revolution." This decree articulated Lenin's policy for redesigning the urban landscape by removing monuments, primarily of tsars, which he called "hideous idols." These monuments were deemed devoid of historic or artistic value and were to be replaced with ones "reflecting the ideas and feelings of the working class of Revolutionary Russia" (Bowlt 1978: 185).[3]

Lenin's decree also included provisions for changing tsarist inscriptions, emblems, and street names. The process of changing street names proceeded at lightning speed (much like today), confounding many urban residents. However, the demolition of tsarist monuments advanced much more slowly than Lenin had planned. By 1919 only one tsarist monument had been removed, and since sculpture was a comparatively underdeveloped art form in Russia and materials were in short supply, fewer monuments than anticipated were erected.[4] In addition, some of the initial monuments were made of plaster of Paris or terra-cotta and quickly crumbled when placed outside in such a harsh climate.

Although Lenin took the task of redesigning the imperial urban landscape to reflect the Revolution and its values very seriously, others did not. In a twist of humor, a group of poets led by Sergei Esenin and Anatolii Mariengof went around Moscow in 1921 pulling down the plates of the new street names and replacing them with ones bearing their own names! (Stites 1989: 66).

Lenin's decree specified that sixty-six "outstanding persons in the field of revolutionary and social activity" would be honored in future monuments. These monuments were to "serve the aim of extensive propaganda rather than the age of immortalization" (Lodder 1983: 53). Although designed and sculpted by various artists, the monuments are characterized by a realistic yet geometricized depiction of various Russian and European "cultural heroes." They also had small plaques with biographical information, referred to as "agitational inscriptions," fulfilling their didactic obligations to the masses. Designed as political events, the ceremonial unveilings, many of which were held on Sunday mornings to substitute for the ritual of churchgoing, were accompanied by speeches, music, and other means of performing propaganda. The stable of sixty-six figures slated to be rendered in monument included Russian and foreign revolutionaries and social activists, writers and poets, philosophers and scholars, composers and performers.[5]

The plan of monumental propaganda was implemented in Kyiv by the May 7, 1919, decree of the Council of People's Commissars. One of the first monuments removed in 1917 was the statue of Stolypin, the reformist chairman of the Council of Ministers under Tsar Nicholas II. Monuments to Tsars Nicholas I, Alexander III, and two to Alexander II were also dismantled. By 1923 a total of eight monuments had been removed in Kyiv.

Of the thirteen monuments erected in 1918 in response to the Plan, one was to Taras Shevchenko, a gifted Ukrainian artist and poet born into serfdom. On the merits of his talent and his tragic life, Shevchenko was popularly embraced in the late nineteenth century as the Ukrainian national poet and the mythic father of the Ukrainian nation. For the Bolsheviks, Shevchenko was an exemplary victim of imperial oppression, serving ten years in internal exile for his "revolutionary democratic" ideals. The early Soviet leaders used the monument to Shevchenko to demonstrate their sensitivity to national differences in contrast to the cultural imperialism and intolerance of the tsars, who were noted for such discriminatory policies as banning the printing of any written material in the "peasant dialect" of Ukrainian.

In 1922, as the economic situation began to improve after the end of the civil war, there was a resurgence of monumental propaganda. The constructivist movement propelled forward the introduction of new forms of public space. In the mid-1920s, constructivist artists volunteered their skills to the new regime and began to create decorative art forms designed to "enlighten" the masses. The artists were committed to changing not only ideological superstructures, institutions, and political apparatuses but social relationships and patterns of everyday practice as well. Constructivist design of urban public space attempted to bridge the gap between science and utopia, the real and the ideal, the experienced and the alleged. The constructivist movement influenced creation in many artistic spheres, notably theater, architecture, poster art, and literature.[6]

The creation that came to define the constructivist movement was Tatlin's Monument to the Third International. Maiakovskii celebrated it as the first monument without a beard because of its nonrepresentational nature.[7] Tatlin's creation, with its celebration of the power of science and technology to enlighten, remains, however, an exemplary monumental depiction of the utopian ideal of the Revolution to create a "new man" capable of selflessly dedicating himself to building an ideal society.

The constructivist movement's avant-garde and experimental creations came under increasing fire in the late 1920s. Party leaders charged that their work embodied revolutionary content but in a form inaccessible to the masses. Stalin's policy of socialist realism in art, which condemned representation deemed "untruthful," was articulated in 1932 and formally institutionalized in 1934.[8] Monuments and other art forms were saddled in a more direct and unambiguous way with the didactic function of educating the masses in the spirit of socialism. Andrei Zhdanov criticized constructivism for its depiction of "nonexistent life with nonexistent heroes . . . that spirited the reader away from the contradictions and oppression of life to an unreal world, to a world of utopias."[9] The goal of socialist realism was to transform consciousness through the "truthful depiction" of life and history in art. The aesthetic value of a work of art was increasingly determined by its ideological and political effectiveness, a critical shift that reached its apex under Stalin, yet persisted as official Soviet policy until 1991.

Conformity and Commonality of Space

Over time the cultural diversity of the Soviet population was to some degree neutralized by state-sponsored efforts to standardize urban public space. For Soviet citizens, regardless of whether one was in Irkutsk, Kyiv, or Almaty, the uniformity of Soviet-designed urban space created a sense of cultural and historical commonality. The stunningly formulaic nature of Soviet urban planning, the small stable of approved cultural heroes and historical events honored in monuments everywhere, and the specifically Soviet architectural styles that changed with political leaders, all contributed to a feeling of familiarity and belonging in a country that spanned eleven time zones.

One need only think of the highly successful film made in the 1970s, *Ironiia Sud'by* (Irony of Fate), which was so popular when it was released that it is now ritually shown every New Year's Day on television to mass audiences across the former Soviet Union. The film depicts a homeward-bound man, who intoxicated after a drinking session with his buddies in the bath house, is mistakenly put on a plane to Leningrad. When he lands in Leningrad, he believes he is home in Moscow. He tells the taxi driver his address. This exact address exists in Leningrad, too. The neighborhoods, streets, and the apartment house seem familiar, and he continues to think that he has arrived home. When he gets to the apartment, of course, his standard key works in the standard door. The layout of the apartment is the same too. The furniture, the bookshelves, and the pull-out couch all look familiar. Relieved that he is finally home, he lies down to rest before meeting his girlfriend for dinner. The plot thickens when the real owner of the Leningrad apartment arrives and the hero comes to learn that although everything appears the same, he is hundreds of miles away from home. This film was such a smash hit because it touched a raw nerve in the vast majority of the population who experienced the classic Soviet reaction of "laughter through tears" when faced with the all-too-familiar cookie-cutter conformity of the cities they have built and inhabit.[10]

In towns across the land, Soviet citizens could expect to find a monument to Lenin in the central square, a principal thoroughfare named Lenin Street, and rings of *novi budivli* or gray apartment blocks in the outskirts. Monuments and styles of architecture varied with each political leader. Apartment buildings were described in terms of the political period in which they were built; indeed, those buildings erected under Khruschev were called *khrushchoby*, which is a pun on *trushchoby*, which is Russian for "shacks." With every shift, each political leader cast his personal stamp on the urban landscape. Soviet-designed urban space created a sense of cultural and historical commonality across republics and contributed to the underpinnings of a Soviet identity. For a great many Ukrainians, a trip to a Turkic-speaking Islamic Central Asian country, the "near abroad," is not as "foreign" as a trip to a Western European country which shares a similar Judeo-Christian heritage. Soviet-designed urban space, by etching a shared historical experience on the monuments, architecture, and place-names, is one of the many factors that creates a sense of being at home in the face of numerous linguistic, religious, and cultural differences.

The Icon of Socialism

The most valued of all icons during the Soviet period was, of course, Vladimir Il'ich Lenin. Lenin is the personification of the Russian Revolution. Hence his portrait appeared, among other places, in government offices, classrooms, and on banknotes. Every village, town, and city paid tribute to the great leader by erecting full-length monuments to him, by sculpting busts, and by naming the major thoroughfares, soccer stadiums, and mountains after him.[11] The police across the Soviet Union referred to the Lenin monument as "post number one": it was inconceivable not to have a Lenin monument in the most visible place in the heart of every town.[12]

Particularly under Stalin, Lenin was consistently sculpted with a particular expression on his face (earnest) and with slight variation on a single pose (standing tall and strong). His hand was often reaching out in a visionary gesture of leading the way. Over time, except for the major Soviet holidays (May Day and Great October Revolution Day) when the Lenin monuments became once again a focal point of commemoration, Lenin steadily lost his aura for most Soviet citizens.[13]

In time, the colossal Lenin towering over pedestrians in the central town square and the Lenin portraits in every office and classroom, much like advertisements in the West, were actively ignored by most Soviet citizens. The incessant portrayals of the benevolent father figure, protector of revolutionary ideals and the Soviet people, in time became visibly invisible as cynicism toward the two-faced nature of the system increased.

Although the monuments blended at times almost imperceptibly into the gray background of the Soviet urban landscape, this does not in any way suggest that they were unimportant. The monument might have become invisible, but the sign was always visible. In peak periods of sharp political, economic, or cultural change, the monuments often became critical sites for expressing opposition to or endorsement of the ruling regime. For example, first during glasnost in western Ukraine, and then in Kyiv in August 1991 following the failed coup, the Lenin monuments became instant targets of anti-Soviet pro-Ukrainian sentiment. By capitalizing on the politically and historically charged symbolism of the Lenin monuments as representations of the Revolution, their actions had echoes which were heard across the Soviet Union.

Now that contemporary social life is characterized by horrifying levels of corruption unimaginable under Soviet rule, a plummeting standard of living, and streets filled with beggars, juvenile delinquents, and "speculators," protest against these failures has, once again, tended to gravitate toward the Lenin monuments (or the empty pedestals where Lenin once stood). Lenin monuments are the sites of choice for anti-reform, anti-Ukrainian, and pro-Soviet agitation.

There is great regional variation across post-Soviet Ukraine in the reactions the Lenin monuments have prompted. Today in Kharkiv, everyone meets behind Lenin's back. It is the traditional place for a rendezvous. Standing over twenty meters high in Dzerzhinsky Square, renamed Independence Square, but still commonly referred to as Dzerzhinsky Square, the massive Lenin monument towers over the heart of the city as traffic and trolleys revolve around him.[14] Lenin stands opposite an imposing Oblast Party Committee building. The immensity of the monument, erected in 1963, is matched only by the expansiveness of the square. Freedom Square is the second largest square in the world after Tiananmen and makes one of the strongest statements about the Bolshevik penchant for megalomania in urban planning.[15]

In discussing desovietizing the urban landscape, Vitalii, a middle-aged man with two children who teaches history, has this to say: "Where do you start? I have such ambivalent feelings. Everything was renamed at least four or five times during the Soviet period. One street, perpendicular to Lenin Street, was renamed Transvaal Street. We didn't know why. We only knew that we were supposed to hate British colonists. Then the same street was renamed for a black South African hero. I don't even remember his name. He was fighting against the British. For us, it had no meaning. I don't know what the street is called now. Since independence they've renamed over a hundred streets. It's so confusing. They should start downtown and steadily work out. But instead they rename as they like."

And what about Lenin in Freedom Square? "If they take him down, who will be the next guy on the pedestal? In some parts of Ukraine they were in a hurry. They didn't have anyone else so they put up Shevchenko. That's not good. But the worst thing of all would be to do nothing." Of course, there are many possible replacements for Lenin. Even during the

In Kharkiv, the second-largest city in Ukraine, the Lenin monument still stands in the middle of the newly renamed "Freedom Square." The square has several buildings erected in a constructivist style, as was fashionable when they were built in the 1920s when Kharkiv was the capital. There are currently no plans to dismantle Lenin.

Soviet period the Ukrainian writers Ivan Franko and Lesia Ukrainka were immortalized in monument. However, Shevchenko is the literary figure with the greatest stature and is widely interpreted as the father of the nation; and therefore, he, at first glance, appears to be the appropriate replacement for discarded Lenins.

A paradoxical situation arises. When urban streets and squares are arbitrarily renamed and monuments hastily replaced at the whims of government bureaucrats, the result is disorientation and alienation among the fatigued residents of the city. Yet precisely because Vitalii wants the signs in the urban landscape to be relevant to their lives and have meaning (not like the unknown South African hero), he would like to see changes made. In order for the populace to approve of and embrace such changes, place-names and monuments will have to be in some way connected to personal experience by depicting events and figures that are meaningful. It is important to note that changes to monuments and street names have occurred primarily in cities, rather than rural areas. During this phase of intense change, haphazard renaming and alteration of monuments will only randomly be embraced to the extent that it is even undertaken. If a revised, coherent narrative of the Ukrainian historical experience eventually emerges, however contested and fragmentary, it is very likely that some of the quick replacements will be unmade and remade again.

The Fate of Lenin

In Kharkiv, off to the side of Freedom Square near the Lenin monument and within earshot of the metro, is an improvisational speakers' corner of sorts. A crowd of varying size is always there. Independent individuals and representatives of various political parties gather day in and day out, rain or shine, to rant, propagandize, and promote their complaints or solutions to the current social ills. The plethora of speakers extolling a barrage of opinions, perspectives, and agendas has not changed the fact that Communists are still squarely holding the reins of power in this region. With much of the population still reeling in disbelief over the split with Russia, there is no graffiti on this Lenin and there has been no serious talk about removing him.

In contrast, the Lenin monument in Kyiv was the first victim of the failed putsch in August 1991. During the three-day coup attempt, Kyiv was calm. Kyivans strolled along the Khreshchatyk, ate ice cream, and surveyed the latest books for sale by street vendors. The ordinariness of the situation was extraordinary given the stakes of the struggle being waged in Moscow. The morning after the coup failed, the three million residents of Kyiv awoke to find "satan," "fuck" (in English), and swastikas scrawled all over Lenin. It was a pathetic, sacrilegious, or joyous sight, depending on your perspective. Clearly, this posed a formidable problem for authorities, who were reluctant to let Lenin, desecrated in such vulgar terms, stand on display in the central square, named October Revolution Square, renamed Maidan Nezalezhnosti, which is Ukrainian for "Independence Square."

The first option for quick removal, of course, was to simply dynamite Lenin. However, some Soviet construction was selectively built to withstand the strongest tremors of mother nature and mankind alike. When the Lenin monument was erected in 1946, it was built directly into the largest and busiest metro station in the city, which sprawls out under the monument, the entire square, and along the main boulevard. Should they dynamite Lenin, they would sacrifice the metro station too. This plan was scrapped and Lenin was slowly dismantled block by block until only the pedestal remained.[16]

Katerina Ivanovna, a geographer and director of one of two schools out of the twenty-five in her district retaining Russian as the language of instruction, is somewhat chagrined that Lenin came down. Born and educated in a camp in northern Siberia where her father was a prisoner and her mother was sent to work as a nurse, she has spent nearly all of her fifty-three years in Russia, coming to Kyiv only because her husband, a Ukrainian who had never lived in Ukraine, was assigned to Kyiv by the Russian news agency for which he works. Her only daughter, son-in-law, and grandchild are still living in Russia.

On the recent changes to October Revolution Square, she has this to say:

> To forget everything would be bad. . . . It's part of our history, be it good or bad. There's a tendency to take down all the monuments in order to forget the Soviet period. But you can't change the thinking of a person simply by removing these monuments. To break something is easy, to build something in its place is more difficult. How do you change the thinking? You have to first change the environment in which a person lives. The two are closely related.

In closing, she sighs, "The world will learn from our experiment."

Now, up on the steep embankment, towering over the central square atop the pedestal where Lenin once stood, are advertisements for foreign banks, computers, and financial services.[17] Lenin, a representation of the Revolution and the principle sign of state socialism, has been replaced by signs of capitalist consumerism. One of the critical differences between the two signs is that save for a handful of exceptions, the ads for financial services and luxury items are simply dream images, totally unavailable in material form, for the most of the population. State socialism was, of course, readily available to all. New signs of capitalist consumerism, struggling to dislodge and overtake the old signs of Soviet ideology, are inscribed in public space and onto a population newly divided into "haves" and "have nots."

Not all renaming efforts have been successful. After the Revolution,

Khreshchatyk was renamed Vorovskii Street. The new name never caught on and it reverted back to Khreshchatyk. Officially reverting back to Khreshchatyk from Vorovskii Street represents one of the few examples of official renaming capitulating to popular use. Given the Soviet penchant for frequent renaming, many place-names were popularly referred to by a previous name, partially out of habit and partially to stem confusion. Good maps are a rarity so it takes time for people to learn the new names. Dzerzhinsky's name was attached to streets, squares, and metro stations, and although as the founder of the forerunner of the KGB he is a widely hated figure, it is not uncommon to hear his name used to refer to a particular place.

Further down Khreshchatyk, is Lenin Street, renamed Bohdan Khmelnytsky Street after the Cossack hetman who chased the Poles from Ukraine by forging an alliance with the Russian tsar in 1654, and further still, at the base of Shevchenko Boulevard, named for the Ukrainian national poet, is a small statue of Lenin surrounded by a park and sitting area. Of the three most visible and central signs of Lenin on the Khreshchatyk, two are gone with only this small statue remaining—for now at least.

In L'viv, the sixth-biggest city in Ukraine and the cultural capital of Ukrainian-speaking Ukraine, the Lenin monument was the first one in all of Ukraine to be demolished. It was removed prior to independence in 1990. Following the annexation of this region to Soviet Ukraine during World War II, a huge monument of Lenin was erected in the center of town. The monument was strategically placed to interrupt the view of the splendid nineteenth-century opera house, built when L'viv was part of the Austro-Hungarian empire. Local lore has it that the Soviets built the base of the Lenin monument with the tombstones of Jews, who made up a substantial part of the pre–World War II population in this city (this assertion proved impossible to verify). The popular charge of Soviet brutality toward Jews is noteworthy given this region's history of anti-Semitism and the oft-heard popular categorization of Lenin "as a Jew."

A tremendous eyesore and source of irritation to most residents, Lenin was removed amid celebration of enthusiastic crowds at the earliest opportunity during the hopeful days of glasnost. A lead ball dangling from a crane smashed right into Lenin, instantly converting him to debris. A gaping hole, which was subsequently filled in with water, was left in the monument's wake, making something of a fountain out of Lenin's remains.

The Lenin monument in L'viv was one of the earliest casualties of anti-Soviet agitation in the final years of Soviet rule. Once the Lenin monument was removed, a view of the L'viv Opera House was restored.

Interestingly, however, within eyesight of the original Lenin, just a bit further down the same boulevard, local authorities erected a monument to Shevchenko, the Ukrainian national poet. And still further down the same boulevard just past Shevchenko, there is the monument to Adam Mickiewicz, the Polish national poet. The Polish government erected this monument when, during the interwar period, this region and its capital city L'viv was part of Poland. This means that down the main boulevard in L'viv we have the remains of Lenin, followed in quick succession by a monument to Shevchenko and a monument to Mickiewicz, each man representing a phase (Soviet, post-Soviet, pre-Soviet) of the historical experience of the region. Most agree that the new benevolent patriarchal figure of Shevchenko is represented in the same imposing geometric socialist realist style as Lenin and other revolutionary figures. The critical difference is that in this town Shevchenko, unlike Lenin, is not resented.

By placing a monument to Shevchenko alongside the site of the former monument to Lenin, the past is somehow simplified. By sliding in a

In L'viv, the sixth-largest city in Ukraine and the center of contemporary Ukrainian culture, a monument to Shevchenko was erected near the former site of the Lenin monument. The Soviet tradition of brides being photographed before the monument to Lenin has been reformulated in post-Soviet society. Homage is now paid to Taras Shevchenko, a nineteenth-century poet and Ukrainian national icon.

new ideology, a refashioned cultural hero and father figure of the nation, the past is made desirable and one's own again. This new version of the past can be used to make sense of current hardships and to furnish new meanings to questions of revised individual and national identity.

Furthermore, the Soviet ritual of brides being photographed on their wedding day before Lenin and the habit of laying flowers at the base of the monument on Lenin's birthday or on state holidays continues albeit at the site of Shevchenko, on Shevchenko's birthday, and on December 1 in celebration of the referendum that secured Ukrainian independence. Lenin was removed but an icon of another ideology was quickly erected in his place and the spatial practices embedded in the lived spaces that formed around Lenin continue around Shevchenko.

The persuasive powers of visual representations are complemented by the fact that monuments generate certain spatial practices, which, in turn, are both constrained and produced by the space in which they are performed (Lefebvre 1991: 142–46). These spatial practices become the underpinnings of what Paul Connerton (1991) calls "habit memory," yet another form of recall, which dynamically interacts with various forms of consciousness. Such practices and their sites in public space inform the memories that both structure and are structured by everyday life. This connection to memory in lived spaces can provide the need to see oneself, one's own experiences, in the public sphere in order to make such sites meaningful.

Mukachevo is a town in western Ukraine beyond the Carpathian Mountains in a corner of Europe where the borders of Slovakia, Hungary, Romania, and Ukraine come together. The town is visibly marked by its Hungarian past, although after the breakup of the Austro-Hungarian empire it was part of Czechoslovakia during the interwar period. Capitalizing on the confusion wrought by the war, the nascent Carpatho-Ukraine state was formed in 1938, unifying the ethnically Ruthenian lands. It collapsed one year later under attack by Hungarian forces. Eventually, the entire region was overrun by the Red Army and annexed to Soviet Ukraine in 1944.

Here in Mukachevo the authorities adopted yet another solution to the sticky problem of the persistence of Soviet signs in post-Soviet society. At the base of the former Lenin Street, a beautiful boulevard lined with nineteenth-century buildings and churches, a small monument to Lenin was built in proportion to Mukachevo's nineteenth-century architecture. In this town, close to the Hungarian border with its swirling mix of Ruthenians, Hungarians, Slovaks, Ukrainians, Russians, Jews, and Gypsies, the authorities decided to remove Lenin but they left the empty pedestal. Through his noticeable absence, Lenin is very much present. The glaringly empty space itself testifies at the same time to the past and the new relationship of the present to the past. Rarely is an empty space the solution of choice because the ambiguity of emptiness suggests that established values and norms of behavior are changing but new ones have not yet crystallized. Emptiness shatters constraint and can encourage destructive behavior. In Mukachevo, the present acquires meaning with reference to a ruptured and conflicted past as represented by the empty pedestal where Lenin once stood. Perhaps the monument has been removed but the residents of Mukachevo will continue to see the sign. In every absence, there is the presence of what has been lost.

In Boryspol', a small town not far from Kyiv, the Lenin monument received an altogether different treatment. On his birthday in 1993, Lenin received a coat of gold paint! It was unclear who had sheathed

In Mukachevo, a small town on the Ukrainian-Hungarian border, the Lenin monument was quickly removed following the fall of the Soviet Union, leaving only the empty pedestal.

Lenin in a bright metallic gold reminiscent of the sparkling cupolas of Orthodox churches. The town was abuzz over who had done it and what it meant. Opinion was divided. Some said it was a tribute to Lenin, hence the choice of gold and the gesture of immortality on his birthday, which is celebrated on April 22. Others, mostly the younger residents of Boryspol', rolled their eyes and said the "hooligans" were making fun of him. Bright gold turned Lenin into Soviet kitsch.

My landlady, a sixty-year-old Ukrainian whose father had been a decorated officer in the Red Army, argued that the golden Lenin was neither a tribute nor a mockery. "They painted him gold to keep him from rusting!" she exclaimed. Clearly, she saw pure pragmatism, no symbolism whatsoever, even when I insisted that the brilliance of the gold hardly looked like industrial-strength rustoleum. To her, this was routine maintenance and thank God somebody was maintaining something.[18]

Some months later, this same Lenin was the site of another political statement. Lenin's gold coat was splashed with red paint, a color connoting beauty in Russian culture and the color associated with the Russian Revolution and Soviet symbolism. Again, the perpetrators were unknown. The response to this was to resplash him with even more light blue paint to cover the red paint. The combination of light blue and gold meant that, in essence, Lenin was draped in a makeshift yellow-and-blue Ukrainian flag.[19]

By the time Lenin's birthday rolled around one year later on April 22, 1994, he had been neatly repainted in metallic gold from head to toe once again. None of this was ever reported in the news. Few people were aware of the dialogue taking place literally on Lenin. I knew simply because a friend passed by him every Saturday on her way from Kyiv to her dacha to tend to her garden. She knew this was something that would probably amuse the foreigner.

The various reactions to the central icon of socialism across five cities in post-Soviet Ukraine suggests the variation in attitudes toward the Soviet system. To the local populations the transformations are at best disorienting and often they are simply fatiguing. Although enormous changes have besieged the urban landscape in Kharkiv since the fall of the Soviet Union, especially in the commercial sector in the form of advertisements, redesigned stores, and a multitude of flea markets, the monumental propaganda remains relatively undisturbed and decidedly Soviet. In Kharkiv, as Lenin stands tall and proud, William Faulkner's famous dictum comes to mind: "The past is not dead; it's not even past."

This is in sharp contrast to the political public spheres in Kyiv, L'viv, and Mukachevo, where we see the familiar habit, practiced with stunning frequency under Soviet rule, of erasing discredited historical figures. Of course, for individuals the practice of removing or destroying monuments to disinherited historical figures serves to erode painful and conflicted memories from consciousness. By eliminating reminders to a ruptured past in the form of monuments, political leaders can reinstate an unambiguous, teleological historical interpretation of the nation's past, which is, once again, leading to a "bright future." Nowhere is this more in evidence than in L'viv, where the repugnancy of the past represented by Lenin has been traded in for a resurging one, represented by Shevchenko, a cultural hero who fought for a space in the public sphere for Ukrainian culture and language and for the protection a state apparatus would afford to keep Ukrainian culture flourishing.

And in Boryspol', given the degree to which the shared symbolic vocabulary has withered amid the convulsive changes to the established social order, attempts to use Lenin under a veil of ambiguity and anonymity to make political statements, either pro- or anti-Soviet, often fail because the meanings of the symbols and gestures used are no longer clearly understood. If the sign changes when interpretative categories are not shared (or shared only generationally), its meanings become fractured, reaching different groups with different messages. The Lenin monuments across Ukraine, as they were originally intended by Lenin's own Plan, are still serving the purposes of political education and indoctrination to a new social, cultural, and economic order, albeit initially by prompting disorientation, confusion, and for some, simply fatigue.

Women Warriors and the Nation

The devastation sustained in Ukraine as a result of World War II was on a massive scale: an estimated 5 million were killed, 2 million were deported to camps in Europe, 3.5 million were evacuated to other parts of the Soviet Union and over 10 million were left homeless. Seven hundred fourteen cities and over 28,000 villages were destroyed. In Kyiv alone, 200,000 residents were killed and over 100,000 were deported. Nine hundred and forty buildings were destroyed—nearly all of Khreshchatyk was leveled to the ground—and 40 percent of the city's housing was lost. Because World War II marks a turning point and a great victory which came at a high price, the event was widely commemorated in monuments across Ukraine. In those regions where the destruction was particularly intense, such as around Kyiv, even small towns and villages have a monument to soldiers killed during World War II.

Myroslava Maksymivna, a fifty-five-year-old Ukrainian biologist who lives in Kyiv with her daughter and granddaughter, recalls:

> I was a small child at the time of the war but I remember it well. We left Kyiv for our dacha in central Ukraine, about three hours south of Kyiv. But we weren't much safer there. I remember when the Germans came. They torched the whole village. The houses had thatched roofs and burned very quickly. The whole sky was ablaze. Yes, I saw my whole village burn.
>
> . . . My father was a soldier in the war. He kept a diary, which was forbidden. He served near Stalingrad and Rostov shuttling arms by night on a barge across the Volga River into German-

occupied territory. Thinking, crying out the whole way "For the Motherland! For Stalin!" [Rus., *Za Rodinu! Za Stalina!*] The Twentieth Party Congress was for him a private tragedy.[20] He believed in Stalin, in the Soviet system. He knew about the repressions and was afraid but thought that Stalin didn't know, that his subordinates were working without his knowledge.

The most important event for the USSR was the war. The regime survived for nearly fifty years after the war. The war was a turning point: the Soviet Union could have been ruined but it strengthened itself. The war changed the internal political situation of the country dramatically. Also after the war the West was afraid of the USSR so foreign policy changed drastically too.

In the cities, the monuments to the war often reached grandiose proportions, reflecting its importance in the lives of individuals and its relevance for the Soviet state. Unlike other monuments, the World War II monuments distinguish themselves by their location at the site of actual historical events. In this way, the monument becomes a surrogate experience for those without memories of the war. For example, on the banks of the Dnipro River in Kyiv is the infamous monument to World War II built in 1980. Alongside the monument is a rich array of gold-domed churches of the Kievo-Pechers'ka Monastery built in the eleventh century.[21] The cupolas of the Orthodox churches are lorded over by the monument, a highly masculinized buxom warrior woman in a flowing gown holding a sword and shield, emblazoned with the Soviet star, crest, and hammer and sickle, raised high above her head.[22] This monument is one of the dominant and defining elements of the landscape in the Ukrainian capital.

Officially, the monument is known as *Mat' Rodina*, which literally means "Mother Motherland," yet the reference is to the allegorical "Mother Russia." The monument is popularly referred to as the "baba." *Baba* is a derogatory word used to connote a peasant woman (or any adult female). Its negative connotations come from the wretched, impoverished, and oppressive conditions in which peasant women lived, subordinated to their husbands, the Church, and the police.[23] Throughout formal and informal interviews, I never heard a single favorable word uttered with reference to this monument, only complaints about the preposterous amounts of money spent on something as "useless" and as "horrible."

Beneath the *Mat' Rodina* built right into the pedestal of the monument is an expansive museum showcasing the achievements of the Great Patriotic War, as World War II is called in official Soviet discourse. Maps on the walls indicate the key battles fought, the number of casualties incurred, and the shifting lines of the front. This museum celebrates the ability of the Soviet people to unite against and defeat a common enemy. With a bounty that included newfound respect for the Soviet system and considerable territory annexed into its orbit, the war was something of a validating experience for the system and for the sacrifices Soviet citizens had made to build it.

Outside the museum and off to one side is a large open-air museum exhibiting the progress of Soviet military weapons and machinery, from cars that needed to be cranked to tanks that float. Some of the tanks and planes used during World War II are also exhibited. Never far off and always within view are the cupolas of the monastery. That weapons of destruction are revered next to a sacred and historic place of learning doesn't appear to be a paradox more troubling than the others for those Kyivans out for a stroll to reminisce or to simply to escape the noise and rigor of city life.

While the monument esplanade enshrines Soviet military might and victory, it also represents the Soviet state. Much like the state apparatus itself, the monument was designed to inspire fear and awe. The statue of the gigantic and muscular warrior woman was positioned where it would have maximum visibility and would dwarf all else in its presence. Because such a monument, hated for its grotesqueness, is made to represent what is for many an intensely heartfelt and meaningful event, the legitimacy of this monument, and by extension the Soviet state, is undermined by a passively aggressive cynicism toward the system.

Testifying to the tragic side of the victory is the Babyi Yar memorial in Kyiv. While Mat' Rodina trumpets victory, Babyi Yar commemorates victimization. Set on the site of the massacre of approximately 200,000 Jews from 1941 to 1943, a grassy, gaping ravine encircled by a path dotted with benches is all that is left to testify, in its enormity and anonymity, to the staggering number of bodies beneath the soil. The first line of the celebrated Evgenii Yevtushenko's poem "Babii Yar" reads: "No monument stands over Babii Yar."[24] In its emptiness and stillness, the powerful commemorative value of this anti-monument monument was articulated. Yet after Yevtushenko brought attention to this, and perhaps because of it, Soviet authorities erected an immense socialist realist monument in

1976 in the middle of the ravine. Three plaques, written in Ukrainian, Russian, and Hebrew, acknowledge the hundreds of thousands killed at this site from 1941 to 1943.

The grandeur of victory and the suffering of near defeat are commemorated in Mat' Rodina and Babyi Yar. Regardless of the price paid, victory prevailed. It catapulted the country to superpower status, unified the population, and held the system intact for another forty-six years. For these reasons Soviet leaders immortalized the war in ever-present grandiose monuments. Concerned over potential popular negative reaction, post-Soviet leaders have not attempted to formally alter monuments to World War II. Much like the state calendar and textbook accounts, the war remains an event with mythic and sacred meaning capable of transcending mere state boundaries.

Axioms of Soviet Life

Although Lenin was the personification of the Russian Revolution, in many other instances Soviet leaders chose to use allegory to represent historical events and the values of the Soviet system. "People's friendship" was a tenet of Soviet ideology that stressed "internationalism" as the cultural basis for the Soviet people. The concept of people's friendship was inscribed on the urban landscape in a multitude of forms, in monuments, in street names, and in "Houses of Friendship," which served as Soviet cultural centers.

In Kyiv, at the end of Khreshchatyk, the main artery of the city, just behind the Philharmonic Concert Hall overlooking the Dnipro River, is a massive monument offered in the spirit of "people's friendship." When the sky is clear, many people can be found strolling the plaza and taking in the view of the river. Street vendors, lined up near the monument, offer matrioshkas, postcards, and paintings for sale to a steady stream of Kyivans and the few tourists who trickle in.

The monument celebrates the union of Ukraine with Russia. The union is represented by a large silver arc which stretches across an expansive plaza, offering a spectacular view of the river and of a new district of the city filled with *novi budivli*, or "new" gray apartment blocks, which are now twenty to thirty years old. Squarely under the arc stand two robust, muscular, young men holding a banner overhead with the Soviet star, crest, and hammer and sickle emblazoned on it.[25]

The monument to "People's Friendship," located at the end of Khreshchatyk, Kyiv's main boulevard, and overlooking the Dnipro River, was intended to celebrate the unification of Ukraine with Russia, as symbolized by the expansive arc and statue of two robust young men joining hands in a sign of strength and victory.

Inscribed on the pedestal on which the young men stand, first in Russian and then in Ukrainian, are the words "In celebration of the Unification of Ukraine with Russia." Slightly off to the right of the monument stands a collection of greater-than-life Ukrainian folkloric figures, featuring the obligatory mother and child and bandura player. A small wall near the figures indicates both in Russian and in Ukrainian that the figures were erected in 1957 to commemorate the fortieth anniversary of the founding of the Soviet Union.

The collapse of the Soviet Union opened borders and lines of communication to the West. It also created new borders almost as impenetrable as the former iron curtain was. Two years after independence, the exchange rate was one ruble to four kupons and a first-class train ticket from Kyiv to Moscow cost less than a New York City subway token. The following year, the rate was one ruble to 25 kupons and each train ticket cost $20, or an average monthly salary. The rate of exchange remained very unfavorable to the holder of kupons and the price of a ticket for the thirteen-hour ride to Moscow has continued to soar. (Since the introduction of an official currency, the hryvnia, in late 1996, the exchange rate has stabilized.) For many, travel to Russia remains as unaffordable and nearly as difficult to secure as travel to Eastern Europe.

Fewer and fewer Russian newspapers, magazines, books, and television programs are making their way into Ukraine, exacerbating an already sizable information vacuum brought on by rising prices and a breakdown in distribution networks. In response to the new political borders and the *disunification* of Ukraine from Russia, someone ingeniously removed the "with Russia" part of the inscription and now the monument reads: "In Celebration of the Unification of Ukraine." With this minor ironic adjustment, the monument comments on current political conditions. For some, the unshackling of Ukraine from Russia was a long-time dream. Although individuals are unable to mark independence and the withering of Soviet ideology by dismantling the monument, at least they can alter the framework in which it is read by altering the inscription.

"Peoples friendship" was an axiom of multinational Soviet life and a tenet of the ideological propaganda used to meld highly diverse people into the *sovetskii narod*. As Iakiv Samiilovych, a retired professor of economics who taught in L'viv, claims, "Moscow wanted to create a single indivisible empire." Born in a shtetl in Lublin, Poland, he fled in 1938 to Brest, Belarus, where he studied economics. After World War II ended, he went to L'viv State University to teach because L'viv was closest to Poland.

> The key factor that explains today's mess is the fact that everything in Soviet society was based on lies. They spoke of "people's friendship" but as a Jew they placed terrible restrictions on me. They called me a "cosmopolitan." The power structure didn't trust me because I was a Jew. Jews were a third sort in the USSR but when I was abroad I had to say that I was happy living in the Soviet Union.[26] They said we had socialism but we didn't have socialism. They said we had social security but we didn't have that either. Politics here was all based on lies. That's why we split up the way we did.

He is referring to the eruption of armed conflicts in many of the fifteen former Soviet republics. Yet the representation of people's friendship in highly visible monuments across the former Soviet Union, such as this one in Kyiv, keep the concept and what Iakiv Samiilovych called the "lies of the system" alive in the memories of Soviet-turned-Ukrainian citizens. Although memory is a fundamental component of an individual's sense of self, history cannot be reduced to memory, nor can identity be specified in terms of history alone. As the new signs of the post-Soviet urban landscape are read, they will influence the terms and categories in which history, both personal and collective, will come to be understood. As a permanent marker on the urban landscape, this monument testifies to another way of life and, for some, to an enduring unity with friends and relatives to the north.

Building Consensus

The urban landscape and the monuments adorning it were utilized by the Soviet leadership as an ideological terrain upon which power relations were inscribed. The strength of the image conveyed in monument was intended to represent the strength of Soviet rule. Through strategic placement of monuments, ritualized mass demonstrations, and the practice of renaming streets and towns according to political fashion, Soviet authorities inscribed signs onto the urban landscape to represent themselves, the Soviet people, and, above all, their power and right to rule.

Amid social turmoil and economic chaos, the monuments to Lenin, military might, and peoples' friendship appear as haunting vestiges of a shattered and shattering world. The Soviet penchant for forcing the past into a coherent and teleological schema has exacerbated the inherent confusions and uncertainties of the present. This tension imposes itself on historical understanding and in the process reworks the internal relation between past and present. The forces that held memory at bay by attempting to stifle and redirect it out of the public sphere have broken down. This rupture has catapulted the pain from memories of personal and historic trauma to the forefront once again, imposing itself on historical interpretation and political discourse, now that the collapse of the Soviet Union has created new political conditions conducive to this. The confluence of official historical narrative and its representations combines with individual memories on an individual level to become a discursive terrain for reconfiguring selfhood and identity. On a collective level the overlap between official historical narrative and individual experience embedded in memories can be used to produce a consensus of collective experience.

Memories metamorphose in tandem with our understanding of a collective past as represented in dominant historical discourses, which in Soviet society often assumed a summary form in monuments. Because these monuments no longer hold sway over the collective imagination, they assume a colossal importance didactically.[27] In these monuments history survives, a history that testifies not to what one has lived through but to what one has died through, representing an endless succession of wanton death and destruction brought on by the Revolution, the civil war, the Famine, the Stalinist repressions, World War II, and Chernobyl, to name only the most piercing of events. The dream images of monuments commemorate the suffering of the living and their rulers' illusions of grandeur and mass deception. They are haunting reminders of the popular saying, "Tak zhyty ne treba" (You mustn't live like this).

For a population that has been russified and sovietized, the prospect of now being ukrainianized can seem daunting. For those who have long awaited the institutionalization of a Ukrainian national culture under its own state, the feelings are one of elation, relief, and disappointment. The confusion and paradoxes of the present and the categories used to fashion a new sense of self and a new nation in the post-Soviet world acquire meaning only with respect to a ruptured and conflict-ridden narrative of the past. The past acquires increased salience as a way to read meaning into present predicaments and uncertainties. Monuments are an ideological terrain that local populations use to represent themselves to themselves and to others, highlighting the distinctiveness of their historical experience. In this sense, the private sphere of individual recollection intersects with the public sphere and public remembering. The events embodied in monuments will correspondingly influence the relational nature of memory by shaping which events from individual and collective experience are remembered, how, and by whom. It is within this gray area of overlap that a consensus of collective historical experience of Soviet power is produced. The sense of commonality born of consensus and reflected in state-sponsored historical narrative could become part of the foundation of a sense of nationhood and contribute to the construction of inclusivist forms of national identity.

A newly institutionalized Ukrainocentric perspective on historical interpretation of the Soviet period must engage the representations of official Soviet narrative. The results of this exchange will continue to manifest themselves in signs in urban space. The signs emerging from this encounter will be read alongside the old signs of Soviet ideology, new signs of capitalist consumerism, and above all, signs of confusion. The cult of monuments developed by the Soviet leadership to foster a revolutionary consciousness suited to the social, political, and economic order they sought to establish lives on. But not even something carved in stone is stable. Rather, monuments and other signs in the urban land-scape are a means to preserve, contest, or reformulate representations of a particular historical experience. The metamorphosis of the meaning of these representations of the past informs the terms and categories in which individuals remember the Soviet experience and set the parameters of a national culture to support a national identity in the quest to strengthen the nascent Ukrainian state.

Afterword

After the unexpected failed coup attempt in Moscow sent crowds into the streets in celebration of the imminent demise of the Soviet Union, I was struck by totally different expressions on familiar faces. Friends whom I had known for years I now saw for the first time jubilantly beam with joy. Many confessed that they never thought they would live to see the end of the communist regime, which they had come to hold in such contempt, nor the emergence of an independent Ukrainian state, which many had dreamed of since the rebellious days of youth. The optimism and enthusiasm that had been growing during glasnost, spurred on by each new revelation of past and present transgressions of the ruling elite, had finally culminated in the desired end: a chance to start over, to eliminate the hurtful and destructive practices of a condemned system, and to regain one's rightful place as Europeans and capitalize on the good life that such a new destiny and identity promised. All those dreams harbored in secret suddenly appeared as potential realities when impediments erected by the system seemed doomed to imminent collapse.

Even as I left Ukraine in early September 1991, the experience was entirely different from other departures. Previously, because of complicated procedures involved in obtaining letters of invitation and visas, one could never be certain to make it back to see friends again. It was inconceivable to maintain contact by sending letters directly or, worse, telephoning. I was always haunted by fears that those who befriended me would get in trouble and, indeed, one did. And yet, all that fear of state reprisal for something as simple as friendship vanished after the failed coup. I departed promising to write, to stay in touch, and we even began talking of arranging visits to the United States. It was on this buoyant, hopeful note that I left Kyiv and ecstatic friends in September 1991.

This is why I was amazed when I returned only one year later to embark on the research that would eventually inform this book and found that much of that enthusiasm had evaporated. Save for intellectuals and the most savvy of entrepreneurs, hope for positive change that would bring forth meaningful improvements in individuals' lives had withered. All those dreams formulated under an oppressive regime of being able to travel, to read what one wanted, to pursue a more fulfilling career, and, perhaps most important of all, to live without humiliation, had become a burden as it became more and more apparent that the unthinkable had occurred: in many respects the new social order was far crueler and more unpredictable than the old. For many, individually held dreams of a truly bright future became a burden as they slipped further and further from grasp.

When I left Ukraine again in 1994, much of the Soviet system had deteriorated and the process of global integration had begun. Although hyperinflation had been tamed and some individuals had managed to parlay the changes into improvements in lifestyle and career, many were left disoriented and disconcerted. Why, in three short years, had the mood tumbled for most from the heights of jubilation to tired resignation and fear of the future? Although the new Ukrainian state might have shown itself capable of protecting aspects of Ukrainian culture, it became obvious that it was unable to protect its citizens from crime, poor health, vanishing employment opportunities, and most poignant of all, from despair. The breakdown of a rule-laden, rigid bureaucracy had left in its wake a vacuum where a darwinian struggle for survival had emerged. Left to fend on their own, many became vulnerable to organized crime, abdication of state responsibilities, and that most noxious byproduct of capitalist systems, unemployment and poverty.

I mention this mood of burden because it struck me as one of the most powerful forces stifling motivation and constraining individual agency during the period in which I conducted this fieldwork. I have tried to illustrate the ways in which individuals and groups have negotiated, endorsed, or challenged aspects of the new Ukrainian state's efforts to direct historical revision. This overall mood of disillusionment in the early years of independence was a formidable backdrop against which this process was unfolding. Dismay over the new paths to social mobility, such as trading and organized crime, and a redesigned social contract that crushed bonds of solidarity as it ushered in an atomized struggle for survival hardly seemed part of the so-called transition to a democratic state and a market-oriented economy during the heady years of glasnost.

I don't mean to suggest that many people regret the fall of the Soviet system (although some do), but rather that most failed to fully anticipate the tremendous disruption this would cause in everyday living and in proposed life course trajectories. The hidden costs have proven to be formidable. As the familiar practices of everyday life vanished into memory, unrelenting improvisation made it increasingly difficult to discern what was emerging to take its place. Because the repositioning of Ukraine into a world capitalist economy called for collective and personal redefinition, it was linked to the constitution of new cultural values and practices, and in the end, to the constitution of a new nation.

Many anthropological studies have examined the dissolution of cultural identities caused by imperial expansion. Alternatively, here we witness a process of remaking identities caused by imperial collapse, a process that must be understood in terms of its global, historical context. Remaking cultural identities is not purely a matter of invention as some would have us believe, but rather a reversal of the practice of being defined by others to shouldering the responsibility of self-definition. To use history as a discourse for identity, as Appadurai (1981) has argued, previously existing cultural elements must be harnessed to the process. By analyzing which aspects of Soviet culture retain relevancy and meaning, we see not only the destruction of previous forms of cultural identity, but the psychological aftermath of their destruction as well.

To reinstitute a sense of stability, continuity, and hope, cultural and political leaders turned to history. The past takes on a marked salience when meanings, categories, and concepts in the present appear opaque. The past becomes a resource used to forge meaning in the present. By rendering the past less ambiguous, the unpredictability of the present can be somewhat quelled. In this way, the present acquires meaning only in terms of a ruptured and tragic past.

I have argued in this book that the unifying phase of nationalism as it is unfolding in post-Soviet Ukraine has hinged on attempts to create a historically based sense of national identity out of the ruins of an internationalist socialist culture. Redefinition of collective and individual experience occurs in historically, spatially, and socially determined circumstances and at certain sites of experience. School curricula and textbooks, festivals to promote mass culture, commemorations and the state calendar, monuments and urban public space, as we saw, are some of the most salient sites where the new Ukrainian state has tried to articulate a national history, using historical representations, myth, and symbolism to reframe the Ukrainian nation. The socialization received at school is a means of instilling a sense of historical and national consciousness in young minds. The liminal periods delivered by festivals and commemorations create the potential to alter historical consciousness. Similarly, names and monuments in urban space inform the frameworks, categories, and periods within which we recall lived history, both personal and collective.

Taken together, these sites begin to structure the temporal and spatial terrains and, by extension, the commonality of a people living under a particular state. Ukrainians become marked as a people, separate and distinct from others whose social life unfolds in a different space to a different rhythm. There is nothing particularly unique about this overall process. When empires or large states splinter, new, postcolonial states almost always engage in such national (re)narration in an effort to create a revised sense of national identity to legitimate new political realities and to grapple with the dissent it inspires. Indeed, all states to some degree engage in such efforts because power, and especially the power of the state, must be expressed in symbolic forms (see Kertzer 1988).

After having analyzed some of the sites at which attempts are made to institutionalize a new national culture and the relevance of such a process for perceptions of legitimacy and state stability, we can now ask how this adds to our understanding of the experience of socialism and what this suggests about the nature of the Ukrainian state and popular attitudes toward it. Clearly, the pace and nature of the process of producing and institutionalizing a post-Soviet national culture operates in tandem with the Soviet state and its legacy, for as Breuilly has argued, the nature of the preexisting state dictates which form a nationalist ideology or movement will take (1988: 361).

The process described and analyzed thus far in a formerly Soviet context differs from other colonial experiences in essentially three ways. First and most significant, this process is occurring as massive political, economic, social, cultural, and demographic changes are simultaneously engulfing the region. This, obviously, creates formidable social tension brought on by insecurity and unpredictability. Faltering industrial and agricultural sectors and a breakdown in transportation networks and social services have prompted a sharp decrease in the standard of living for large segments of the population. Consumed with meeting basic human needs for survival, individuals are overwhelmed by the feeling of being railroaded by the changes, rather than having an active role in directing them.[1]

Second, as we saw, under Soviet rule control of the historical narrative was blatant and unapologetic. Professional historians were straddled with rigid guidelines admitting some topics for historical inquiry, eliminating others, and as a result, over time the credibility of official historiography was undermined. The blatant manipulation of historical accounts had two consequences. Artistic depictions of historical events were often seen as more truthful, more reflective of a lived reality, because the interpretative aspects of artistic renditions allowed more to slip by the censors. Such rigid censorship also gave memory heightened importance for recording the past. Memories of lived experience become essential in reconstructing collective experience when official, credentialed sources have been so discredited.

Third, efforts to institutionalize a national culture inevitably trigger some degree of dissent. As a result, a dialogue of sorts develops between the state and its citizenry as various individuals or social groups object to the version of history that the state is attempting to institutionalize. Under Soviet rule this popular response was particularly covert and coded so as to elude state retribution for challenging the state's authority, and this, as we saw, contributed to the flourishing of a culture of fraud. Massive efforts were made to suppress any organized challenges to state-driven narratives. Ongoing, individualized battles with an uncooperative bureaucracy cultivated practices of deceit as individuals bent, twisted, and manipulated rules and regulations in the course of everyday living and hardened the habit of the "two personalities" syndrome, or secretly knowing one thing but saying another.[2]

James Scott has written that "the more menacing the power, the thicker the mask" (1990: 3). Historical representations that are powerfully conditioned and crafted into a narrative of collective historical experience constitute what he has called a "public transcript," or an attempt to legitimate current power relations. Rarely is a public transcript simply accepted. Rather, it inevitably triggers a response, albeit often a response that finds expression "off stage" as Scott would say, or out of the public sphere where it cannot issue a direct challenge to established power relations by confronting the validity of the public transcript. By examining the discrepancies between "public transcripts" and "hidden transcripts," or coded commentaries on public transcripts, one sees the contradictions and tensions among different groups of individuals to redistribute power, wealth, and status of certain cultural products and identities (1992: 4). Memories tend to inform the alternative or hidden transcripts of disenfranchised individuals just as official historiography is part of the public transcript asserted by the state to explain and naturalize power relations.

However, the dynamics governing the confrontations between public transcripts and hidden transcripts have entirely changed. Opposition in post-Soviet society is far more vocal, uninhibited, and less monolithic. It relies less on nonwritten, nonverbal forms of individually expressed opinions. Educators form private schools; the Chervona Ruta festival has been deliberately held in highly russified areas with the intention of provoking—and overcoming—resistance to ukrainianization; groups stage their own commemorations when they are absent from the state calendar; and monuments are dismantled and erected in response to local demands for change. In each of these instances, responses draw less on a well-known hidden transcript of anti-Soviet sentiment and increasingly on Ukraine's legacy of statelessness. The specifics of local reactions are in part a byproduct of this legacy and in part a regional reaction to the Soviet state and to the specific historical experiences that emerged from the confrontation of these populations and the Soviet state.

At this vulnerable point of the country's development, parallel processes on the subnational level are under way. The reevaluation of each region's historical experience creates the possibility of redefining key moments of Soviet rule and using this to both articulate a regional identity and to issue a critique of a unifying national historical narrative. The specific historical experiences of various regions have led to the formation of different cultural values, political orientations, and a multitude of localized identities, such as Crimean, Donbas, and Transcarpathian. Demarginalizing one group by creating state-sponsored representations of "our past" inevitably disenfranchises other groups. Regional identities were fueled by divergent experiences of Soviet rule and have spurred the creation of new histories challenging the legitimacy of nationalist, unofficial-turned-official historical representations.

The scope of the change, compounded by conflicting attitudes reflecting worship of the state and suspicion of its power, the desire for its protection and fear of its intrusive regulation combine to make it difficult to predict how Ukrainian statehood will develop. The Soviet system created a sense of nationality whose meaning varied greatly, from intellectuals with a highly defined nationalized self who supported Rukh, to many in eastern and southern Ukraine, who saw their Ukrainian nationality as a bureaucratic designation not necessarily indicative of a linguistic or cultural identity. This book has looked at the sites at which the state attempts to convert the meaning of historical events into personal events and turn a national identity into a personal identity. The state is not always successful. Increasingly in the former Soviet context, individuals, who are now faced with a plethora of new influences, values, and choices, respond by launching a counterdiscourse, by appropriating other events, another understanding of what the nation is and who its members are.

During this period of intense transformation, some rely on received Soviet concepts and practices to forge meaning in their lives. Others look to new groups embracing different value systems to furnish narratives to explain their collective past in an effort to provide comfort in the present and hope for the future. One thing is clear—the path that Ukraine and other formerly socialist states have embarked upon, much like in 1917, is likely to trigger global consequences. Hybrid forms of economic, political, social, and cultural life are likely to emerge from the meshing of vastly different cultural systems. In this context, at a minimum, one must be prepared to witness and analyze the unexpected.

Notes

Introduction

1. Other anthropological studies that address the combined themes of the state and nationalism or the constitution of nationhood include Handler 1988, Kapferer 1988, Borneman 1992, and Watson 1994.

2. Hobsbawm (1990: 182–83), Verdery (1996: 34 and 207), and Borneman (1992: 284) note a similar loss of the state's monopoly on the use of violence. A growing literature on the mafia in formerly socialist societies testifies to the extent that criminal organizations challenge state structures' control over the means of violence. See Verdery 1996: 216–20.

3. Andreas Kappeler (1994) also begins his account of Ukrainian history with the same phrase, highlighting Ukraine's history of statelessness and its openness to a myriad of cultural influences.

4. Soviet-created notions of nationality present a challenge to theories of nationalism that rest on a correspondence between nation and state. The very statelessness of Ukraine did not hinder a national culture from developing. This hybrid situation and the paradoxes it creates are rarely accommodated in the literature on nationalism and colonialism. Malkki's study (1995) of how Hutu refugees in exile, without a state and without even a territorial base, developed a national culture based on a consensus of collective historical experience embodied in narrative also serves to challenge accepted relations between nation and state.

5. Gellner (1983: 1), Breuilly (1982: 3), and Hobsbawm (1990: 9) employ a similar definition of nationalism.

6. To commemorate the second anniversary of the Chernobyl disaster, Zelenyi Svit proposed holding a memorial rally in Kyiv but permission was denied. They held it anyway and remarkably few repercussions ensued, spurring them on still further. For a discussion of Zelenyi Svit and the relationship of the environmental movement to the nationalist ascendancy in Ukraine, see Dawson 1996, esp. pp. 71–82. The environment also played a key role in the struggles for independence in Central Asia and in Lithuania. See Roi 1992 and Dawson 1996: 34–63.

7. The contribution of the Ukrainian diaspora, located primarily in Canada, the United States, and Australia, has been very significant in supporting Ukrainian churches and Ukrainian cultural institutions, both during Soviet rule and during this critical transition period. Unfortunately, a complete detailing of diasporic participation in the Ukrainian cultural revival is beyond the scope of this study. See Kuropas 1991 and Subtelny 1991 for studies of how immigrants kept links to Ukraine and maintained Ukrainian cultural practices and values as a meaningful part of their everyday lives.

8. Lina Kostenko, one of the most beloved poets in Ukraine, asserts that these two events, the Famine and Chernobyl, are the most crucial for defining the Ukrainian experience of Soviet rule. See Kostenko 1993: 2. Also see Petryna 1995: 196–220. She

points to the widespread perceptions of the centrality of these two events in shaping the history of Ukraine in the twentieth century.

Chapter 1: Nationality in Soviet and Post-Soviet Ukraine

1. Russian Independence Day has since been renamed *Den' Rossii* (Russia Day) and is now celebrated on June 12.

2. I provide this and other discursive and administrative terms in Russian because they are so closely linked with the Soviet system, which used Russian as the lingua franca. In Ukrainian, Soviet people would be *radians'kyi narod*.

3. Even the Russian Republic was referred to as "Rossiiskii," not "Russkii." This important distinction, which is religiously observed by most Russian politicians, acknowledges the multinational composition of the population by purposefully not referring to it as "Russian" and using the non-ethnically based term "Rossiiskii." Unfortunately, both terms are usually translated into English as "Russian," masking the discursive recognition of the vast cultural and linguistic diversity of the population of the Russian Republic, now the Russian Federation.

4. Verdery (1996: 62) and Borneman (1992: 18–19), two anthropologists from whom I have taken inspiration, employ a similar definition of nationality. Also see Hobsbawm 1991: 18–20.

5. Although there was debate about the origins of nations and their relative importance, Lenin and Stalin were in agreement on one key point: national identification should be merged with territorial definition.

By 1928, in part as a result of the 1926 census, political units based on group size were set up to match ethnic units. Ethnic units were described as peoples (*narody*), smaller or less developed peoples (*narodnosti*), nationalities (*natsional'nosti*), nations (*natsii*), and tribes (*plemena*). Based on such loose distinctions, political units were established: republics, autonomous republics, national *okrug*s, national *raion*s, national soviets, national executive committees (*tuzriki*), native soviets (*tuzemnye sovety*), down to emcampment committees (*lagerkomy*) (Slezkine 1994: 427–30). Each group, regardless of size, was encouraged to develop its own autonomous culture within its borders. Ethnographers contributed to the institutionalization of ethnicity by establishing categories and classifying peoples according to demographic size and cultural development, all of which was used to determine state funding for national educational and cultural institutions (Slezkine 1991 and Grant 1995). Nineteenth-century Western anthropologists engaged in a similar enterprise for European empires. See Stocking 1987 and 1983 and Asad 1988.

6. *Vsesoiuznaia perepis' naseleniia 1926 g.* (All-union population census, 1926), vol. 17, Moscow 1929, p. 98, italics in original; cited in Bilinsky 1964: 413.

7. Ibid., Instruction No. 10, p. 98, italics in original; cited in Bilinsky 1964: 413–14.

8. It is interesting to note the parallels to another multicultural society, the United States, which also embraces citizenship and an elected identity (Hispanic, Native American, etc.) as constitutive of social identity. Correspondingly, many of the same tensions ensue.

9. Of all the former Soviet republics, only Armenia has a demographically insig-

nificant minority. All other new states have at least one sizable minority in addition to the titular nationality group. This is evidence of the arbitrariness of Soviet borders concerning "national" republics and the extent of ethnic mixing and mobility during the Soviet period.

10. In the *Communist Manifesto*, Marx wrote, "National differences and antagonisms between peoples are vanishing gradually from day to day owing to the development of the bourgeoisie, to freedom of commerce, to the world market, to uniformity in the mode of production and in the conditions of life corresponding thereto" (1989: 128).

Indeed, the structural requirements of an industrialized economy demand mobile populations, a high rate of literacy, and something of a mass culture, all of which facilitate assimilation and chisel away at cultural differences. Industrialization, however, also generates inequality. When patterns of inequality and economic exploitation mirror ethnic divides, as they often did in the Russian empire and in the Soviet Union, the process of assimilation is significantly slowed and national differences can even become enhanced and entrenched. The priority Marx gave to class and economic inequality as divisive forces, perhaps led him to underestimate the balkanizing power of nationality and the extent to which it can serve as an alternative base for opposition.

11. For a historical overview of the evolution of intellectual thought on the relationship of the "two Russian nationalities," meaning Ukrainians and Russians, see Lindenheim and Luckyj 1996, esp. the essays by Kulish, Kostomarov, Nechui-Levytsky, and Malaniuk. Dzyuba (1974) analyzes the dynamics of russification on Ukrainian culture under the Soviet regime.

12. Quotations are drawn from several sources. One-hundred-forty interviews were formally conducted at prearranged times and were tape-recorded. Thirty-five life histories were gathered and fifty-seven open-ended questionnaires were collected from members of the intelligentsia inquiring how they understood the problems in the country, if they supported a Ukrainian cultural revival, and if so, how and to what degree. In addition, numerous interviews were conducted in a spontaneous, semi-structured fashion without being tape-recorded. I recorded these exchanges in my field notes as we spoke or directly following the interview. By making the decision not to tape-record, in many instances, I believe I received a more frank and extensive response to my questions. The names of all informants have been fictionalized. In choosing pseudonyms I have tried to reflect the language in which the informant referred to him- or herself and chose to speak.

13. This opinion became less common after the Russian aggression in Chechnya escalated in 1995.

Chapter 2: The Rise of Nationalist Opposition

1. Signs of change reflecting these new policies and priorities initially came in the form of new editorial appointments at several influential periodicals. Two appointments were especially notable. In early 1986 Vitalii Korotych, a Ukrainian writer and poet from Kharkiv, Ukraine, became the editor of what was to become the wildly popular Moscow-based news and general interest weekly magazine *Ogonëk* (Little Fire). Y. Yakovlev became the editor of *Moskovskii Novosti* (Moscow News), an influential daily newspaper. Both men were respected for their efforts to bring non-Soviet influences

and perspectives to bear on the Soviet media. Their appointments were the beginning of a sea change in Soviet journalism, a shift away from merely toeing the Party line. See Davies 1989 for an overview of how this relaxing of state censorship fueled a popular interest in history and Ries 1997 for how the everyday lives of Moscovites were dominated by conversation of newfound freedoms discussed in the press.

2. David Marples has written extensively on the social impact, broadly defined, of the Chernobyl accident. See Marples 1986 for technical details on the actual occurrence of the accident and for efforts to evacuate the contaminated zone. Marples (1988) addresses how the impact of the accident was initially understood and has affected everyday life in Ukraine and (1991) analyzes the political ramifications of the accident.

3. In 1991 the International Atomic Energy Agency and six other United Nations agencies studied rates of cancer and birth defects among 825,000 people who live in the most contaminated regions of Ukraine, Belarus, and Russia. Even though the study omitted consideration of two of the most affected groups, the "liquidators" or emergency clean-up crew, of whom thirty-one died immediately, and the estimated 116,000 to 135,000 residents who were evacuated from the twenty-mile zone (Marples 1988: 31), it nonetheless offered evidence that there was no increase in radiation-related illnesses such as thyroid cancer, birth defects, or leukemia among the population living near the reactor because of the accident. Consideration of "liquidators" was not undertaken because information regarding their contamination, decontamination, and overall health remains classified. Soviet authorities did acknowledge that 237 firemen became ill with "radiation sickness" but they assert that 209 of them were eventually "cured" (Marples 1988: 35). These figures are viewed with skepticism in the West, yet without more complete information it is impossible to challenge them.

Consideration of the evacuees from the twenty-mile zone was omitted at the request of Soviet authorities (See Dickman 1991: 335). Although the team considered it likely that there would be an increase in the number of thyroid cancers in the next five to ten years, they maintained that many of the health effects were not radiation-induced but rather caused by stress. They traced the sources of stress to official withholding of details of the accident, lack of health education, and needlessly evacuating populations who were exposed to "an absurdly low threshold" of radiation (Dickman 1991: 335). These findings were instantly challenged by many Western scholars and environmental organizations, charging that the team had a pro–atomic energy bias.

At a conference organized in Vienna to commemorate the tenth anniversary of the accident, a commission made up of members from the International Atomic Energy Agency, the World Health Organization and the European Commission continued to maintain the same position regarding the public health consequences of the accident.

Recently, Marples (1995) wrote, "The anticipated spate of leukemias has not yet materialized, and several observers have pointed out that thyroid gland cancer among children—currently the most prevalent Chernobyl-related disease—is usually not fatal. Because of the time lag since Chernobyl, it is often very difficult to attribute illness even among "liquidators" directly to radiation from Chernobyl. A critical concern has been the psychological consequences of the accident, which have been immense and which the authorities have in general failed to deal with adequately."

4. Dawson's 1996 study of environmental activism concludes that the antinuclear protests were in fact more reflective of demands for national sovereignty rather than of

strongly held environmental principles. The key environmental organization, Zelenyi Svit (Green World), was far stronger, as evidenced by the number of environmental clubs registered under the Zelenyi Svit umbrella, in western Ukraine, a region of the country with a history of nationalist activism, than it was in the highly industrialized eastern regions. Indeed, Dawson refers to the environmental movement in Ukraine as "little more than a surrogate for hidden nationalist demands" (1996: 7). This is how she explains the virtual collapse of environmental protest after Ukrainian independence. Motyl (1993) also discusses the political implications and uses of the Chernobyl accident by nationalist opposition leaders.

5. Chernobyl means "wormwood." In the Book of Revelation, there is reference to a "star from heaven" burning like a lamp: "And the name of the star is called Wormwood; and the third part of the waters became wormwood; and many men died of the waters because they were made bitter" (Revelation 8:11). The Chernobyl plant was located on the Prypyat River. Two writers in particular, Oles Honchar and Iurii Shcherbak, noted this biblical reference to wormwood, and it quickly became known the world over. Given the religious revival that arose shortly after the accident, propelled by the Millennium of Christianity celebration in 1988, some began to interpret the accident as predestined because of this biblical reference.

6. Two other notable films (both Russian) are *Chernobyl: Dva tsvieta vremeni* (*Chernobyl: Two Colors of Time*), which documented the clean-up effort, and *Chernobyl: Osen' 1986* (*Chernobyl: Fall 1986*), which featured the entombment of the disabled reactor.

7. Cited in Onyshkevych 1989: 151. Onyshkevych gives an overview of the different artistic genres that engaged the accident and its aftermath. Bahry 1989 gives a broad illustration of the themes that dominated discourse during glasnost.

8. See Kuzio and Wilson 1994 and Motyl 1990 for a discussion of the dynamics of mass politics and protest in the late 1980s which helped usher in independence.

9. For example, the release of Tengiz Abuladze's film *Repentance* was a sensation for its searing allegorical portrayal of Stalin's despotism. Stalinist repression was also illustrated by Anatolii Rybakov's book, *The Children of the Arbat*, published in 1987, twenty years after it was written.

Specifically affecting Ukraine were the spate of films on Chernobyl mentioned earlier. *Holod-33* was a moving black-and-white film depicting the famine. There was also a strong tendency to re-release the known and highly respected works of Ukrainian historians such as Hrushevsky and Vynnychenko as well as the ethnographic writings of Kulish and Kostomarov.

10. By 1987 the weekly newspaper of the Writers' Union, *Literaturnaia Gazeta* (Literary Newspaper), had a circulation of 3.1 million and, especially in provincial towns, the public complained that not enough copies were printed. *Novii Mir* (New World), a literary monthly, saw its circulation rise from 495,000 to 1,150,000 in one year from 1987 to 1988. Post-Soviet economic changes have caused circulation rates to plummet once again.

11. The relevance of memory as an object of scholarly inquiry arose again in the 1970s as historians increasingly recognized the merits and legitimacy of oral history, which uses memories as its documents. See Passerini 1987, Thompson 1988, and Vansina 1985.

12. Following Davis and Starn (1989) and Nora (1984, 1989), and Le Goff (1992), I am concerned with the interdependence and tension between history and memory. Many anthropological studies have examined the role of history in nationalist struggle, yet there remain very few ethnographic studies addressing this dynamic within Soviet society. Verdery (1991a), Borneman (1992), and Watson (1994) all address such questions within the Eastern European context.

13. Verdery (1996: 96–97) notes the common tendency of East European national histories to position themselves as "victims" of oppression inflicted by a larger state or a barbaric "other." She cites the claim of noted Romanian writer Mircea Eliade that "few peoples can claim that they had so much ill fortune in history as the Romanian people" (1996: 96), among other examples of nationally victimized histories recanted throughout Eastern Europe. See Subtelny 1993: 33–54 for an overview of the common biases of contemporary Ukrainian historians and an analysis of the dilemmas and impediments to reorienting away from the stance of "defending Ukrainian historical truth."

14. Renan writes, "L'oubli et je dirai même l'erreur historique, sont un facteur essentiel de la formation d'une nation et c'est ainsi que le progrès des études historiques est souvent pour la nationalité un danger" (cited in Hobsbawm 1990: 12). Other studies of institutionalized remembering and forgetting under socialism include Grant's 1995 study of the Nivkhi experience of Soviet rule and Watson 1994, which attempts to portray patterns of institutional and historical manipulation and individual recollection as a form of resistance in socialist societies.

15. Historians estimate that between 35,000 and 50,000 Jews died in pogroms in 1919–20 (Subtelny 1994: 363–64). Although the White Volunteer Army was partially responsible, the Directory's forces, which were technically under the command of Symon Petliura, also participated.

16. The Famine was not by any means limited to Ukraine. There was also widespread starvation in Kazakhstan as Party agents tried to round up nomadic herders and peasants into collective agricultural and livestock farms (see Olcott 1981). Areas in southern Russia were also affected. In terms of sheer numbers, however, more Ukrainians died because of the Famine than any other nationality. Coercive measures in grain collection were particularly extensive in Ukraine, and the Russian-Ukrainian border was vigilantly guarded against importation of grain or significant quantities of food stuffs.

The Famine has become the subject of much scholarly inquiry, particularly the debate over the number of casualties it triggered. Wheatcroft (1990: 358), using census data, estimates the death-toll at four to five million; Mace (1986: 50) asserts that five to seven million deaths is a conservative estimate of the casualties sustained in Ukraine alone; and Conquest (1986: 306) estimates eight million total victims of the Famine, five million of whom were specifically in Ukraine. Conquest, however, counts separately another 6.5 million victims of dekulakization, ultimately making his estimates highest of all.

17. Widespread resistance to collectivization and dekulakization took many forms. Some peasants slaughtered their livestock or burnt their crops to avoid turning them over to the authorities. Many peasants fled to the cities. To stem the tide, the authorities forced some peasants to enter collective farms by razing their homes and destroying

their property. Stalin blamed the "excesses" of collectivization on overzealous local officials.

18. In 1929 there were 607,000 workers in heavy industry in Ukraine. In 1930, 80 percent of the new recruits who worked in the Donbas coal mines were Ukrainian peasants. By 1933 the number had risen to 1.1 million, the majority of whom were former peasants, now working in coal and metallurgical enterprises (Krawchenko 1985: 129). See Kuromiya 1988: 213–26 for an overview of the transformation of the labor market during the Famine and Liber 1992 and Krawchenko 1985: 116–20 for the specific ramifications of industrialization for the Ukrainian peasantry.

19. See Le Goff 1989 for a discussion of the importance of studying the manipulation of memory in a context, much like late-Soviet Ukraine, where social memories are primarily oral or where a collective memory is being recorded.

20. Maurice Halbwachs was a pioneer theorist of what he called the "social frames of collective memory" (1975, 1980). He argued that individual memory is present-oriented, structured by membership in social groups, and essentially an instrument of reconfiguration. Halbwach's seminal contribution came when he cogently argued for the ability of social milieus and social practice to structure and inform what had been considered a purely individual and self-contained faculty. When memories did not find some form of externalization, they withered, he argued.

21. A great number of studies on memory of Holocaust survivors exist which attempt to analyze this paradox. Among the best are Langer 1991, Felman and Laub 1992, and Young 1993.

22. Results of March 1991 referendum: 70.2 percent of the Ukrainian population supported what was labeled the "Gorbachev union," or preserving the USSR as a "renewed federation of equal sovereign republics." A second question asked whether one was in favor of a union "on the basis of the Ukrainian declaration of sovereignty." Republic-wide support averaged 10 percent higher for a confederation than for the Gorbachev union.

23. Over 90 percent of the total population voted to support independence. Support was lowest in Crimea where 54 percent voted for Ukrainian independence.

Chapter 3: On Being Soviet

1. "Moi adres ne dom, ne ulitsa. Moi adres Sovetskii Soiuz. . . . Segodnia ne lichnoie glavnoie, a svodka rabochego dnia." This song was one of the many penned by David Tuchmanov, a composer who now lives in Hamburg, Germany and makes his living as a restaurant pianist.

2. Grant's 1995 study of the Nivkhi of Sakhalin Island argues that many Nivkhi came to think of themselves as Soviet after the traditions and way of life upon which a Nivkhi identity depended were destroyed. For those who physically could not be taken for Russian and whose ethnic identity had been erased, forgotten, or otherwise made unavailable, a Soviet identity, as Soviet leaders intended, was all that was left.

3. See Pesman 1995 for a discussion of the numerous ways the corresponding Russian verbs and adjectives which trace their origins back to the central role of *krutit'-sia* reflect the role of this concept in daily life in post-Soviet society.

4. Because of the tendency to have one child per family, quite often people have

no brothers or sisters and only one child. As a result, many build relationships with friends, colleagues, and neighbors that are characterized by and referred to in kinship terms. Adopting family members compensates for small family sizes and serves to enhance the links of cooperation and dependence. The most widespread means of creating fictive kin is through *kumivstvo*, or according a friend the status of god-father (*kum*) or god-mother (*kuma*). The *kum* designation elevates the level of commitment and reciprocity between individuals and families.

5. Anthropologists have long documented these influential forms of nonmonetary exchange and their effects on social relations. Such exchange systems tend to predominate in nonmarket economies. See Mauss 1990, Malinowski 1961, and for a more recent study of the "gift economy" in China, Yang 1994.

6. Even after independence, in the cities the Russian names of Soviet-created bureaucracies fulfilling quintessentially Soviet functions were generally used.

7. Eventually, she did trade this apartment for another one with an improved location, which she now rents to one of the biggest international accounting firms. In the end, all the bureaucratic machinations contributed to procuring a steady, non-work-based form of hard currency income. Handsomely worth the effort, Nina thinks, in spite of the fact that she immigrated to the United States and now lives in Lexington, Kentucky.

8. Kornai (1980: 65–108) discusses the structure of socialist economics and provides insights to why the economic relations put in place by the socialist system in terms of production and distribution have at times proved to be incompatible with basic capitalist practices. Verdery (1996: 204–28) takes inspiration from this and suggests that perhaps the "transition" is not moving from socialism to capitalism but rather the possibility strongly exists that unexpected economic relations and practices, based perhaps on feudalism, are emerging.

9. To facilitate economic relations, on the occasion of the 300th anniversary of the unification of Ukraine and Russia, Khrushchev transferred Crimea, a region with an ethnically Russian majority, as a sign of "friendship among peoples," to the Ukrainian Soviet Socialist Republic on February 19, 1954. The republic to which Crimea belonged was considered at that time no more than a bureaucratic detail. Given Crimea's dependence on Ukrainian resources, particularly water, the administration of a planned economy was simplified by the transfer.

10. Ukraine is made up of twenty-four oblasts and one autonomous republic, Crimea. By far the most tense and complicated region in Ukraine is Crimea, a small peninsula with colossal historic, strategic, and sentimental value. First, the imperial aristocracy, and then the Communist Party officials, built sumptuous palaces and dachas there. Offering the sea, a mountainous terrain, lush vegetation, and a temperate climate, the region has a magnetic appeal.

Sevastopol emerged as the main naval port and the home of the Black Sea Fleet in the early nineteenth century. During the Crimean War and both World Wars, the port attained almost mythic status for its military might. The signature song of the town says it all: "Legendary Sevastopol, / Beyond reach of enemies, / Legendary Sevastopol, / The city of Russian sailors."

Many Russian political leaders and most of the Russian populace have difficulty imagining Crimea as the "near abroad." Tatiana Tolstaya, a renowned author and social critic, recently wrote, "This territory—the Crimea—has no relation to Ukraine. Russia won it at war in the eighteenth century, and Khrushchev illegally transferred it to Ukraine in 1955, as Vladimir Lukin, a historian, member of parliament, and former Russian ambassador to Washington, once confirmed to me in a conversation. The signing of the agreement on the transfer took place *before* the then Supreme Soviet voted its formal agreement, which violated even "despised" Soviet laws" (*New York Review of Books* 44, no. 7: 13–14). Reasoning likes this is used to buttress the claim that the Crimea "illegally" became part of Ukraine and therefore the agreement should not be considered valid and Crimea should be returned to Russia. At least four separate groups lay claim to this valued peninsula: the Crimean Tatars, the Russian Federation, the Ukrainian State, and a Crimean separatist movement.

11. See Verdery 1996: 206 for an expanded discussion of how the practice of rationing with coupons bound individuals to their place of residence or workplace simply to procure goods. Similarly, the practice served to exclude undesirable competitors for scarce goods and created a fortress mentality.

Chapter 4: Educational Reform

1. To collect data on how the teaching of Ukrainian history has changed, I spent between one and three weeks at fifteen public schools in L'viv, Kyiv, and Kharkiv (and in two rural schools for comparison). Massive changes in public education were swiftly initiated by government decree following independence in 1991 in order to ukrainianize the first post-Soviet generation. I observed the initial implementation of these vast curricular changes in 1992–93. Through interviews and observation in the classroom, I was able to record the reactions of students, parents, teachers, and administrators to these changes. In each of the three aforementioned cities I visited Russian language schools, schools that were changing from Russian to Ukrainian as the medium of instruction, and Ukrainian language schools. I also conducted interviews and observed in five private schools, three of which I describe here.

2. Contemporary efforts to ukrainianize the educational system are not new in Ukraine, but rather, represent another phase in an ongoing effort. One of the central demands made after the failed Revolution of 1905 by Ushinskyi and Korf, two of the more vocal Ukrainian educational reformers, was to institute primary education in Ukrainian in Ukraine. As of 1914, only half of the school-age children in the empire received any formal education (see McClelland 1979). Rural areas were particularly underserved. Of the 577 secondary schools in Ukraine in 1914, only twenty were in rural areas (Prokofieva et al. 1967: 326). This is in stark contrast to the near universal literacy in Ukraine today. Aside from this critical difference, there are similarities in the projects to Ukrainianize public education.

3. For a discussion of the workings of pre-perestroika schools, especially the role of ideology in socialization and of how ideology informed the curriculum of secondary schools, see Bereday et al. 1960, Dunstan 1978, and Pearson 1990. Pearson (1990) examines changes in the educational system from the 1960s to the 1980s, paying particular attention to how the system became dysfunctional. She analyzes the sources of youth alienation, disrespect for authority, and family breakdown.

4. See Pennar et al. 1971 and Prokofíeva et al. 1967 for a historical overview of how Soviet education policy was received and implemented in each of the republics. See esp. Pennar et al. 1971: 297–310 for an analysis of how the educational system was viewed as the "center of Russian influence" in Central Asia and how this bred alienation and served to discourage students from pursuing higher education in this region.

5. "Ukraina XXI Stolitta: Derzhavna Natsional'na Prohrama 'OSVITA' " (The state national program of education), report issued by a commission of the Ministry of Education, Kyiv, Ukraine, 1992, p. 3.

6. Officially, reform efforts in the late 1980s centered on enhancing individuality while still championing economic collectivism in spite of the fact that the simultaneous propagation of such ideals was already showing strain. See *Uchitel'skaia Gazeta*, April 1990, p. 1. "Humanism" was also held up as a guiding principle of educational reform. One of the most notable changes occurred in 1990 when teachers were officially allowed to teach history from a variety of perspectives, although to some degree this was no doubt already occurring after Gorbachev's famous call in 1988 to fill in the "blank spots" of Soviet history. See *Uchitel'skaia Gazeta*, December 28, 1989

7. "Ukraina XXI Stolitta," p. 4. Most political rhetoric still refers to "the people of Ukraine" as opposed to the "Ukrainian people," a distinction with colossal ramifications for a multiethnic population. This document is laced with references to the latter.

8. In a parallel move to desovietize schools, in 1992 a government decree was issued stating that each school had to remove all Soviet propaganda, portraits of Lenin, slogans, etc. As there was nothing to replace them with—save a few portraits of Taras Shevchenko, the Ukrainian national poet—some teachers refused. This is particularly true in rural areas where, materially speaking, schools are much more modest than in urban areas. The enforcement of such decrees has become random and ineffective. Of course, nearly all school interiors are decorated with mosaics and mural paintings depicting socialist realist themes, such as Lenin leading children further down the path to communism, members of the Pioneer youth organization busily at work, and kitschy nature scenes, and these all remain.

9. Arel (1995a: 174–77) argues that such reform has important political implications. I would add that the reforms of the educational system, both implemented and pending, most likely contributed to the strong showing of support for Leonid Kuchma in the presidential elections in 1994. At the time, Kuchma's knowledge of Ukrainian was rudimentary although he was diligently studying the state language of the country of which he was soon to become president. Arel notes that "russophones," meaning Russian-speaking ethnic Russians and ethnic Ukrainians, supported independence on the basis of non-national appeals to the "people of Ukraine." Yet moves to derussify the curriculum deprives them of "part of their identity, a bicultural identity in many cases bequeathed to them by many generations" (1995a: 175).

10. By 1994 the Ukrainian state television channel began to abandon the prominent folklore component in its programming realizing that it was driving viewers to the Russian channels. Prime time programming on the Ukrainian state channel is now filled with soap operas purchased from the West, such as "Dynasty" and "Santa Barbara," which are dubbed into Ukrainian.

11. For example, one school in Kyiv had ninety students in the eleventh grade and four teachers who needed the eleventh grade textbook. The school had two copies.

Another school had only seventeen copies for nearly one hundred students and these were kept locked in the library to prevent theft.

12. Pavlyshyn (1991) argues that the same is true for the recasting of Ukrainian literature. Glasnost, rather than bringing forth new ideas and theories on the literary process, has swept in an atmosphere dominated by efforts to produce the definitive new textbook on the history of Ukrainian literature (1991: 14–15). Efforts to revise text-books are overshadowed by the need for "national consensus in education" and the revalidation of claims for "Ukrainian national self-assertion" and debates over how much of the socialist frame of reference should be maintained in school and university pedagogy. Under such circumstances, he argues, there is little hope of charting new literary territory or of moving beyond received ideas. Quite the same critique could be made of pedagogical historiography.

13. See page 214, note 16, for an overview of how Western historians have inter-preted the severity of the Famine.

14. These schools should not be confused with the specialized schools (*spetsshkily*) created during the Soviet period to offer an intensive program of study in a particular discipline. Although admission to these schools was quite competitive, in style, method-ology, and overall curricula, these specialized schools differed little from standard state schools. They in no way offered an alternative to standard schools, merely an intensive, specialized program of study. See Dunstan 1978 for an overview of specialized educa-tion in the Soviet Union and esp. pp. 197–208 for a discussion of how specialized schools differ from "mass schools."

15. Dr. Olena Bilous, the rector of the Ternopil Institute of Economics and Entre-preneurship, is studying the phenomena of private education in Ukraine. These statis-tics come from an interview she gave to the *Ukrainian Weekly*, February 2, 1997, p. 8.

16. For overviews of the status of private education in specific countries, see McLean and Voskresenskaya 1992: 86 for Russia; Kozakiewicz 1992: 95–96 for Poland and von Kopp 1992: 107–9 for Czechoslovakia. The trend has been particularly note-worthy in Poland. In 1989 there were only thirty-two secular private high schools. One year later two hundred had been created. This does not even take into account the formidable presence of Catholic schools (Kozakiewicz 1992: 95–96).

17. Generally, Western historians have argued that the three eastern Slavic peoples (Ukrainians, Russians, and Belarusans) share a common origin and only began to di-verge after the Mongol invasions of the thirteenth century. See Subtelny 1994 and Magocsi 1996 for a comprehensive overview of Ukrainian history and a discussion of Kievan Rus' and how this period relates to subsequent historical development.

18. In Western Ukraine, where four indigenous denominations, the Uniate or Ukrainian Catholic Church, the Ukrainian Autocephalous Orthodox Church, the Ukrainian Orthodox Church–Kyiv Patriarchate and the Russian Orthodox Church, or as it is sometimes called, Ukrainian Orthodox Church–Moscow Patriarchate, plus a multitude of sects, have followers, the policy often simply involves strongly encourag-ing students to attend the church of their choice.

19. This school, like many of these new elite schools, marks its distinctiveness by referring to itself as a "collegium." Others use the European terms "gymnasium" or "lycée." To ensure confidentiality of the interview respondents, the names of all private schools have been changed.

20. The Kyiv Mohyla Academy reopened in 1992 on the historic site of the original seventeenth-century monastery with substantial funding from the Ukrainian diaspora and other Western sources such as the Soros Foundation. During Soviet rule, several buildings in the monastic complex were destroyed. Others eventually became the Navy's training center for *politruki*, or "political commissars." It was their job to ensure that the Party maintained control over the naval forces. In a post-Soviet world, these naval officers are now called "psychological counselors." In a Felliniesque twist, until September 1993, these uniformed naval officers trained in Party doctrine and Marxist-Leninist ideology walked the halls of the Academy side-by-side with aspiring Ukrainian nationalist leaders. By 1996, Kyiv Mohyla Academy had 900 students and offered one of the most ambitious university programs of study in Ukraine.

21. Soviet policy has been inconsistent concerning single-sex education. Following the Revolution of 1917 the spirit of women's emancipation ushered in an era of coeducation. However, under Stalin, this policy came under reconsideration. In 1943 a decree was issued ordering restitution of single-sex education. Single-sex education was implemented in the cities but in rural areas this was fraught with logistical complications, such as shortages of additional school buildings and teachers. In 1954 Khrushchev decreed that coeducation would be reintroduced the following year, and since then only physical education and domestic science classes have remained single sex.

22. The revival of national traditions is seen as inseparable from redefining the role of women in society to be in keeping with mythologized ideals of motherhood and a glorification of the domestic sphere. This trend is quite dominant throughout the former Soviet bloc. See Verdery 1996: 61–82 for an insightful overview and Funk and Mueller 1993 for a collection of essays detailing changes in gender roles in specific Eastern European countries and the former Soviet Union. See Marsh 1996 for changes in post-Soviet Russia and Ukraine and Rubchak 1996 for post-Soviet Ukraine specifically. Rubchak claims women's associations in post-Soviet Ukraine have made such themes as family, self-sacrifice, and the importance of revitalizing national traditions central. Judging by the published statements of these associations, the needs of women are unequivocally subordinated to the needs of the nation. Often laced with religious references, the leaders of women's associations see women as the vehicle by which the "moral spirit" of the Ukrainian people will be restored.

Chapter 5: Festivals

1. In 1991 I attended the Chernova Ruta Festival. Information on other Chernova Ruta festivals mentioned in this chapter was obtained through interviews, press reports, and other published sources.

2. See Bahry 1994 for an overview of contemporary rock music in Ukraine as well as a discussion of the 1989 Chervona Ruta Festival. Ramet (1994) and Cushman (1995) address the interconnections between rock music and cultural change in Eastern Europe and Russia respectively. Slobin (1996) analyzes how various musical genres are a reflection of cultural change in Eastern Europe and a force prompting reexamination of received values and practices formed under a socialist regime.

3. Taras Kurchyk, "My zabuly vse" (We have forgotten everything), from the

album *Pop Muzykanty* (Pop Musicians) (Toronto-Kyiv: Kobza, 1989); translated in R. Bahry 1994: 254.

4. Ibid., p. 256.

5. Following is the Ukrainian text as transcribed from the Snake Brothers' album *My Khloptsi z Bandershtadtu*, recorded in 1991 and distributed by Audio Ukraina: "Zasnuly hnani i holodni / Khto buv nikym toi stav nichym / Tse bude zavtra a s'ohodni / Ne khochesh spaty to lezhy i movchy / A na Ukraini lad i spokii / Shchebeche soloveiko / Z namy Partiia i Boh."

6. "My khloptsi z Bandershtadtu / Khodymo do tserkvy / Shanuiemo bat'kiv / Nikhto tak iak my ne vmie huliaty / Poky surmy ne zahraly / Baraban ne zbyv / Ie khto hovorit' bandyty, khulihany / Z toho bolota / liudei ne bude." This text is also transcribed from the Snake Brothers' album *My Khloptsi z Bandershtadtu*, recorded in 1991 and distributed by Audio Ukraina.

7. Victor Turner, building on the work of van Gennep and his schema of a tripartite ritual process involving separation-transition-reintroduction, further theorized on the nature of the transition phase of ritual. He described it as a liminal, or betwixt or between phase during which a feeling of communitas or "communion of equal individuals" emerges (1967: 96). The dialectical process of social life, he reasoned, suggests that communitas and social structure, or transitions and states, are mutually constituting and interdependent.

Chapter 6: Commemoration and the State Calendar

1. I was fortunate to have been in Ukraine in the summers of 1990 and 1991 when numerous pro-Ukrainian independence demonstrations took place which drew heavily on historical representations. This provided a solid basis of comparison with the state-sponsored and popular ceremonies and demonstrations I observed, and when possible videotaped, after independence from 1992 to 1995. The unsanctioned popular commemorations I observed include Great October Revolution Day in Kyiv (1992), May Day in Kyiv (1993 and 1994), the anniversary of the Chernobyl nuclear accident in L'viv (1993), a pro-Soviet, pro-Russian demonstration in Sevastopol (1993), and an anti-Ukrainian demonstration in Kharkiv (1993). For data on commemorations I did not personally witness, I rely on interviews and press reports.

2. The role of commemoration in shaping collective memories and historical consciousness has received quite a bit of scholarly attention in the past decade. Notable studies that address the interrelationship among commemoration and history and community and identity formation include Bodnar 1991, Butler 1989, Connerton 1989, Gillis 1994, and Mosse 1990.

3. For a discussion of attempts following the French Revolution to construct a more secular calendar by making adjustments to the temporal framework of daily life, see Zerubavel 1981: 70–100 and 1977.

4. The most notable works on commemoration in the USSR are Binns 1979 and 1980 and Lane 1981. Binns argues that rather than a mere reflection of Marxist-Leninist ideology and a crass display of state power, the Soviet ceremonial system was actually the result of a negotiation over time between individual and group appropriations of ceremony and state efforts to generate patriotism and allegiance. Lane provides an

extensive historical and descriptive account of the development of the Soviet state calendar.

5. Narkompros was the People's Commissariat of Enlightenment and was responsible for art, propaganda, and education. Proletkult was an organization devoted to working-class culture, which was defined as "proletarian" and "collective."

6. Durov was making a pun on the well-known Marxist slogan "Workers of the World Unite!"

7. By 1929, Lenin's rather tolerant Law on Religion was under revision. Religion steadily became equated with opposition to the revolution. Religious people, beliefs, practices, etc., were repeatedly the butt of satirical and agitational humor. The show trials of 1929 and 1930 and a wave of religious persecution eventually established atheism as the official doctrine of the land.

8. It also became the custom to schedule cultural performances and amateur events with revolutionary themes around the Great October Revolution anniversary celebrations. For example, the initiation rituals into the Pioneers, the children's youth organization of the Communist Party, were frequently held on the eve of the November 7th commemoration, both drawing on and adding to the importance of the anniversary.

9. The process of removing the overtly religious and sacred components from such life cycle rituals as weddings, baptisms, and funerals and in their place developing secularized rituals to echo socialist ideology was a remarkable feat of Soviet society. Unfortunately, a description and analysis of these secular rituals is beyond the scope of this book. For an overview of such rituals in the USSR, see Lane 1981.

10. Hrytsenko (n.d.) details how Shevchenko was transformed into a champion of the Soviet cause and achieved mythic status as a hero of the people in commemoration and, as we will see in the next chapter, in monument too. Although a nationalist leader to many, from the beginning, Bolshevik leaders embraced Shevchenko as a symbol of the people's resistance to oppressive tsarist rule and advanced a cult of "Red Shevchenko." Nationalist leaders now struggle to peel away the various roles and myths, such as proletarian hero, that Shevchenko was cast into. Grabowicz (1982) analyzes how myths were forged from Shevchenko's life by groups often pursuing contradictory aims.

11. For an overview of Rukh's building momentum during this period and especially the organization's efforts to forge a nationalist historiography using commemorations and anti-commemorations, see Kuzio and Wilson 1994: 99–121.

12. The World Bank Report on Poverty in Ukraine (Report No. 15602-UA) details the difficulty the beleaguered Ukrainian state is having in maintaining payments to victims of the Chernobyl disaster and their families promised during Soviet rule. Furthermore, the report suggests that limited government funds could perhaps be better spent on means-tested forms of public assistance, which none of the Chernobyl benefits currently are. The tenth anniversary of the accident only revived fears and memories of the disaster. Talk of reducing social assistance benefits to victims to include only the truly needy remains a topic too politically sensitive to broach.

13. Dawson's study of eco-nationalism concludes that the environmental movement in Ukraine grafted itself onto the nationalist movement agitating for indepen-

dence. Once independence was achieved, the environmental movement lost much of its political force and popular appeal (1996: 81).

14. As part of the commemoration of the fiftieth anniversary of the Famine, a substantial oral history project was undertaken in North America among immigrants from Ukraine to record the last living memories of the Famine of 1932–33. The project was directed by James Mace and resulted in a three-volume compilation of interviews of eyewitness testimony to the Famine. See Mace and Heretz 1990.

15. In referring to the guilt the world has before Ukrainians, Drach is alluding to several Western journalists, in particular William Duranty of the *New York Times*, who under close supervision visited Ukraine while the Famine was claiming hundreds of lives per day and later reported that there was no famine. The Ukrainian diaspora has long suspected that these reporters chose to only see and report on the impressive pace of modernization because of their Soviet sympathies. Without acknowledgment of the Famine from Soviet authorities or from Western reporters, there was virtually no international aid forthcoming to alleviate the suffering of the Ukrainian peasantry.

16. This point about the involvement of local Ukrainians in creating and sustaining conditions that contributed directly to the famine is also documented in the oral histories presented in Mace and Heretz 1990.

17. The phrase "Banderite trident" refers to Stepan Bandera, the leader of the Organization of Ukrainian Nationalists, an armed force that originally collaborated with the Nazis during World War II against the Soviet Red Army before they turned against both foreign armies. Bandera was eventually exiled and died in Munich in 1959.

"Petliurite flag" refers to Symon Petliura (1879–1926) who was the president of the Directory of the Ukrainian People's Republic and the commander of its armed forces. The Ukrainian People's Republic was an independent state, declared during the confusion and chaos of the civil war following the Revolution of 1917. Petliura's regime came to an end after he forged an alliance with the Ukrainian-Galician (UHA) armies against the Red Army. Surrounded by the Red Army and facing imminent defeat, he fled to Warsaw in 1920 and lived out the rest of his life in exile. Perhaps more than any other individual, Petliura has personified the struggle for Ukrainian independence. Petliura is also associated with the vicious pogroms committed by the UNR troops in 1918–20.

18. On September 29–30, 1941, approximately 34,000 Jews were led to the Babyi Yar valley, shot, and left for dead in an enormous ravine. By the end of World War II, over 150,000 Jews were executed at this ravine. Execution was the most frequent method for exterminating Jews in central and eastern Ukraine. The massacres at Babyi Yar represent the single most devastating event for Kyiv's Jewish population. In 1976 a monument was erected to honor the "Soviet citizens" who died at Babyi Yar.

19. See Anderson 1991: 9–10 for an interesting discussion of the unifying appeal and symbolism of monuments to an unknown soldier and an eternal flame. He links such symbolic monuments to an individual's ability to "imagine" him- or herself as part of a national community to which they feel a certain allegiance.

20. These quotations are taken from the "The 50th Anniversary of the Formation of the Ukrainian Insurgent Army," *Ukrainian Quarterly* 48, no. 2 (summer 1992): 133.

21. See "Holidays for Everyone" (*Sviata glia vcikh*), *Den'*, May 7, 1997, p. 4.

22. The Ukrainian word for holiday, *sviato*, is related to *sviatyi*, meaning "holy" or "sacred."

23. See Zerubavel 1981: 101–37 for a discussion of how such cultural institutions as the sabbath serve to maintain qualitative distinctions between sacred and profane temporal domains. Zerubavel also discusses how sacred concepts of time shape fundamental categorical distinctions and structure everyday practices in a multitude of contexts.

24. The relationships of the various churches in Ukraine to each other and to the state is beyond the scope of this study. Suffice it to say that the fragmentation in religious affiliation potentially can create and sustain intra-ethnic tensions. Yet the splintering of the Orthodox churches and the increasing number of Protestant denominations, and a host of apocalyptic sects and exotic cults suggests that any one church will have difficulty establishing itself as *the* national church.

25. Verdery (1996: 53–55) notes how the arrhythmic nature of commemoration under socialism mimicked the arrhythmic production patterns of slacking and storming. Furthermore, she notes that a consequence of socialism's arrhythm was an undermining of a sense of "normal" by instituting uncertainty and unpredictability in everyday life.

Chapter 7: Urban Landscape

1. I have taken the phrase "empire of signs" from Roland Barthes's (1970a) book of the same name. Barthes argues that culture functions as a semiotic system of signs and, much like a text, can be read and mined for meaning. Elsewhere, he makes the same case for an urban semiotics by reading the signs inscribed in urban space as a means of analyzing culture. See Barthes 1970b: 11–13. For a critique of the space as text metaphor see Lefebvre 1991.

2. The spelling of the city's name in Russian and Ukrainian using the Cyrillic alphabet is the same, although the pronunciation varies slightly from one language to the next.

3. Originally published in *Isvestiya VTsIK*, Moscow, April 14, 1918

4. The Orthodox Church equated sculpture with idols and pagan magic and placed a ban on sculpture in churches prior to the Revolution.

5. Two women were approved for commemoration in monument, Sofiia Perovskaia, an accomplished terrorist in the People's Will Party, and the German communist Rosa Luxemburg. See Bonnell 1991: 267–88 for an interesting discussion of female allegorical images symbolizing such concepts as "freedom" and "liberty" in monument and early Soviet political art.

6. In experimental theater, V. E. Meierkhol'd, one of the movement's most effective proponents, used "scaffoldings" instead of traditional sets for his actors, who frequently wore overalls and practiced his acting technique of "bio-mechanics." In literature, the constructivists advocated the "technical rigging" of culture, as exemplified by I. L. Sel'vinskii's poem "The Thief" (1922), written entirely in the vernacular of criminals. See Hedgbeth 1975: 23–36 and Deak 1975: 7–22 for a discussion of transgressions of established art forms during this period.

7. Referred to as "engineering art," Tatlin's monument was hailed for its unifica-

tion of art and industry in celebration of technology. Consisting of two separate spirals built around a diagonal axis and adorned with three vertically stacked rooms of glass all spinning at different speeds, the monument looked like a cross between the Leaning Tower of Pisa and the Eiffel Tower. Both technological difficulties and an overly grandiose scheme for erecting it across the expansive Neva River in Petrograd impeded the monument's realization, and ultimately it was never built. See Lodder 1993.

8. In 1934 the Union of Soviet Writers statue defined socialist realism as follows: "It demands of the artist the truthful, historically concrete representation of reality in its revolutionary development. Moreover, the truthfulness and historical concreteness of the artistic representation of reality must be linked with the task of ideological transformation and education of workers in the spirit of socialism" (cited in Tertz 1965: 716).

9. This quotation is from Andrei Zhdanov's speech to the first Congress of Soviet Writers. See Bowlt 1976: 293.

10. In all fairness, the same could be said of suburbs across America, so many of which revolve around shopping strips and malls filled with chain stores. The tendency toward conformity in urban planning, be it propelled by the capitalist economies of scale in the United States or the socialist economies of central planning in the USSR, is undeniable, suggesting that perhaps in large and diverse countries a sense of familiarity born of conformity in the urban landscape is not altogether unwelcome.

11. However, the highest mountain in the Soviet Union, located in Central Asia, was renamed "Peak Communism."

12. I learned this one night while walking around Kharkiv with friends. There are a number of kiosks selling an eclectic array of goods on the main square. Judging by the shattered glass that one frequently sees in the morning, kiosk break-ins are a recurring problem. I assumed that the police officers standing about were there to protect the kiosks against thieves. My comment elicited wide eyes of wonder and peals of laughter. "The police are here to protect Lenin! As for the kiosks, it's their problem if they get ripped off!" said Slava, one of the few entrepreneurs born of the break-down of the Soviet system, with a smirk on his face. Slava has a post-Soviet profession: he matches new companies with investors and helps them all plow through the morass of government regulation. The idea that the police would actually protect private property or individual investment struck Slava as touchingly naive.

13. Only among the generations over sixty years of age, and especially among those who had prestigious professions, did I find some people who, although thoroughly critical of the Soviet system, refused to criticize Lenin. They preferred instead to heap blame on Stalin and his sinister regime to explain the many ills of Soviet society. Trotsky asserted that Stalin staged a counterrevolution, corrupting and contorting many of the original values and plans of the Bolsheviks. See Trotsky (1972). Many educated elite over sixty, who comparatively speaking, lived quite well under the Soviet system, subscribe to this view. This interpretation has been repeated by many Western historians. See Davies 1989.

14. Felix Dzerzhinsky was the founder of the Cheka (secret police) during the civil war and one of the Party's best organizers. The Cheka eventually evolved into the KGB. In 1924, he became chairman of the Supreme Economic Council, where he, under the directives of Stalin, effectively pushed for rapid industrialization.

15. Prior to the Revolution, Kharkiv, the largest city of eastern Ukraine and the capital of Soviet Ukraine from 1917 to 1934, had only three monuments: one to the Russian poet Pushkin; one to Gogol, who was from Ukraine and used Ukrainian themes in some of his short stories, which were written in Russian; and one to the founder and namesake of Kharkiv University, V. H. Karazin. See Leibfreid et al. 1987: 13.

16. The Lenin monument, built in the central hall of the Guggenheim-like honey comb Lenin Museum in Kyiv, is another instance of Soviet construction built to last until the end of time. The museum closed briefly in fall 1991 and reopened as *Ukrainskii Dim*, Ukrainian House, designed to showcase contemporary Ukrainian art. They had succeeded in removing almost all of Lenin from the central hall of the museum. However, the pedestal was most likely built right into the foundation. When the museum reopened, the remains of the Lenin monument, which presumably could not be removed, were boxed up, coffin-like, and covered with a banner reading "Ukrainian House."

This was brought to my attention when two artists, both of whom had spent considerable time in the building when it exhibited Leninism and even more now that it exhibits art, were arguing over whether the monument had been a full statue of Lenin or simply his head. Neither could remember Lenin's form clearly, although they were both certain that it was Lenin. The signifier was lost in memory, although the signified was easily retrieved.

17. For several months in late 1992, adding to the surrealism, there was even an ad encouraging Ukrainians, at the height of the Serbo-Croatian war, to deposit their savings in a Zagreb bank.

18. Judging by the fact that monuments to other Soviet heroes, who now inspire divided opinions among an increasingly vocal population, have also been subsequently painted gold, I think it is safe to conclude that local authorities ordered the "golden Lenin." Although some I spoke with were convinced that only the authorities could have painted Lenin gold, others were uncertain. It is difficult to say who the subsequent painters were. The amorphous nature of agency is reflected in language: the invisible hand of "they" is constantly evoked as people dispense with a subject and say simply "they painted him" or "they took him down."

19. The symbolism of the Ukrainian flag is popularly explained as yellow for the wheat fields of the former "breadbasket of Europe" and blue for the sky.

20. At the Twentieth Party Congress Khrushchev made his "secret speech" where he condemned the cult of personality of Stalin and the excesses of Stalinist rule.

21. In 1926, the monastery was converted to a museum. Only during World War II was the monastery, like many other churches across Ukraine, opened up and allowed to function once again. The monastery was in full operation from 1942 until it was reverted to a museum once again in 1961. Today, some parts of the museum are still open but all the churches not under renovation are being used for religious purposes once again.

22. The sword and shield are the emblems of the KGB.

23. For a discussion of the term as well as the use of women in Soviet propaganda see Bonnell 1991: 267–88 and Stites 1986.

24. This poem, written in Russian, was one of five Yevtushenko poems upon which Dmitrii Shostakovich based his Thirteenth Symphony.

25. The male depiction of republics was relatively rare, given the prevalence of war memorials commemorating patriotism and sacrifice in which the homeland is nearly always allegorically represented as female.

26. "Abroad" in this narrative means other Eastern European socialist countries. Although it was difficult to travel to Eastern Europe, it was far easier to arrange than travel to Western countries, which was, of course, a rare privilege accorded to only very few trusted Party cadres.

27. See Buck-Morss 1990: 159 for a discussion of the mythic elements of cultural objects.

Afterword

1. See the World Bank Poverty Report No. 15602-UA, issued June 27, 1996, for a detailed account as to who has suffered poverty in post-Soviet Ukrainian society and to what degree and the means by which this poverty is manifest.

2. Verdery evokes the notion of "social schizophrenia" as a means to describe the bipolarity that the socialist system bred in individual psyches (1996: 94).

References

Aksyonov, Vasilii
1983 *Island of Crimea: A Novel*. Translated by Michael W. Heim. New York: Random House.

Amin, Shahid
1995 *Event, Metaphor, Memory: Chauri Chaura, 1922–1992*. Berkeley and Los Angeles: University of California Press.

Anderson, Benedict
1991 *Imagined Communities: Reflections on the Origin and Spread of Nationalism*. London: Verso.

Appadurai, A.
1981 "The Past as a Scarce Resource." *Man*, n.s., 16: 201–19.

Apple, Michael W.
1990 *Ideology and Curriculum*. 2d ed. New York: Routledge.

Arel, Dominique
1995a "Ukraine: The Temptation of The Nationalizing State." In Vladimir Tismaneanu, ed., *Political Culture and Civil Society in the Former Soviet Union*. Armonk, N.Y.: M. E. Sharpe.

1995b "Language Politics in Independent Ukraine." *Nationalities Papers*. 23 (3): 597–622.

1995c "The Russian Factor and Territorial Polarization in Ukraine." Paper presented at the conference "Peoples, Nations, Identities: The Russian-Ukrainian Encounter," Columbia University, September 22, 1995.

Armstrong, John
1990 *Ukrainian Nationalism*. Englewood, Colo.: Ukrainian Academic Press.

Asad, Talad, ed.
1988 *Anthropology and the Colonial Encounter*. Atlantic Highlands, N.J.: Humanities Press.

Bahry, Donna
1993 "Society Transformed? Rethinking the Social Roots of Perestroika." *Slavic Review* 52 (3): 512–54.

Bahry, Romana M., ed.
1989 *Echos of Glasnost in Soviet Ukraine*. North York, Ontario: Captus University Publications.

1994   "Rock Culture and Rock Music in Ukraine." In Sabrina Petra Ramet, ed., *Rocking the State: Rock Music and Politics in Eastern Europe and Russia*. Boulder, Colo.: Westview Press.

Balzer, Marjorie Mandelstam
1981   "Rituals of Gender Identity: Markers of Siberian Khanty, Ethnicity, Status, and Belief." *American Anthropologist* 83 (4): 850–67.

Barthes, Roland
1970a   *L'Empire des Signes*. Paris: Gallimard.

1970b   "Semiologie et Urbanisme." *Architecture d'Aujourd'hui*, December 1970–January 1971, pp. 11–13.

Battaglia, Debbora
1990   *On the Bones of the Serpent: Person, Memory, and Mortality in Sabarl Island Society*. Chicago: University of Chicago Press.

Battaglia, Debbora, ed.
1995   *Rhetorics of Self-Making*. Berkeley and Los Angeles: University of California Press.

Beezley, William H.
1994   "The Porfirian Smart Set Anticipates Thorstein Veblen in Guadalajara." In William H. Beezley, Cheryl English Martin, and William E. French, eds., *Rituals of Rule, Rituals of Resistance*, Wilmington, Del.: : Scholarly Resources.

Benjamin, Walter
1968   "Theses on the Philosophy of History." In *Illuminations*, translated by Harry Zohn, edited by Hannah Arendt. New York: Schocken.

Benson, Susan Porter, Stephen Brier, and Roy Rosenzweig, eds.
1986   *Presenting the Past*. Philadelphia: Temple University Press.

Bereday, George Z. F., William W. Brickman, and Gerald H. Read, eds.
1960   *The Changing Soviet School: The Comparative Education Society Field Study in the U.S.S.R.* Boston: Houghton Mifflin.

Bhabha, Homi K.
1990   *Nation and Narration*. New York: Routledge.

Bilinsky, Yaroslav
1964   *The Second Soviet Republic: The Ukraine after World War II*. New Brunswick, N.J.: Rutgers University Press.

Binns, Christopher
1979   "The Changing Face of Power: Revolution and Accommodation in the Development of the Soviet Ceremonial System, I." *Man* 14 (4): 585–606.

1980   "The Changing Face of Power: Revolution and Accommodation in the Development of the Soviet Ceremonial System, II." *Man* 15 (1): 170–87.

Blanchot, Maurice
1986   *The Writing of the Disaster*. Translated by Ann Smock. Lincoln: University of Nebraska Press.

Bloch, Marc
1989   *The Feudal Society*. Chicago: University of Chicago Press.

Blumberg, Hans
1985   *Work on Myth*. Translated by Robert M. Wallace. Cambridge, Mass.: MIT Press.

Bodnar, John
1991   *Remaking America: Public Memory, Commemoration, and Patriotism in the Twentieth Century*. Princeton, N.J.: Princeton University Press.

Bonnell, Victoria E.
1991   "The Representation of Women in Early Soviet Political Art." *Russian Review* 50 (3): 267–88.

1988   "The Representation of Politics and the Politics of Representation." *Russian Review* 47 (3): 315–22.

Borneman, John
1992   *Belonging in the Two Berlins: Kin, State, Nation*. New York: Cambridge University Press.

Bourdieu, Pierre
1967   "Systems of Education and Systems of Thought." *International Social Science Journal* 19: 338–58.

1973   "Cultural Reproduction and Social Reproduction." In Richard Brown, ed., *Knowledge, Education and Cultural Change*. London: Tavistock Publications.

1988   *Homo Academicus*. Translated by Peter Collier. Stanford, Calif.: Stanford University Press.

1990   *In Other Words*. Stanford, Calif.: Stanford University Press.

1991   *Outline of a Theory of Practice*. Translated by Richard Nice. Cambridge: Cambridge University Press.

Bourguet, Marie-Noelle, Lucette Valensi, and Nathan Wachtel, eds.
1990   *Between Memory and History*. New York: Harwood Academic Press.

Bowlt, John E.
1978   "Russian Sculpture and Lenin's Plan of Monumental Propaganda." In Henry A. Millon and Linda Nochlin, eds., *Art and Architecture in the Service of Politics*. Cambridge, Mass.: MIT Press.

Bowlt, John E., ed.
1976   *Russian Art of the Avant-Garde: Theory and Criticism, 1902–1934*. Translated by John Bowlt. New York: Viking Press.

Boyarin, Jonathan
1992 *Storms from Paradise*. Minneapolis: University of Minnesota Press.

Boyarin, Jonathan, ed.
1994 *Remapping Memory: The Politics of TimeSpace*. Minneapolis: University of Minnesota Press.

Breuilly, John
1982 *Nationalism and the State*. New York: St. Martin's Press.

Bridenthal, Renate, and Nancy Koonz, eds.
1977 *Becoming Visible: Women in European History*. Boston: Houghton Mifflin.

Bromley, Julian, and Viktor Kozlov
1989 "The Theory of Ethnos and Ethnic Processes in Soviet Social Sciences." In *Comparative Study of Society and History* 31 (3): 425–38..

Bromwich, David
1992 *Politics by Other Means: Higher Education and Group Thinking*. New Haven, Conn.: Yale University Press.

Brubaker, Rogers
1994 "Nationhood and the National Question in the Soviet Union and Post-Soviet Eurasia: An Institutionalist Account." *Theory and Society* 23 (1): 47–78.

Buck-Morss, Susan
1990 *The Dialectics of Seeing: Walter Benjamin and the Arcades Project*. Cambridge, Mass.: MIT Press.

Burawoy, Michael, and Janos Lukacs
1992 *The Radiant Past: Ideology and Reality in Hungary's Road to Capitalism*. Chicago: University of Chicago Press.

Burke, Peter
1989 "History as Social Memory." In Thomas Butler, ed., *Memory: History, Culture and the Mind*. New York: Basil Blackwell.

Chatterjee, Partha
1986 *Nationalist Thought and the Colonial World*. Minneapolis: University of Minnesota Press.

1993 *The Nation and Its Fragments: Colonial and Postcolonial Histories*. Princeton, N.J.: Princeton University Press.

Clark, Katerina
1981 *The Soviet Novel: History as Ritual*. Chicago: University of Chicago Press.

Clements, Barbara Evans
1985 "The Birth of the New Soviet Woman." In Abbott Gleason, Peter Kenez, and Richard Stites, eds., *Bolshevik Culture: Experiment and Order in the Russian Revolution*. Bloomington: Indiana University Press.

Cohen, David William
1994   *The Combing of History*. Chicago: University of Chicago Press.

Comaroff, Jean
1985   *Body of Power, Spirit of Resistance: The Culture and History of a South African People*. Chicago: University of Chicago Press.

Comaroff, Jean, and John Comaroff
1991   *Of Revelation and Revolution: Christianity, Colonialism, and Consciousness in South Africa*. Chicago: University of Chicago Press.

Comaroff, John, and Paul C. Stern
1994   "New Perspectives on Nationalism and War." *Theory and Society* 23 (1): 147–50.

Combs-Schilling, M. E.
1989   *Sacred Performances: Islam, Sexuality, and Sacrifice*. New York: Columbia University Press.

Condee, Nancy, ed.
1995   *Soviet Hieroglyphics: Visual Culture in Late Twentieth-Century Russia*. Bloomington: Indiana University Press.

Connerton, Paul
1991   *How Societies Remember*. Cambridge: Cambridge University Press.

Conquest, Robert
1986   *The Harvest of Sorrow: Soviet Collectivization and the Terror-Famine*. New York: Oxford University Press.

Corrigan, Philip Richard D., and Derek Sayer
1985   *The Great Arch: English State Formation as Cultural Revolution*. New York: Basil Blackwell.

Cullerne Brown, Matthew, and Brandon Taylor, eds.
1993   *Art of the Soviets: Painting, Sculpture and Architecture in a One-Party State, 1917–1992*. Manchester: Manchester University Press.

Cushman, Thomas
1995   *Notes from Underground: Rock Music Counterculture in Russia*. Albany: State University of New York Press.

Davies, R. W.
1989   *Soviet History in the Gorbachev Revolution*. Bloomington: Indiana University Press.

Davis, Natalie Zemon, and Randolph Starn
1989   "Introduction [to Special Issue on Memory and Counter Memory]." *Representations* 26 (spring 1989): 1–6.

Dawson, Jane
1996   *Eco-Nationalism*. Durham, N.C.: Duke University Press.

Deak, Frantisek
1975   "Russian Mass Spectacles." *Drama Review* 19 (2): 7–22.

Deutsch, Karl
1953   *Nationalism and Social Communication: An Inquiry into the Foundations of Nationality*. Cambridge, Mass.: Technology Press of MIT.

Dickman, Steven
1991   "Chernobyl Effects Not as Bad as Feared: Study Finds No Cancer or Birth Defects; Two Key Populations Omitted, Though." *Nature* 351 (6): 325.

Dominguez, Virginia R.
1989   *People as Subject, People as Object: Selfhood and Peoplehood in Contemporary Israel*. Madison: University of Wisconsin Press.

Drach, Ivan
1993   "To the Famine-Genocide of 1933." Translated by R. K. Stojko-Lozynskyj. *Ukrainian Quarterly* 40 (4): 357–61.

Duncan, James, and David Ley, eds.
1993   *Place/Culture/Representation*. London: Routledge.

Dunstan, John
1978   *Paths to Excellence and the Soviet School*. Atlantic Highlands, N.J.: Humanities Press.

Durkheim, Emile
1965   *The Elementary Forms of the Religious Life*. Translated by Joseph Ward Swain. New York: The Free Press.

1984   *The Division of Labor in Society*. Translated by W. D. Halls. New York: The Free Press.

Dzyuba, Ivan
1974   *Internationalism or Russification?* New York: Monad Press.

Ehrenburg, Ilya
1962   *People and Life, 1891–1921*. New York: Knopf.

Entrikin, J. Nicholas
1991   *The Betweenness of Place: Towards a Geography of Modernity*. Baltimore, Md.: Johns Hopkins University Press.

Felman, Shoshana, and Dori Laub
1992   *Testimony: Crises of Witnessing in Literature, Psychoanalysis, and History*. New York: Routledge.

Fentress, James, and Chris Wickham
1992   *Social Memory*. Oxford: Blackwell.

Fitzpatrick, Sheila
1978   *Cultural Revolution in Russia, 1928–31*. Bloomington: Indiana University Press.

1979   *Education and Social Mobility in the Soviet Union, 1921–34*. New York: Cambridge University Press.

Foucault, Michel
1972   *The Archaeology of Knowledge and the Discourse on Language*. Translated by A. M. Sheridan Smith. New York: Pantheon Books.

1977a   *Language, Counter-Memory, Practice: Selected Essays and Interviews by Michel Foucault*. Edited by Donald F. Bouchard. Ithaca, N.Y.: Cornell University Press.

1980   *Power/Knowledge: Selected Interviews and Other Writings, 1972–1977*. Edited by Colin Gordon. New York: Pantheon Books.

Fox, Richard G.
1985   *Lions of the Punjab: Culture in the Making*. Berkeley and Los Angeles: University of California Press.

Fox, Richard G., ed.
1990   *Nationalist Ideologies and the Production of National Cultures*. Washington, D.C.: American Anthropological Association.

Funk, Nanette, and Magda Mueller, eds.
1993   *Gender Politics and Post-Communism: Reflections from Eastern Europe and the Former Soviet Union*. New York: Routledge.

Funkenstein, Amos
1989   "Collective Memory and Historical Consciousness." *History and Memory* 1 (spring–summer 1989): 5–26.

Gauthier, Stephen
1979   "The Popular Base of Ukrainian Nationalism in 1917." *Slavic Review* 38 (1979): 30–47.

Geertz, Clifford
1973   *The Interpretation of Cultures*. New York: Basic Books.

Gellner, Ernest
1983   *Nations and Nationalism*. Ithaca, N.Y.: Cornell University Press.

1987   *Culture, Identity, and Politics*. Cambridge: Cambridge University Press.

Giddens, Anthony
1991   *Modernity and Self-Identity: Self and Society in the Late Modern Age*. Stanford, Calif.: Stanford University Press.

Gillis, John R., ed.
1994   *Commemorations: The Politics of National Identity*. Princeton, N.J.: Princeton University Press.

Goldman, Wendy Z.
1993   *Women, the State, and Revolution: Soviet Family Policy and Social Life, 1917–1936*. New York: Cambridge University Press.

Grabowicz, George G.
1982   *The Poet as Mythmaker: A Study of Symbolic Meaning in Taras Ševčenko*. Cambridge, Mass.: Harvard University Press.

Grant, Bruce
1995   *In the Soviet House of Culture: A Century of Perestroikas*. Princeton, N.J.: Princeton University Press.

Grant, Nigel
1968   *Soviet Education*. Baltimore, Md.: Penguin Books.

Grossberg, Lawerence, Cary Nelson, and Paula A. Treichler, eds.
1992   *Cultural Studies*. New York: Routledge.

Groys, Boris
1992   *The Total Art of Stalinism: Avant-garde, Aesthetic Dictatorship, and Beyond*. Translated by Charles Rougle. Princeton, N.J.: Princeton University Press.

Habermas, Jürgen
1988   "Concerning the Public Use of History." *New German Critique* 44 (spring–summer 1988): 40–50.

Hajda, Lubomyr, and Mark Beissinger, eds.
1990   *The Nationalities Factor in Soviet Politics and Society*. Boulder, Colo.: Westview Press.

Halbwachs, Maurice
1980   *The Collective Memory*. Translated by Francis Ditter and Vida Y. Ditter. New York: Harper & Row.

1975   *Les Cadres Sociaux de la Mémoire*. New York: Arno Press.

Handler, Richard
1988   *Nationalism and the Politics of Culture in Quebec*. Madison: University of Wisconsin Press.

Hann, C. M.
1993   *Socialism: Ideals, Ideologies, and Local Practice*. London: Routledge.

Hans, Nicholas
1963   *The Russian Tradition in Education*. London: Routledge & Kegan Paul.

Harvey, David
1989   *The Urban Experience*. Baltimore, Md.: Johns Hopkins University Press.

Hedgbeth, Llewellyn
1975   "D.E." *Drama Review* 19 (2): 23–36.

Herzfeld, Michael
1982   *Ours Once More: Folklore, Ideology, and the Making of Modern Greece*. Austin: University of Texas Press.

1991   *A Place in History: Social and Monumental Time in a Cretan Town*. Princeton, N.J.: Princeton University Press.

Hobsbawm, E. J.
1990   *Nations and Nationalism Since 1780: Programme, Myth, Reality*. Cambridge: Cambridge University Press.

Hobsbawm, E. J., and Terence Ranger, eds.
1983   *The Invention of Tradition*. Cambridge: Cambridge University Press.

Hosking, Geoffrey A.
1989   "Memory in a Totalitarian Society: The Case of the Soviet Union." In Thomas Butler, ed., *Memory: History, Culture and the Mind*. New York: Basil Blackwell.

1990   *The Awakening of the Soviet Union*. Cambridge, Mass.: Harvard University Press.

Hroch, Miroslav
1985   *Social Preconditions of National Revival in Europe: A Comparative Analysis of the Social Composition of Patriotic Groups among the Smaller European Nations*. Translated by Ben Fowkes. Cambridge: Cambridge University Press.

Hryshev'skyi, Mykhailo
1919   *Kul'turno-Natsional'nyi Rukh na Ukraini v XVI–XVII Vitsi*. Vyd. 2. Kyiv: Dniprosoiuz.

1941   *A History of Ukraine*. Edited by O. J. Frederiksen. New Haven, Conn.: Yale University Press.

Hrytsenko, Oleksandr
1994   *Kul'turna Politika: Kontseptsii i Dosvig*. Kyiv: I.D.U.S.
n.d.   "Our Song, Our Wisdom: National Mythologies and Civil Religion in Ukraine." Unpublished manuscript.

Hrytsenko, O. A., ed.
1995   *Stan Kul'turnoi Sferi ta Kul'turnoi Politiki v Ukraini: Analitichnii Ohliad*. Kyiv: IKP UTsKD Ministerstva Kul'turi Ukraini.

Humphrey, Caroline
1983   *Karl Marx Collective: Economy, Society, and Religion in a Siberian Collective Farm*. Cambridge: Cambridge University Press.

Husband, William B.
1991a   "Secondary School History Texts in the USSR: Revising the Soviet Past." *Russian Review* 50 (4): 458–80.

1991b   "Administrative Perestroika and Rewriting History: The Dilemma of Glasnost in Soviet Education." *Journal of Educational Administration* 29 (4): 7–16.

Isaacs, Harold
1975   "Basic Group Identity: The Idols of the Tribe." In Nathan Glazer and Daniel Moynihan, eds., *Ethnicity: Theory and Experience*. Cambridge, Mass.: Harvard University Press.

Jacoby, Susan
1974   *Inside Soviet Schools*. New York: Hill & Wang.

Johnson, Richard, et al.
1982   *Making Histories: Studies in History-Writing and Politics*. London: Hutchinson.

Jones, Anthony, ed.
1994   *Education and Society in the New Russia*. Armonk, N.Y.: M. E. Sharpe.

Kapferer, Bruce
1988   *Legends of People, Myths of State: Violence, Intolerance, and Political Culture in Sri Lanka and Australia*. Washington, D.C.: Smithsonian Institution Press.

Kappeler, Andreas
1994   *Kleine Geschichte der Ukraine*. Munich: C. H. Beck

Keith, Michael, and Steve Pile, eds.
1993   *Place and the Politics of Identity*. London: Routledge.

Kenez, Peter
1985   *The Birth of the Propaganda State: Soviet Methods of Mass Mobilization, 1917–1929*. Cambridge: Cambridge University Press.

Kertzer, David I.
1988   *Ritual, Politics, and Power*. New Haven, Conn.: Yale University Press.

Kline, George, ed.
1957   *Soviet Education*. New York: Columbia University Press.

Kohut, Zenon E.
1986   "The Development of a Little Russian Identity and Ukrainian Nationbuilding." *Harvard Ukrainian Studies* 10 (3–4): 559–76.

1994   "History as Battleground: Russian-Ukrainian Relations and Historical Consciousness in Contemporary Ukraine." In S. Frederick Starr, ed., *The Legacy of History
in Russia and the New States of Eurasia*. Armonk, N.Y.: M. E. Sharpe.

Kolasky, John
1968   *Education in the Soviet Union: A Study in Discrimination and Russification*. Toronto:
Peter Martin Associates.

Kolomayets, Marta
1993   "Ukraine's People Recall National Tragedy of Famine-Holocaust." *Ukrainian
Weekly*, September 19, 1993, p. 1.

1995   "Chernova Ruta Festival Rocks Sevastopol—and Black Sea Fleet." *Ukrainian
Weekly*, July 2, 1995, p. 10.

Kornai, Janos
1980   *Economics of Shortage*. New York: North-Holland.

Kostenko, Lina
1993   "Chernobyl in the Dose of Historical Consciousness." *Literatura Ukraina* 39
(4552): 2.

Kotkin, Stephen
1991   *Steeltown, USSR: Soviet Society in the Gorbachev Era*. Berkeley and Los Angeles:
University of California Press.

Koval', M. V., S. V. Kul'chyts'kyi, and Iu. A. Kurnosov, eds.
1992   *Istoriia Ukrainy*. Kyiv: Raiduha.

Koval', M.V., S. V. Kul'chyts'kyi, Iu. A. Kurnosov, and V. H. Sarbei, eds.
1991   *Istoriia Ukrainy*. Kyiv: Osvita.

Kovalenko, Lidiia, and Volodymyr Maniak
1991   *Holod 33: Narodna Knyha Memorial*. Kyiv: Radians'kii Pis'mennyk.

Kozakiewicz, Mikolaj
1992   "Educational Transformation Initiated by the Polish Petestroika." *Comparative
Education Review* 36 (1): 91–100.

Krawchenko, Bohdan
1985   *Social Change and National Consciousness in Twentieth-Century Ukraine*. London:
Macmillan.

Kristeva, Julia
1980   *Desire in Language: A Semiotic Approach to Literature and Art*. New York: Columbia University Press.

1993   *Nations without Nationalism*. New York: Columbia University Press.

Kuchler, Susanne
1988   "Malangan Objects, Sacrifice and the Production of Memory." *American Ethnologist* 14 (4): 625–37.

Kuchler, Susanne, and Walter Melion, eds.
1991   *Images of Memory: On Remembering and Representation*. Washington, D.C.: Smithsonian Institution Press.

Kuebart, Friedrich
1989   "The Political Socialisation of Schoolchildren." In Jim Riordan, ed., *Soviet Youth Culture*. Bloomington: Indiana University Press

Kulchytsky, George P.
1993   "Western Relief Efforts During the 'Stalin Famine.'" *Ukrainian Quarterly* 49 (2): 152–64.

Kuromiya, Hiroaki
1988   *Stalin's Industrial Revolution: Politics and Workers, 1928–1932*. Cambridge: Cambridge University Press.

1995   "Ukraine and Russia in the 1930s." Paper presented at the AAASS convention, October 27, 1995.

Kuropas, Myron B.
1991   *The Ukrainian-Americans: Roots and Aspirations, 1884–1954*. Toronto: University of Toronto Press.

Kuzio, Taras, and Andrew Wilson
1994   *Ukraine: Perestroika to Independence*. New York: St. Martin's Press.

Laclau, Ernesto
1990   *New Reflections on the Revolution of Our Time*. London: Verso.

Lamphere, Louise, ed.
1992   *Structuring Diversity: Ethnographic Perspectives on the New Immigration*. Chicago: University of Chicago Press.

Lane, Christel
1981   *The Rites of Rulers, Ritual in Industrial Society: The Soviet Case*. Cambridge: Cambridge University Press.

Lane, David
1992   *Soviet Society Under Perestroika*. New York: Routledge.

Langer, Lawrence L.
1991   *Holocaust Testimonies: The Ruins of Memory*. New Haven, Conn.: Yale University Press.

Lefebvre, Henri
1991   *The Production of Space*. Translated by Donald Nicholson-Smith. Cambridge, Mass.: Basil Blackwell.

Le Goff, Jacques
1992   *History and Memory*. Translated by S. Rendall and E. Claman. New York: Columbia University Press.

Le Goff, Jacques, ed.
1989   *L'Etat et les Pouvoirs*. Paris: Seuil.

Leibfreid, A.U., et al., eds.
1987   *Khar'kov: Arkhitektura, Pamiatniki, Novostroiki*. Kharkiv: Prapor.

Lenin, V. I.
1968   *Critical Remarks on the National Question*. Moscow: Progress Publishers.

Lévi-Strauss, Claude
1966   *The Savage Mind*. Chicago: University of Chicago Press.

Liber, George O.
1992   *Soviet Nationality Policy, Urban Growth, and Identity Change in the Ukrainian SSR, 1923–1934*. New York: Cambridge University Press.

Lindheim, Ralph, and George S.N. Luckyj
1996   *Toward an Intellectual History of Ukraine: An Anthology of Ukrainian Thought from 1917 to 1995*. Toronto: University of Toronto Press.

Lissyutkina, Larissa
1993   "Soviet Women at the Crossroads of Perestroika." In Nanette Funk and Magda Mueller, eds., *Gender Politics and Post-Communism: Reflections from Eastern Europe and the Former Soviet Union*. New York: Routledge.

Lodder, Christina
1983   *Russian Constructivism*. New Haven, Conn.: Yale University Press.

1993   "Lenin's Plan for Monumental Propaganda." In Mathew Cullerne Brown and Brandon Taylor, eds., *Art of the Soviets: Painting, Sculpture and Architecture in a One-Party State, 1917–1992*. Manchester: Manchester University Press.

Lowenthal, David
1985   *The Past Is a Foreign Country*. Cambridge: Cambridge University Press.

Luxemburg, Rosa
1976   *The National Question: Selected Writings*. Edited by Horace B. Davis. New York: Monthly Review Press.

Lynd, H. M.
1958   *On Shame and the Search for Identity*. New York: Science Editions.

MacAloon, John, ed.
1984   *Rite, Drama, Festival, Spectacle: Rehearsals Toward a Theory of Cultural Performance*. Philadelphia: Institute for the Study of Human Issues.

Mace, James
1986   "The Famine of 1933: A Survey of Sources." In R. Serbyn and B. Krawchenko, eds., *Famine in Ukraine, 1932–33*. Edmonton, Alberta: Canadian Institute of Ukrainian Studies.

1993   "How Ukraine Was Permitted to Remember." *Ukrainian Quarterly* 49 (2): 121–51.

Mace, James, and Leonid Heretz, eds.
1990   *Oral History Project of the Commission on the Ukraine Famine*. Washington, D.C.: U. S. Government Printing Office.

Magocsi, Paul Robert
1996   *A History of Ukraine*. Toronto: University of Toronto Press.

Maier, Charles S.
1988   *The Unmasterable Past: History, Holocaust, and German National Identity*. Cambridge, Mass.: Harvard University Press.

Malinowski, Bronislaw
1961   *Argonauts of the Western Pacific*. New York: E. P. Dutton.

Malkki, Liisa
1990   "Context and Consciousness: Local Conditions for the Production of Historical and National Thought Among Hutu Refugees in Tanzania." In Richard G. Fox, ed., *Nationalist Ideologies and the Production of National Cultures*. Washington, D.C.: American Anthropological Association.

1995   *Purity and Exile: Violence, Memory, and National Cosmology among Hutu Refugees in Tanzania*. Chicago: University of Chicago Press.

Markovits, Andrei, and Frank E. Sysyn, eds.
1982   *Nationbuilding and the Politics of Nationalism: Essays of Austrian Galicia*. Cambridge: Harvard University Press.

Markus, Vasyl
1985   *Religion and Nationalism in Soviet Ukraine after 1945*. Cambridge, Mass.: Ukrainian Studies Fund, Harvard University Press.

Marples, David R.
1986   *Chernobyl and Nuclear Power in the USSR*. New York: St. Martin's Press.

1988   *The Social Impact of the Chernobyl Disaster*. Edmonton: University of Alberta Press.

1991   *Ukraine Under Perestroika: Ecology, Economics, and the Workers' Revolt*. New York: St. Martin's Press.

1995   "Analysis: A Nuclear Catastrophe in the Making in Former USSR?" *Ukrainian Weekly*, June 25, 1995, pp. 2, 19.

Marsh, Rosalind, ed.
1996   *Women in Russia and Ukraine*. Cambridge: Cambridge University Press.

Marx, Karl
1989   *Manifesto of the Communist Party*. Edited by Frederick Engels. New York: International Publishers.

Mauss, Marcel
1990   *The Gift: Forms and Functions of Exchange in Archaic Societies*. Translated by W. D. Halls. New York: W. W. Norton.

McClelland, James C.
1979   *Autocrats and Academics: Education, Culture, and Society in Tsarist Russia*. Chicago: University of Chicago Press.

McLaren, Peter
1986   *Schooling as a Ritual Performance: Towards a Political Economy of Educational Symbols and Gestures*. New York: Routledge.

McLean, Martin, with Natalia Voskresenskaya
1992   "Education Revolution from Above: Thatcher's Britain and Gorbachev's Soviet Union." *Comparative Education Review* 36 (1): 71–90.

Medvedev, Zhores
1990   *The Legacy of Chernobyl*. New York: W. W. Norton.

Moore, Sally Falk
1987   "Explaining the Present: Theoretical Dilemmas in Processual Ethnography." *American Ethnologist* 14 (4): 727–36.

Moore, Sally F., and Barbara G. Myerhoff, eds.
1977   *Secular Ritual*. Amsterdam: Van Gorcum.

Mosse, George L.
1975   *The Nationalism of the Masses: Political Symbolism and Mass Movements in Germany from the Napoleonic Wars through the Third Reich*. New York: H. Fertig.

1985   *Nationalism and Sexuality: Respectability and Abnormal Sexuality in Modern Europe*. New York: H. Fertig.

1990   *Fallen Soldiers: Reshaping the Memory of the World Wars*. New York: Oxford University Press.

Motyl, Alexander J.
1980   *The Turn to the Right: The Ideological Origins and Development of Ukrainian Nationalism, 1919–1929*. Boulder, Colo.: East European Monographs.

1990   *Sovietology, Rationality, Nationality: Coming to Grips with Nationalism in the USSR*. New York: Columbia University Press.

1993   *Dilemmas of Independence: Ukraine after Totalitarianism*. New York: Council on Foreign Relations Press.

Munch, Ronaldo
1986   *The Difficult Dialogue: Marxism and Nationalism*. Atlantic Highlands, N.J.: Zed Books.

Myerhoff, Barbara
1974   "A Death in Due Time: Construction of Self and Culture in Ritual Drama." In J. J. MacAloon, ed., *Rite, Drama, Festival, and Spectacle: Rehearsals toward a Theory of Cultural Performance*. Philadelphia: Institute for the Study of Human Issues.

Nahaylo, Bohdan, and Victor Swoboda
1989   *Soviet Disunion: A History of the Nationalities Problem in the USSR*. New York: The Free Press.

Nairn, Tom
1977   *The Break-up of Britain: Crisis and Neonationalism*. London: New Left Books.

Nora, Pierre
1984   *Les Lieux de la Mémoire*. Paris: Gallimard.

1989   "Between Memory and History: Les Lieux de Mémoire." *Representations* 26 (Spring 1989): 7–25.

Olcott, Martha Brill
1981   "The Collectivization Drive in Kazakhstan." *Russian Review* 40 (April 1981): 122–42.

Onyshkevych, Larissa, and M. L. Zaleska
1989   "Echos of Glasnost: Chornobyl in Soviet Ukrainian Literature." In Romana Bahry, ed., *Echos of Glasnost in Soviet Ukraine*. York, Ontario: Captus University Publications.

Ortner, Sherry
1984   "Theory in Anthropology since the Sixties." *Comparative Studies of Society and History* 26: 126–66.

Panchyshyn, Andrii
1997.   "Chervona Ruta—Kvitka Pechali." *Den'*, May 14, 1997, p. 7.

Panova, Rossica, Raina Gavrilova, and Cornelia Merdzanska
1993   "Thinking Gender: Bulgarian Women's Im/possibilities." In Nanette Funk and Magda Mueller, eds., *Gender Politics and Post-Communism: Reflections from Eastern Europe and the Former Soviet Union*. New York: Routledge.

Passerini, Luisa
1987   *Fascism in Popular Memory: The Cultural Experience of the Turin Working Class*. Translated by Robert Lumley and Jude Bloomfield. New York: Cambridge University Press.

Passerini, Luisa, ed.
1992   *Memory and Totalitarianism*. Oxford: Oxford University Press.

Pavlyshyn, Marko
1991   "Aspects of the Literary Process in the USSR: The Politics of Re-canonisation in Ukraine after 1985." *Southern Review* 24 (1): 12–25.

Pennar, Jaan, Ivan I. Bakalo, and George Z. F. Bereday
1971   *Modernization and Diversity in Soviet Education: With Special Reference to Nationality Groups.* New York: Praeger Publishers.

Pesman, Dale
1995   "To Survive You've Got to Krutit'sja." Paper presented at the AAASS convention, October 27, 1995.

Petryna, Adriana
1995   "Sarcophagus: Chernobyl in Historical Light." *Cultural Anthropology* 10 (2): 196–220.

Pfaff, William
1993   *The Wrath of Nations: Civilization and Furies of Nationalism.* New York: Simon & Schuster.

Piaget, Jean
1968   *On the Development of Memory and Identity.* Translated by Eleanor Duckworth. Barre, Mass.: Clark University Press..

Potichnyj, Peter J., and Yevhen Shtendera, eds.
1986   *Political Thought of the Ukrainian Underground, 1943–51.* Edmonton, Alberta: Canadian Institute of Ukrainian Studies.

Pred, Allen
1990   *Making Histories and Constructing Human Geographies: The Local Transformation of Practice, Power Relations, and Consciousness.* Boulder, Colo.: Westview Press.

Procyk, Oksana, Leonid Heretz, and James Mace
1986   *Famine in the Soviet Ukraine, 1932–33.* Cambridge, Mass.: Harvard University Press.

Prokof'eva, M. A., P. V. Zimina, M. N. Kolmakovoi, M. I. Kondakova, and N. P. Kuzina
1967   *Narodnoe Obrazovanie v SSSR, 1917–1967.* Moscow: Prosveshchenie.

Ramet, Sabrina P.
1994   *Rocking the State: Rock Music and Politics in Eastern Europe and Russia.* Boulder, Colo.: Westview Press.

Redl, Helen B., ed.
1964   *Soviet Educators on Soviet Education.* Translated by Helen B. Redl. New York: The Free Press of Glencoe.

Ries, Nancy
1997   *Russian Talk: Culture and Conversation during Perestroika.* Ithaca, N.Y.: Cornell University Press.

Riordan, Jim, ed.
1989 *Soviet Youth Culture*. Bloomington: Indiana University Press.

Roi, Yaacov
1992 "Nationalism in Central Asia." In Zvi Gitelman, ed., *The Politics of Nationality and the Erosion of the USSR*. New York: St. Martin's Press.

Rosaldo, Michelle Z.
1980 *Knowledge and Passion: Ilongot Notions of Self and Social Life*. New York: Cambridge University Press.

Rosaldo, Renato
1993 *Culture and Truth: The Remaking of Social Analysis*. Boston: Beacon Press.

Rose, Nikolas
1990 *Governing the Soul: The Shaping of the Private Self*. New York: Routledge.

Rowe, William, and Vivian Schelling
1993 *Memory and Modernity: Popular Culture in Latin America*. London: Verso.

Rubchak, Marian
1996 "Christian Virgin or Pagan Goddess: Feminism versus the Eternally Feminine in Ukraine." In Rosalind Marsh, ed., *Women in Russia and Ukraine*. Cambridge: Cambridge University Press.

Samarin, Vladimir D.
1957 "The Soviet School, 1936–1942." In George L. Kline, ed., *Soviet Education*. New York: Columbia University Press.

Scott, James
1985 *Weapons of the Weak: Everyday Forms of Peasant Resistance*. New Haven, Conn.: Yale University Press.

1990 *Domination and the Arts of Resistance*. New Haven, Conn.: Yale University Press.

Shanin, Teodor
1989 "Ethnicity in the Soviet Union: Analytical Perceptions and Political Strategies." *Comparative Study of Society and History* 31 (3): 409–24.

Shcherbak, Iurii
1989 *Chernobyl: A Documentary Story*. Translated by Ian Press. New York: St. Martin's Press.

Shoemaker, Sydney, and Richard Swinburne
1984 *Personal Identity* Oxford: Basil Blackwell.

Shturman, Dora
1988 *The Soviet Secondary School*. London: Routledge.

Singer, Milton
1955 "The Cultural Pattern of India." *The Far Eastern Quarterly* 15: 23–36.

1972 *When a Great Tradition Modernizes: An Anthropological Approach to Indian Civilization*. New York: Praeger Publishers.

Slezkine, Yuri
1991 "The Fall of Soviet Ethnography, 1928–38." *Current Anthropology* 32 (4): 476–85.

1992 "From Savages to Citizens: The Cultural Revolution in the Soviet Far North, 1928–38." *Slavic Review* 51 (1): 52–76.

1994 "The USSR as a Communal Apartment, or How a Socialist State Promoted Ethnic Particularism." *Slavic Review* 53 (2): 414–52.

Slobin, Mark, ed.
1996 *Retuning Culture: Musical Changes in Central and Eastern Europe.* Durham, N.C.: Duke University Press.

Smith, Anthony D.
1986 *The Ethnic Origins of Nations.* New York: Basil Blackwell.

1991 *National Identity.* Reno: University of Nevada Press.

1992 *Ethnicity and Nationalism.* New York: E. J. Brill.

Soja, Edward A.
1989 *Postmodern Geographies: The Reassertion of Space in Critical Theory.* New York: Verso.

Sollors, Werner
1989 *The Invention of Ethnicity.* New York: Oxford University Press.

Sorokowski, Andrew
1988 *Ukrainian Catholics and Orthodox in Poland and Czechoslovakia.* Cambridge, Mass.: Ukrainian Studies Fund, Harvard University Press.

Starr, Frederick S., ed.
1994 *The Legacy of History in Russia and the New States of Eurasia.* Armonk, N.Y.: M. E. Sharpe.

Stites, Richard
1985 "Iconoclastic Currents in the Russian Revolution: Destroying and Preserving the Past." In Abbott Gleason, Peter Kenez, and Richard Stites, eds., *Bolshevik Culture: Experiment and Order in the Russian Revolution.* Bloomington: Indiana University Press.

1986 *The Women's Liberation Movement in Russia: Feminism, Nihilism, and Bolshevism, 1860–1930.* Princeton, N.J.: Princeton University Press.

1989 *Revolutionary Dreams: Utopian Vision and Experimental Life in the Russian Revolution.* New York: Oxford University Press.

1992 *Russian Popular Culture: Entertainment and Society since 1900.* New York: Cambridge University Press.

Stocking, George
1987   *Victorian Anthropology*. New York: The Free Press.

Stocking, George, ed.
1983   *Observers Observed: Essays on Ethnographic Fieldwork*. Madison: University of Wisconsin Press.

Subtelny, Orest
1991   *Ukrainians in North America: An Illustrated History*. Toronto: University of Toronto Press.

1993   "The Current State of Ukrainian Historiography." *Journal of Ukrainian Studies* 18 (1–2): 33–54.

1994   *Ukraine: A History*. Toronto: University of Toronto Press.

Suny, Ronald Grigor
1989   *The Making of the Georgian Nation*. London: I. B. Tauris.

1993   *The Revenge of the Past: Nationalism, Revolution, and the Collapse of the Soviet Union*. Stanford, Calif.: Stanford University Press.

Swedenburg, Ted
1995   *Memories of Revolt: The 1936–1939 Rebellion and the Palestinian National Past*. Minneapolis: University of Minnesota Press.

Sysyn, Frank F.
1987   *The Ukrainian Orthodox Question in the USSR*. Cambridge, Mass.: Ukrainian Studies Fund, Harvard University Press.

Szporluk, Roman
1975   "Russians in Ukraine and Problems of Ukrainian Identity in the USSR." In P. Potichnyj, ed., *Ukraine in the Seventies*. Oakville, Ontario: Mosaic Press.

1994   "Reflections on Ukraine after 1994: The Dilemmas of Nationhood." *Harriman Review* 7 (7–9): 1–10.

Taussig, Michael
1987   *Shamanism, Colonialism, and the Wild Man: A Study in Terror and Healing*. Chicago: University of Chicago Press.

Tenenbaum, Barbara A.
1994   "Streetwise History: The Paseo de la Reforma and the Porfirian State, 1876–1910." In William H. Beezley, Cheryl English Martin, and William E. French, eds., *Rituals of Rule, Rituals of Resistance*. Wilmington, Del.: : Scholarly Resources.

Tertz, Abram (Andrei Sinyavsky)
1965   "On Socialist Realism." In *The Trial Begins*. New York: Vintage Books.

Thompson, Paul
1988   *The Voice of the Past: Oral History*. Oxford: Oxford University Press.

Trotsky, Leon
1972   *The Revolution Betrayed: What Is the Soviet Union and Where Is It Going?* 5th ed. New York: Pathfinder Press.

Tucker, Robert C., ed.
1975   *The Lenin Anthology.* New York: Norton Books.

Turner, Victor W.
1969   *The Ritual Process: Structure and Anti-Structure.* Chicago: Aldine.

1974   *Drams, Fields, and Metaphors: Symbolic Action in Human Society.* Ithaca, N.Y.: Cornell University Press.

1986   *The Anthropology of Experience.* Urbana: University of Illinois Press.

1987   *The Anthropology of Performance.* New York: PAJ Publications.

Turner, Victor W., ed.
1982   *Celebration: Studies in Festivity and Ritual.* Washington, D.C.: Smithsonian Institution Press.

Vansina, Jan
1985   *Oral Tradition as History.* Madison: University of Wisconsin Press.

Velychenko, Stephen
1993   *Shaping Identity in Eastern Europe and Russia: Soviet and Polish Accounts of Ukrainian History, 1914–1991.* New York: St. Martin's Press.

Verdery, Katherine
1983   *Transylvanian Villagers: Three Centuries of Political, Economic, and Ethnic Change, 1700–1980.* Berkeley and Los Angeles: University of California Press.

1990   "The Production and Defense of 'the Romanian Nation,' 1900 to World War II." In Richard G. Fox, ed., *Nationalist Ideologies and the Production of National Cultures.* Washington, D.C.: American Anthropological Association.

1991a   *National Ideology under Socialism: Identity and Cultural Politics in Ceaucescu's Romania.* Berkeley and Los Angeles: University of California Press.

1991b   "Theorizing Socialism: A Prologue to the Transition." In *American Ethnologist* 18 (3): 419–39.

1996   *What Was Socialism, and What Comes Next?* Princeton, N.J.: Princeton University Press

Vidal-Naquet, Pierre
1992   *Assassins of Memory: Essays on the Denial of the Holocaust.* New York: Columbia University Press.

von Geldern, James
1993   *Bolshevik Festivals, 1917–1920.* Berkeley and Los Angeles: University of California Press.

von Kopp, Botho
1992   "The Eastern European Revolution and Education in Czechoslovakia." *Comparative Education Review* 36 (1): 101–13.

Vynnychenko, V.
1920   *Vidrodzhennia Natsii*. Kyiv: Videp'.

Wagner, Dan
1978   "Memories of Morocco: The Influence of Age, Schooling, and Environment on Memory." *Cognitive Psychology* 10: 1–28.

Wagner, Roy
1980   *The Invention of Culture*. Chicago: University of Chicago Press.

Watson, Rubie S.
1994   *Memory, History, and Opposition under State Socialism*. Santa Fe, N.M.: School of American Research Press.

Weber, Max
1968   *The Methodology of the Social Sciences*. New York: The Free Press.

Wheatcroft, S. G.
1990   "More Light on the Scale of Repression and Excess Mortality in the Soviet Union in the 1930s." *Soviet Studies* 42 (2): 355–67.

Willis, Paul
1977   *Learning to Labor: How Working-Class Kids Get Working-Class Jobs*. New York: Columbia University Press.

1990   *Common Culture: Symbolic Work at Play in the Everyday Cultures of the Young*. Boulder, Colo.: Westview Press.

Wohl, Robert
1979   *The Generation of 1914*. Cambridge, Mass.: Harvard University Press.

World Bank
1996   *World Bank Poverty Report*. No. 15602-UA, June 27, 1996.

Woronowycz, Roman
1997   "Chervona Ruta Festival of Ukrainian Music Rocks Kharkiv for 14 Nights." *Ukrainian Weekly*, June 8, 1997, pp. 10–11.

Yang, Mayfair Mei-hui
1992   *Gifts, Favors, and Banquets: The Art of Social Relationships in China*. Ithaca, N.Y.: Cornell University Press.

Yates, Frances A.
1966   *The Art of Memory*. Chicago: University of Chicago Press.

Young, James E.
1992   "The Counter-Monument: Memory Against Itself in Germany Today." *Critical Inquiry* 18: 267–96.

1993   *The Texture of Memory: Holocaust Memorials and Meaning.* New Haven, Conn.: Yale University Press.

Young, James E., ed.
1994   *The Art of Memory: Holocaust Memorials in History.* Prestel, N.Y.: The Jewish Museum.

Zerubavel, Eviatar
1977   "The French Republican Calendar: A Case Study in the Sociology of Time." *American Sociological Review* 42: 868–76.

1981   *Hidden Rhythms: Schedules and Calendars in Social Life.* Chicago: University of Chicago Press.

Index